Using Tension as a Resource

Using Tension as a Resource

New Visions in Teaching the English Language Arts Methods Class

Edited by
Heidi L. Hallman
Kristen Pastore-Capuana
Donna L. Pasternak

ROWMAN & LITTLEFIELD
Lanham • Boulder • New York • London

Published by Rowman & Littlefield
An imprint of The Rowman & Littlefield Publishing Group, Inc.
4501 Forbes Boulevard, Suite 200, Lanham, Maryland 20706
www.rowman.com

6 Tinworth Street, London SE11 5AL

Copyright © 2019 by Heidi L. Hallman, Kristen Pastore-Capuana, and Donna L. Pasternak

All rights reserved. No part of this book may be reproduced in any form or by any electronic or mechanical means, including information storage and retrieval systems, without written permission from the publisher, except by a reviewer who may quote passages in a review.

British Library Cataloguing in Publication Information Available

Library of Congress Cataloging-in-Publication Data

Names: Hallman, Heidi L., 1976– editor. | Pastore-Capuana, Kristen, editor. | Pasternak, Donna L., editor.
Title: Using tension as a resource : new visions in teaching the English language arts methods class / [edited by] Heidi L. Hallman, Kristen Pastore-Capuana, Donna L. Pasternak.
Description: Lanham, Maryland : Rowman & Littlefield, [2019] | Includes bibliographical references and index.
Identifiers: LCCN 2018058870 (print) | LCCN 2019005337 (ebook) | ISBN 9781475845495 (Electronic) | ISBN 9781475845471 (cloth : alk. paper) | ISBN 9781475845488 (pbk. : alk. paper)
Subjects: LCSH: English teachers—Training of. | English language—Study and teaching. | Teaching—Methodology.
Classification: LCC PE1066 (ebook) | LCC PE1066 .U75 2019 (print) | DDC 428.0071—dc23
LC record available at https://lccn.loc.gov/2018058870

♾ ™ The paper used in this publication meets the minimum requirements of American National Standard for Information Sciences Permanence of Paper for Printed Library Materials, ANSI/NISO Z39.48-1992.

Printed in the United States of America

For English teacher educators,
with whom we share the journey

Contents

Acknowledgments	xi
Editors' Introduction *Heidi L. Hallman, Kristen Pastore-Capuana, and Donna L. Pasternak*	xiii
Part I: Frameworks for English Education	**1**
1 Educating Teachers for Critical Pragmatism: Methods as a "Conceptual Home Base" *Lauren Gatti, Sarah Thomas, Jessica Masterson, Robert Brooke, and Rachael Wendler-Shah*	3
A Response to Chapter 1 *Melissa Schieble*	17
2 Enduring Assignments in the Methods Course: Lesson Planning and Microteaching as Trigger Points for Stimulating Social Justice Teaching *Terri L. Rodriguez*	21
A Response to Chapter 2 *Allison Wynhoff Olsen*	33
3 Exploring Tensions During Critical Conversations About Race in English Education *Amy Vetter and Melissa Schieble*	37
A Response to Chapter 3 *Lauren Gatti*	53

Part II: Practices in English Education   **57**

4 Writing in and for the 21st Century: Crossing Digital and Multimodal Thresholds in ELA Methods Courses   59
Amber Jensen

A Response to Chapter 4   73
Mike Metz

5 Moving Preservice English Teachers From Egocentric to Sociocentric Readings   77
Crag Hill

A Response to Chapter 5   87
Christopher M. Parsons

6 Powerful Influence and Absurd Neglect: The Legacy of Louise M. Rosenblatt in Secondary English Language Arts Methods Courses   91
Sue Ringler Pet

A Response to Chapter 6   101
Crag Hill

7 Teacher Candidates' Perspectives on Tensions Within the Methods-Based Field Experience   105
Christopher M. Parsons

A Response to Chapter 7   117
Laura A. Renzi

Part III: Communities of English Education   **121**

8 English Education Methods Courses as Sites of Induction Into English Teacher Communities of Practice   123
James Cercone and Kristen Pastore-Capuana

A Response to Chapter 8   139
Amber Jensen

9 Tensions in ELA Field Experiences: Service-Learning Initiatives in Rural Contexts   145
Allison Wynhoff Olsen

A Response to Chapter 9   159
Jamie M. Collins

10 A Teaching Mythology: Disrupting the Tutor/Teacher Dichotomy   165
Heidi L. Hallman and Melanie N. Burdick

A Response to Chapter 10   175
Terri L. Rodriguez

Index   179

About the Editors and Contributors 183

Acknowledgments

This project started with a desire to unite those who teach the methods course in English language arts (ELA) teacher education programs. We recognized that there was a need to share what we refer to as *tensions* or *dilemmas* in teaching this course and to make these tensions visible for others in an effort to improve the practice of teaching the English language arts. The concept of tensions arises from the most recent study of English teacher education, *Secondary English Teacher Education in the United States*, and we are indebted to the work of Donna L. Pasternak, Samantha Caughlan, Heidi L. Hallman, Laura Renzi, and Leslie S. Rush for bringing these concerns to the field through their national study.

Through the National Council of Teachers of English's (NCTE) English Language Arts Teacher Educator's (ELATE) Commission on Methods Teaching and Learning, we encountered others who shared this vision to problematize practices currently taught through methods, or pedagogy, courses. In collaboration with members of this commission, this project was born. We are appreciative for the enthusiasm of all the commission members who contributed to this project—from senior scholars in the ELA field to graduate students.

First, we would like to thank those who have contributed their scholarship and expertise to this project. Both the chapter authors and respondents have fostered a rich dialogue about the teaching of ELA methods in today's context. The structure of the book, with responses following each of the chapters, intends to encourage ongoing discussion among readers of the book concerning the issues that are presented in the book.

Thank you to our editors, Sarah Jubar and Emily Tuttle, who assisted us in shaping this project and seeing it to completion. Thank you to Terri Rodriguez, Melissa Schieble, and Sarah Hochstetler, who offered initial feedback and drafts that focused this endeavor in its earliest stages.

Lastly, we would like to acknowledge our families for their support during this project: John Mattes and the Hallman Mattes children; Michael J. Capuana, Sophia M. Capuana, and Michael A. Capuana; and Stanley B. Shulfer.

It is our hope that projects such as this, which are possible only through a high level of engaged collaboration, continue in our field in order to foster vibrant scholarly conversation, advocacy, and change.

Editors' Introduction

Heidi L. Hallman, Kristen Pastore-Capuana, and Donna L. Pasternak

English teacher education is a dynamic field that has continually redefined itself since its inception in the late nineteenth century at a time when only 10% of most high school students—mostly all white, upper-middle-class or wealthy males—went on to college or university (Pasternak, Caughlan, Hallman, Renzi, & Rush, 2018). At that time, colleges long resisted teaching how to teach, with many of their leaders determining that subject matter content knowledge was the only knowledge that mattered (Atkinson, 1897). This opinion persists today (see Kramer, 1991) despite research supporting that teachers with both pedagogical and subject-specific content knowledge are more effective (Ball, Thames, & Phelps, 2008).

Apart from the numbers of all people who now remain in K–12 school and eventually go on to postsecondary education, 52% of all students are projected to be people of color with different cultural, economic, linguistic, racial, and ethnic needs than those learning the English language arts before them (AACTE, 2018). Therefore, school districts have acknowledged a need for a teacher workforce that is responsive to the racial, cultural, ability, economic, and linguistic diversity represented in U.S. classrooms (Sleeter, 2011).

It is important throughout this book that we acknowledge changes in the subject of English language arts in today's K–12 classrooms, as English language arts is characterized by a number of changing foci. The influence of technology, the emphasis on both literacy and literature, the diversity of students within today's K–12 schools, the expansion of field experiences within teacher education programs, and the emphasis on standards and standardization all constitute an ELA that is different today than it was in the field's past (Caughlan, Pasternak, Hallman, Renzi, Rush, & Frisby, 2017).

These changes can best be understood in relation to the 1995 study published as *How English Teachers Get Taught* by Peter Smagorinsky and Melissa Whiting. This national study of English teacher preparation in the United States guided the field for more than twenty years. This, and other large studies from this period (e.g., Applebee, 1996; Nystrand, 1997), provided accounts of how secondary English teaching operated in the United States that are still cited as definitive accounts of how English language arts content is learned and taught today.

However, in the twenty-plus years since the Smagorinsky and Whiting (1995) study, English teacher education programs and coursework have developed in contextually dependent ways that have been driven by institutional, economic, social, and political considerations (Pasternak, Caughlan, Hallman, Renzi, & Rush, 2014). Today, English teacher education programs must pay increased attention to the tensions that have resulted from these new pressures, and teacher educators must be more attentive to their own program commitments and how these are manifested within the education of teachers at their own institutions.

These demographic and content changes then require English teachers to meet the needs of all their students and, hence, for English teacher educators to address those needs in the coursework and experiences they provide to their teacher candidates. Consequently, this book focuses on the tensions that emerge in teaching the ELA methods course within teacher education programs today. Chapters in the book grapple with both the historical legacies that influence the methods/pedagogy course and the contemporary challenges that are components of teaching the ELA methods courses within teacher education programs.

TEACHING OF THE ENGLISH LANGUAGE ARTS METHODS COURSE

Sometimes referred to as the *didactics* or *pedagogy* course in other countries, the subject-specific English language arts methods course in the United States is where prospective teachers learn how to teach the school subject of English language arts: literature, composition, grammar, linguistics, speech, drama, and the multimodal/multiliteracies, as they emerge with literacy advances.

Often situated within the larger context of teacher certification programs within institutions of higher education, the methods course typically exists as one or more classes within a teacher education program. We draw on Pasternak, Caughlan, Hallman, Renzi, and Rush's (2018) definition of the subject-specific methods course as

> primarily focusing on the representation and teaching of English language arts content. A methods course often also involves inquiry into the beliefs or opinions of participants regarding concepts of English language arts at the secondary level, the planning of lessons or courses of study, and classroom management related to content-specific methods. Courses providing background in English content for teacher candidates should not be regarded as methods courses for the purposes of answering these questions if the focus is not on how to teach the content. (p. 25)

The choice to focus this book on the English methods course arose from the belief that the methods course is positioned as the primary site for English teachers' pedagogical content knowledge (Ball, Thames, & Phelps, 2008; Grossman, 1990; Shulman, 1987), a space where prospective teachers develop knowledge, skills, and aptitude for teaching within their content domain. Furthermore, the importance of subject-specific methods, especially in relation to constructivist and social constructivist theories of learning that apply to both learning to teach and the learning of teacher candidates' pupils, is still relevant in today's teacher education programs.

Teachers must understand their subject matter both as disciplinary adepts and as their students experience it, with the goal of moving students toward mastery of relevant academic performances (Darling-Hammond & Bransford, 2005; Dewey, 1902). It is important that teachers use their relatively brief time in professional education to develop metacognition and effective practices specific to the disciplines they will teach in their classrooms.

The methods course in English teacher education programs bears key responsibility for helping teacher candidates address current issues in ELA and classroom contexts. The English methods course is where teacher candidates take the content they have learned about literature, linguistics, writing, and so forth, and turn the focus of that content to teaching secondary students. At the time of the publication of Smagorinsky and Whiting's study (1995), ELA programs predominantly had one three-credit methods course that was required of their certification of teacher candidates, in a few cases abetted by specific courses about the teaching of writing, literature, language, young adult literature, and related topics. The default course, then, was a comprehensive, subject-specific methods course that covered the teaching of all aspects of ELA content.

Now, programs vary as much in their requirements of methods courses as they do in the types and numbers of programs they have in general (Pasternak et al., 2018). The default of one subject-specific methods course, common in earlier generations and assumed in the design of Smagorinsky and Whiting's study, is no longer the standard. In the current era, bachelor's programs, as well as the other levels of certification, require four or more credits of methods courses (Pasternak et al., 2018). Although a greater percentage of bachelor's programs require seven or more hours of ELA methods, only alternative certification programs deviate from this standard, with some not requiring a subject-specific methods course at all. This shift may be indicative of how the program defines a subject-specific methods course, as discussed above.

A need for attention to a program's commitments has been the catalyst for this book, a commitment often determined by its resources, faculty expertise, or infrastructure. In the chapters that follow, English teacher educators hone in on tensions, commitments, and future directions for English teacher education by highlighting the issues that current English teacher educators confront in educating future teachers of English.

Collectively, the chapters in the book work to highlight tensions that English teacher educators face in teaching the English language arts methods course. In so doing, chapters focus on describing a "tension" or "dilemma" that the chapter author has faced when teaching the middle/secondary ELA methods course. To foster discussion about these tensions, the book provides critical responses to each chapter from another English educator as a way to problematize how English language arts methods courses are taught in various teacher education programs throughout the United States and how context can underscore the physical, theoretical, or philosophical commitment a program makes to the future teachers it educates.

It is the examination and discussion of a program's framework, practices, or communities that clarifies how vibrant and dynamic English teacher education is as a field. It is our hope that such a format encourages a view of how English teacher education is context dependent and ever changing.

OVERVIEW OF BOOK

Frameworks for English Education

The opening section of the book begins with chapters that pose important questions and considerations about how we approach teaching English language arts within methods courses. Chapter 1, "Educating Teachers for Critical Pragmatism: Methods as a 'Conceptual Home Base,'" by Lauren Gatti, Sarah Thomas, Jessica Masterson, Robert Brooke, and Rachael Wendler-Shah, explores the contrasts that sometimes occur between how preservice teachers are guided within university-based methods courses and what teaching methods and models they may encounter in middle/secondary school sites. Through the concept of *critical pragmatism*, a stance that embodies a commitment to democracy and justice enacted through practical means, the chapter suggests ways to assist preservice teachers in working productively to address these mismatches.

The response to this chapter, written by Melissa Schieble, underscores the need for preservice teachers to be keenly aware of the dimensions of the local context in which they teach. Schieble points out practical ways that teacher educators can assist preservice teachers in developing this kind of awareness.

Chapter 2, "Enduring Assignments in the Methods Course: Lesson Planning and Microteaching as Trigger Points for Stimulating Social Justice Teaching," by Terri Rodriguez, addresses the critical question of what social justice teaching is, what it looks like in practice, and how best to prepare teachers for this goal. Through a case study of one English language arts methods course, this chapter examines how opportunities are both afforded and missed for teacher candidates to develop and practice the knowledge, skills, and dispositions associated with social justice teaching.

The response, authored by Allison Wynhoff Olsen, expands upon the sometimes "missed opportunities" that Rodriguez discusses in the chapter, and urges teacher educators to adopt practices that urge them to adopt change in their pedagogy.

Chapter 3, "Exploring Tensions During Critical Conversations About Race in English Education," by Amy Vetter and Melissa Schieble, poses another framework that can engage preservice ELA teachers in teaching for social justice. This chapter explores ways in which English preservice teachers engage in critical conversations during an English language arts methods course. Specifically, the chapter authors explore how preservice teachers discussed one specific tension related to responding to racialized jokes and name-calling in and outside the classroom.

The chapter's response, written Lauren Gatti, builds upon the idea that, as teacher educators, we are able to interrupt these moments through the choices we make in facilitating conversations.

The opening three chapters intend to foster a view of frameworks that shape how we approach teaching the English language arts methods course. Each of these chapters, through frameworks of critical pragmatism, social justice teaching, and critical conversations, engenders an approach to ELA that values teacher and student agency. Such frameworks become new ways of seeing a changing discipline, and we value each for the proactive stance they take with working with both teachers and youth.

Practices in English Education

The second section of the book explores which pedagogical practices teacher educators choose to teach in the ELA methods course. With limited resources, time, and expertise, many English teacher educators select the content that scholarship demonstrates best supports a future teacher of English in a program. Decisions need to be made as to which concepts, skills, and dispositions are integral to the development of a teacher candidate. These choices are often difficult to make and are often dependent upon the expediency of the changing nature of the field itself. What do we keep, abandon, and hold on to?

In Chapter 4, "Writing in and for the 21st Century: Crossing Digital and Multimodal Thresholds in ELA Methods Courses," Amber Jensen examines the modes of academic writing valued by the discipline but considers the value of other modes not thought of as authentic writing. She notes there is a presumption that it is the English teacher's role to teach academic writing, a mode of writing that has its place but not the practicality of other modes favored outside academia. Jensen makes the case that preservice teachers must become advocates for 21st-century writing practices and, in doing so, explores how preservice teachers grapple with the habits of mind that will underscore their decision making as how to teach writing in their own classrooms.

Mike Metz's response addresses the need for preservice teachers to navigate a field that is continually changing, calling into question the prescriptive nature of writing assessments that privilege academic writing but do not account for creativity.

In Chapter 5, "Moving Preservice English Teachers From Egocentric to Sociocentric Readings," Crag Hill examines how to support preservice teachers to read texts in multiple ways, learning to support their future students to see differing viewpoints and use multiple perspectives to analyze a text that will enrich a reading and support future teachers to understand the simultaneous, synergistic nature of reading a text that expands worlds.

Chris Parsons's response questions how these concepts could be supported across disciplinary reading and how an English teacher might address teaching reading in this way.

In Chapter 6, "Powerful Influence and Absurd Neglect: The Legacy of Louise M. Rosenblatt in Secondary English Language Arts Methods Courses," Sue Ringler Pet grapples with the legacy of Rosenblatt as a staple of the ELA methods class. She details Rosenblatt's marginalization and misrepresentation over the years and makes a case for her continued prominence in the ELA methods course.

Crag Hill's response outlines a method with which to mitigate Rosenblatt's marginalization and misrepresentation. Moreover, he extends the knowledge base of teacher candidates as they explore close reading and New Criticism in relation to reader response.

In Chapter 7, "Teacher Candidates' Perspectives on Tensions Within the Methods-Based Field Experience," Chris Parsons discusses the tensions teacher candidates experience as they move theory into practice as they engage in field experiences that are concurrent with the ELA methods class.

Laura Renzi asks a series of questions that push us to think about moving theory to practice and the circumstances that support teacher candidates to adapt the *practice* lessons created in the methods class into learnable moments with K–12 students.

These four chapters critically explore which content is included in an ELA methods course, the ramifications of including it, and the awareness to keep the content dynamic and relevant to an ever-changing but sometimes stagnating field (Pasternak et al., 2018). Moving from teaching writing to the acts of reading and to how to read and whose theories and practices to follow, these chapters lead us to consider the communities of practice we ask teacher candidates to join to remain relevant.

COMMUNITIES OF ENGLISH EDUCATION

The third section of the book explores new visions for how English educators can situate the methods course within communities beyond their immediate institutions. These new models of community-based English education create opportunities for preservice teachers to learn and gain experience through purposeful engagement with professional development networks, service-learning partnerships, and innovative contexts for field placements.

In Chapter 8, "English Education Methods Courses as Sites of Induction Into English Teacher Communities of Practice," James Cercone and Kristen Pastore-Capuana outline how they developed the methods course as a place where preservice teachers enter into the larger English education community of practice (CoP) and how these experiences affected learning and teacher identity development. By reconceptualizing English education programs as "regional hubs," in-service and preservice teachers collaborate to reflect on coursework, develop curriculum, and engage in clinically rich practices that extend beyond methods. Amber Jensen's response to this chapter examines the potential challenges of this approach, such as workload and competing demands on English educators, while offering entry points to create meaningful cross-level and cross-institutional connections for programs that do not have an already established CoP in place.

In Chapter 9, "Tensions in ELA Field Experiences: Service-Learning Initiatives in Rural Contexts," Allison Wynhoff Olsen explores a three-year initiative to develop local and digital service-learning collaborations throughout her program's English language arts methods courses. Specifically, she discusses the tensions that emerge as preservice teachers collaborate with in-service teachers and students across contexts to investigate how prolonged engagement with these networks promotes reflection while mitigating rural teacher isolation.

Jamie Collins's response to Chapter 9 encourages English teacher educators to strategically create spaces in methods courses where preservice teachers engage in professional dialogue about balancing the academic and emotional demands of teaching.

In Chapter 10, "A Teaching Mythology: Disrupting the Tutor/Teacher Dichotomy," Heidi Hallman and Melanie Burdick explore tutoring and service learning in the methods field experience requirement. Advocating for early and diverse field experiences, the authors discuss how strategically reconceptualizing work in the field helps preservice teachers inquire into different teacher roles, relationships, and identities to question the *teacher as authority* conception.

In the response to Chapter 10, Terri Rodriguez iterates the need to reimagine field experience contexts to include nontraditional sites while examining the complex process of interrupting long-standing teaching mythologies.

As a collection, these 10 chapters and responses point to a way forward for English teacher educators to root methods coursework in meaningful clinical practice that extends beyond any given semester and provides support and professional development for teachers throughout their careers. Contextualizing this approach within a community-based, clinical framework suggests a reframing of English teacher education as a sociocultural process that draws heavily from established theoretical work in the field. In doing so, the link between clinical experiences and community-based approaches to preservice and in-service teacher education is clear.

REFERENCES

American Association of Colleges of Teacher Education. (2018). *Colleges of Education: A National Portrait*. Washington, D.C.: AACTE.

Applebee, A. N. (1996). *Curriculum as conversation: Transforming traditions of teaching and learning*. Chicago: University of Chicago Press.

Atkinson, F. W. (1897). *The Professional Preparation of Secondary Teachers in the United States*. Presented to the University of Leipzig for the degree of Doctor of Philosophy.

Ball, D. L., Thames, M. H., & Phelps, G. (2008). Content knowledge for teaching: What makes it special? *Journal of Teacher Education, 59*, 389–407.

Caughlan, S., Pasternak, D., Hallman, H. L., Renzi, L., Rush, L., & Frisby, M. (2017). How English language arts teachers are prepared for 21st century classrooms: Results of a national survey. *English Education, 49*(3), 265–297.

Cercone, J. (2009). We're smarter together: Building professional social networks in English education. *English Education, 41*(3), 199–206.

Conference on English Education. (2008). What do we know and believe about the roles of methods courses and field experiences in English education? Position statements. Retrieved from http://www.ncte.org.

Darling-Hammond, L., & Bransford, J. (2005). *Preparing teachers for a changing world: What teachers should learn and be able to do*. San Francisco: Jossey-Bass.

DeStigter, T. (1998). A good gang: Thinking small with preservice teachers in a Chicago barrio. *English Education, 31*(1), 65–87.

Dewey, J. (1902). *The child and the curriculum*. Chicago: University of Chicago Press.

Grossman, P. L. (1990). *The making of a teacher: Teacher knowledge and teacher education*. New York: Teachers College Press.

Hallman, H. L., & Burdick, M. N. (2011). Service-learning and the preparation of English teachers. *English Education, 43*(4), 341–368.

Kramer, R. (1991). *Ed school follies: The miseducation of America's teachers*. New York: Free Press.

Nystrand, M. (with Gamoran, A., Kachur, R., & Prendergast, C.). (1997). *Opening dialogue: Understanding the dynamics of language and learning in the English classroom*. New York: Teachers College Press.

Pasternak, D. L., Caughlan, S., Hallman, H., Renzi, L. and Rush, L. (2014). Teaching English language arts methods in the United States: A review of the research. *Review of Education, 2*(2), 146–185.

Pasternak, D. L., Caughlan, S., Hallman, H. L., Renzi, L., & Rush, L. S. (2018). *Secondary English teacher education in the United States: Responding to a changing context*. New York: Bloomsbury.

Popkewitz, T. (1994). Professionalization in teaching and teacher education: Some notes on its history, ideology, and potential. *Teaching and Teacher Education, 10*(1), 1–14.

Rush, L. S. (2009). Developing a story of theory and practice: Multigenre writing in English teacher education. *Teacher Educator, 44*(3), 204–221.

Shulman, L. S. (1987). Knowledge and teaching: Foundations of the new reform. *Harvard Educational Review, 57*, 1–22.

Sleeter, C. E. (2011). An agenda to strengthen culturally responsive pedagogy. *English Teaching: Practice and Critique*, 10(2), 7–23.

Smagorinsky, P., & Whiting, M. E. (1995). *How English teachers get taught: Methods of teaching the methods class*. Urbana, IL: Conference on English Education and National Council of Teachers of English.

Smith, E. R., & Anagnostopoulos, D. (2008). Developing pedagogical content knowledge for literature-based discussions in a cross-institutional network. *English Education, 41*, 39–65.

Part I

Frameworks for English Education

Chapter One

Educating Teachers for Critical Pragmatism

Methods as a "Conceptual Home Base"

Lauren Gatti, Sarah Thomas, Jessica Masterson, Robert Brooke, and Rachael Wendler-Shah

In exploring how differences in curriculum in the middle and high school grades affect approaches to secondary English education, a central tension must be acknowledged: Teacher educators tend to educate preservice teachers for an idealized educational landscape—one in which they enjoy hearty amounts of both professional autonomy and institutional support—when in reality, public education has largely embraced the categorical opposites: curricular standardization and institutional opposition to new initiatives (i.e., Kim, 2018). What, then, are English teacher educators to do about this discrepancy? How are they to respond to curricular demands about which they might have grave concerns?

In this chapter, we authors detail the changing curricular emphases for middle and secondary literacy and English courses in the Crestview School District (all district, school, and teacher names are pseudonyms) and discuss how the awareness and understanding of these emphases has shifted the English teacher education program's approach to English teacher education at Great Plains University (GPU), the flagship university located in the same city. Additionally, the authors explain the goals of their English education program at GPU, namely, its focus on certifying critical, creative, and pedagogically flexible teachers.

Because the sorts of curricular changes occurring in local contexts are not separate from larger currents of educational reform, the situation described in this chapter is likely not unique; as such, we build on Smagorinsky, Cook, and Johnson's (2003) scholarship outlining how shifting the focus from theory-practice divides to conceptual development might afford teacher educators an opportunity to consider how programs might cohere around particular commitments and concepts for teaching.

Specifically, we advance the concept of *critical pragmatism*, a stance that embodies a commitment to democracy and justice enacted through practical means that other English teacher educators, faced with similar challenges, might find helpful.

TOWARD A CONCEPTUAL HOME BASE

In their work on concept development and learning to teach, Smagorinsky, Cook, and Johnson (2003) illustrate how Vygotsky's (1987) notion of concepts might enable a more robust and less binary (theory versus practice) approach to teachers' development. In his work, Vygotsky (1987) understood the development of thinking by delineating between concepts, pseudo-concepts, and complexes. Concepts, the most robust and sophisticated of the three, is "the height of intellectual activity because formal, abstracted knowledge of a situation enables one to reapply it to a new situation" (Smagorinsky, Cook, & Johnson, 2003, p. 1403).

A teacher education program, then, should be concerned with the ways in which the different parts of the program—coursework, field experiences, and so forth—help students develop unified concepts around a particular approach to teaching (discussion-based teaching or constructivism, for example). This is often very difficult to do given the common fragmentation of teacher education programs (see Zeichner & Gore, 1990).

Drawing from their research on learning to teach, Smagorinsky, Cook, and Johnson (2003) found that "while students in the elementary program at the same university all espoused constructivism . . . we found no consistent terms coming from the secondary English cohort to characterize their approach to teaching" (p. 1422). In other words, the participants in their study were exposed to constructivism throughout their program, but without shared understandings and definitions of this concept, students could not appropriate the concept of constructivism in ways that would enable them to apply it to new and different settings. Thus, there was "no unified concept of teaching" (p. 1422).

Approaching a teacher education program as a "conceptual home base" (Smagorinsky, 2002) is an important and promising way to reduce the likelihood that novice teachers enter the profession lacking a unified concept of teaching:

> We used the term *conceptual home base* to describe a community of practice whose ideas are powerful enough to inspire ideological loyalty and enduring,

if ever-developing, beliefs about teaching. As we have argued, the university may serve as practitioners' conceptual home base if it effectively teaches conceptions that its graduates find powerful and useful in the classroom. (Smagorinsky, Cook, & Johnson, 2003, p. 1428)

Embracing this notion of a conceptual home base for teachers first entails examining the ways in which concepts are (or are not) enacted in K–12 classrooms at present. This concept is detailed in the following section in discussion of the educational landscape within the Crestview School District, with particular attention paid to the cognitive dissonance experienced by GPU preservice teachers.

ACCOUNTABILITY-CENTERED EDUCATION IN MIDDLE AND HIGH SCHOOL ENGLISH CLASSES

The Crestview School District serves upward of 40,000 students and is well regarded nationally for its success in providing a high-quality educational experience for students. This success is especially notable given that parents and guardians in the district are able to freely select the public schools their children will attend. The district is the second largest in the state, and it is increasing in diversity, with 33% minority students and 46% of students enrolled in the free and reduced-lunch program. Students in the district speak more than 50 different languages, with a particular prevalence of Spanish, Arabic, Kurdish, and Karen.

The district offers both traditional schools and small focus programs, such as a science-focused Zoo School, that allow for active and portfolio-based learning. Additionally, the state is one of the few in the nation that has refused to formally adopt the Common Core State Standards (CCSS). Instead, the state has adopted a set of English/language arts standards that meet and exceed the CCSS in coverage. These standards are assessed within the state's new five-point assessment program for schools. Student performance on curricular goals, including reading and writing, are one of the items on the five-point program.

In recent decades, the city of Crestview has welcomed thousands of refugees from all over the world, and the Crestview School District has adopted policy changes and programs to better serve this population of students, some of whom have had limited experiences with formal schooling but are nonetheless held to district-wide graduation requirements.

In the name of ensuring students are making progress toward educational goals, the district has enacted a set of practices that require that teachers adopt common texts and assessments. The data-driven nature of these practices go hand in hand with the work of school-based professional learning communities (PLCs), which comprise small groups of teachers of the same content who meet weekly to discuss trends in the student data they've collected and report this data to the district.

Although these initiatives have been implemented with the best of intentions, and with student learning at their center, they bear a striking resemblance to the "accountability regimes" (Biesta, 2004) that affect public education elsewhere in the country. In the following section, we explore how GPU's preservice teachers and program graduates encounter, understand, and challenge conceptions of literacy and the larger purposes of English in Crestview's middle and high school classrooms.

LEARNING TO TEACH ENGLISH IN THE CRESTVIEW SCHOOL DISTRICT

On the Crestview School District's official website, the English language arts coordinators acknowledge the centrality of English language mastery to learning in schools. Their mission invokes democratic aims and economic realities and underscores a commitment to educating informed citizens who are capable of critical analysis.

These stated goals are not altogether distinct from the GPU English education program; indeed, they are quite complementary. However, the ways in which these goals are (and are not) actualized in classrooms are another matter. As LeAnn, a preservice teacher completing a practicum at a local middle school in the Crestview district, recalled, "A girl yesterday was like, 'Can't we just like get up and move?' And I was just like, 'Yeah! I would love to.' [*Exhales*] I don't know, I just . . . some of the lessons that you know, it's been a lot of worksheets so far. So . . . not my biggest . . . thing, but I don't know."

Central to Crestview's middle school English curriculum is a focus on the elements of fiction. The common assessment used by the district that the preservice teachers who are placed in "nondifferentiated" (i.e., not advanced) middle school classrooms are also required to use is a plot diagram, the separate parts of which all students are expected to memorize. This triangular plot diagram requires students to identify basic elements of literature: setting, rising action, climax, falling action, resolution, and theme. As a result, the reading process is reduced to observing art as a fill-in-the-blanks formula.

Moreover, the intensifying pressure to produce high scores on this assessment has led some teachers to adopt a rote, almost myopic focus on teaching these skills in isolation. Charlotte, another GPU preservice teacher, illustrated this phenomenon in the context of her own practicum experience.

> At [my middle school], we had the elements of fiction chart that you have to do for all English classes in seventh grade, and it was so boring and I know that they have to know it because they have to do some district- or state-type

thing where they have to be able to fill one out. But the way that my [cooperating teacher] went around doing it . . . she just would always give the worksheet and [say], "Okay, start filling it out." And I know I don't want to do that.

For Charlotte, a budding recognition of the pressures faced by her cooperating teacher, as well as a conscious decision to act *differently* in her own classroom, is apparent in these reflections.

At the high school level, many GPU preservice teachers and recent program graduates teach remedial reading classes, which educate students to pass the Graduate Demonstration of Reading (GDR), a reading proficiency assessment that, as the name implies, is a requirement for graduation districtwide. The tiered reading classes, which individually focus on literal, inferential, or critical comprehension, feature frequent summative assessments in addition to test preparation in advance of the GDR.

Brie, a preservice student in English education at GPU, completed her fall practicum in two reading classes at two different high schools within the Crestview school district. In her weekly reflections, the cognitive dissonance she experienced between the reading curriculum she was required to teach and the approaches to teaching reading that she was learning in her methods class became increasingly apparent. Below, she discusses the disconnect between the approach to teaching reading comprehension detailed in Kylene Beers's (2003) *When Kids Can't Read: What Teachers Can Do* and that of the reading classes she observed:

> "Comprehension as a process, not a product" (Beers, 2003, p. 139). I don't know if I'm entitled to this opinion since I've only seen a glimpse of reading classrooms and curriculum from our practicum, but I believe our district has this totally backwards. Beers has detailed so many prereading, during reading, and now postreading strategies for students who struggle [with] reading.
>
> The Beers text excites me and yet leaves me feeling frustrated and confused with what is actually happening in reading classes in our district. The curriculum could provide many opportunities for these strategies, which are intended to engage students in reading in addition to giving them reading supports, but instead it is heavily focused on comprehension as the product.
>
> Our students spend entire class periods answering multiple choice comprehension questions following a nonfiction article to practice for the GDR weekly. They spend entire blocks writing literal, inferential, and critical essays over books they have not read. And I attribute this to the approach the district has taken and the inflexibility teachers have to put *reading* first in the *reading* classroom.

Taken together, the construction of reading comprehension as a product in high school reading classes (which builds on the frequency of worksheets students experience in their middle school English classes) promotes a narrow view of literacy that exists in tension with the goals of the GPU English education program. Given the aforementioned Crestview district goals, which prominently feature democratic aims and underscore a commitment to educating informed citizens who are capable of critical analysis, a dissonant juxtaposition exists. While the district claims it values a critical engagement with text toward amplified democratic participation, its practices reinforce the opposite.

This is not a function of different commitments on behalf of the district and GPU's English education program, nor is it a function of different motives wherein one group values student learning and engagement and the other does not. But at the same time, the differences in approach are real and, in many instances, substantial. Given these tensions, what are the ways forward for English teacher educators? How might these differences be addressed?

A WAY FORWARD: CRITICAL PRAGMATISM IN THE ENGLISH METHODS CLASS

The tension highlighted is a complex one. As such, the response from teacher educator programs must be similarly multifaceted. In our case, numerous adaptations have been made to better educate English education students for the realities of the classrooms they will likely enter. In an effort to build partnership and coherence between the district and the university, GPU faculty members connect with district personnel responsible for secondary English professional development decisions to see which texts will be used that academic year with Crestview's English teachers. When possible, GPU chooses that text for inclusion for methods.

For example, when the district selected Kylene Beers and Robert Probst's (2012) book, *Notice and Note: Strategies for Close Reading*, GPU English education students also read this book at the start of their semester. This shared text allowed for practicum students and Crestview cooperating teachers to begin their semesters together with a shared language for teaching close reading strategies. Additionally, the English education faculty at GPU works intentionally to cultivate and maintain strong, positive relationships with district teachers and administrators through regular meetings and coordination efforts.

However, the momentum and increasing intractability of the data-driven curricular reforms in the Crestview School District has meant that the two-course methods sequence at GPU has necessarily begun to operate as a crucial site for developing in its preservice teachers a stance of *critical pragmatism*, which serves as the conceptual home base for the GPU English education program.

This concept, derived from Cornel West's (1989) formulation of *prophetic pragmatism*, posits that preservice teachers must be "future-oriented" in their efforts and outlook, and must act in ways that advance the "moral aim of enriching individuals and expanding democracy" (West, 1989, p. 5). In West's view, change requires a clear-eyed view of the nature and status of social injustice at present (what he terms bearing "prophetic witness"), while still moving forward despite seemingly insurmountable challenges ("tragicomic hope") (West, 2004).

The critically pragmatic teacher, in the view of the GPU English education instructional staff, is one who is able to thoughtfully navigate the accountability demands in public education and works to strike a democratic balance between complying with district demands and actively interrogating the assumptions from which they emanate. The critically pragmatic teacher, then, walks the line between compliant subject and inquisitive agent.

The commitment to critical pragmatism is evident in three key practices of the GPU English education program: explicit instruction in planning justice-oriented lessons; the assignment of regular, critical reflections that engage educational theories and issues of practice; and a commitment to an ongoing dialogue between GPU preservice teachers and graduates of the program who currently serve as English teachers in the Crestview School District. Each of these practices will now be described in turn.

Lesson Planning in Critical, Creative, Ethical, and Caring Ways

Within our English education program at GPU, extended discussions about the program's core values have taken place over the past six years among a cadre of instructors in the English and education departments. Through these conversations, and influenced by the scholarship of philosopher Daniel Lipman (2003), they have developed four domains of teacher practice that constitute the pillars of the program. These domains concern the *critical*, *creative*, *ethical*, and *caring* dimensions of the work of teaching, and relatedly, they emphasize a sociocultural, constructivist approach to teaching and learning.

Within each domain, preservice teachers are taught to approach lesson planning by accounting for several generative questions. Perhaps most importantly, the observation protocol that the GPU faculty has developed is grounded in these domains (see Table 1.1). This protocol was intended to concretize and make visible the ways in which day-to-day teaching practices—facilitating discussion, framing a lesson's import, and so forth—are linked to central concepts of GPU's program, namely, critical pragmatism.

Beyond the program-wide, recursive usage of these teaching domains, preservice teachers learn the orientation of critical pragmatism through taking part in a range of field experiences that are coordinated with a number of

Table 1.1. Abridged Observation Protocol at GPU

Domain	Central questions	Resources for development
Critical	Is the larger purpose (i.e., the *why?* or *so what?*) of the lesson's topic explicit, engaging, and relevant?	Applebee, A. (1996). *Curriculum as Conversation*.
	Is the topic presented in a way that invites authentic thinking and problem solving?	Appleman, D. (2015). *Critical Encounters in High School English: Teaching Literary Theory to Adolescents*.
	Are students asked to consider multiple points of views, definitions, and/or perspectives?	Hillocks, G. (1995). *Teaching Writing as Reflective Practice*.
		hooks, b. (2009). *Teaching Critical Thinking: Practical Wisdom*.
Creative	Does the lesson create purposeful and relevant space for visual, verbal, or kinesthetic invention?	McCallum, A. (2012). *Creativity and Learning in Secondary English: Teaching for a Creative Classroom*.
	Does the lesson tap into more than one way of understanding an issue?	Robinson, K. (2001). *Out of Our Minds: Learning to Be Creative*.
	Do students have enough time to engage the creative process (to prepare, elaborate on their ideas, reach insight, revise, and reflect)?	Serafini, F. (2013). *Reading the Visual: An Introduction to Teaching Multimodal Literacy*.

Domain	Central questions	Resources for development
Ethical	Is the lesson constructed with a range of learners (and learners who have different levels of motivation and ability) in mind?	Beers, K. (2003). *When Kids Can't Read: What Teachers Can Do.*
		Gallagher, C., & Lee, A. (2008) *Teaching Writing that Matters: Tools and Projects that Motivate Adolescent Writers.*
	Does the lesson invite authentic, structured, and sustained student conversation about a text?	
		McCann, T. M., Johannessen, L., Kahn, E., & Flanagan, J. (2006) *Talking in Class: Using Discussion to Enhance Teaching.*
	Is the lesson designed to foreground student voice, application, and experimentation?	
Caring	Is the classroom a space of warmth, safety, and stimulation?	Fay, J. & Funk, D. (1995). *Teaching with Love and Logic.*
	Does the teacher notice and effectively attend to relational aspects of teaching and learning during difficult classroom occurrences? Do the difficulties turn into teachable moments?	hooks, b. (1994) *Teaching to Transgress: Education as the Practice of Freedom.*
		Noddings, N. *The Challenge to Care in Schools* (2005) and *Caring: A Relational Approach to Ethics and Moral Education* (2003).

local school districts and are explicitly connected to their methods coursework. These field experiences include an informal eight-week practicum with English language learners (ELLs) at a linguistically diverse high school (16 hours), a virtual partnership with a rural district in the state (14 hours), and a reading and writing partnership with students in a 10th-grade classroom at a culturally and socioeconomically diverse high school (18 hours).

The coordinated field experiences and courses that undergraduates experience in the program reflect a larger collaborative effort on behalf of the faculty from both the GPU English and the teacher education departments, as well as advanced doctoral students who coordinate and teach in the program. Through this collaboration, instructors work to frame lesson planning at all stages of the program as an act of critical pragmatism.

Critical Notebook Reflections in Methods I

The methods courses not only provide a crucial site in which preservice teachers are acquiring and honing their pedagogical content knowledge but also offer a space where cognitive dissonance experienced by students like Brie, LeAnn, and Charlotte can be drawn out and overtly discussed. As students begin to piece together the local realities of teaching English, methods courses prioritize this intellectual development.

One way in which this development is encouraged is through using weekly reflections (called Notebooks) that require students to synthesize their field experiences alongside educational theory and scholarship. The specific topics are up to preservice teachers to decide for themselves; the only general requirement is that they are one to two single-spaced pages in length, and that they explicitly engage key concepts presented in course readings and their own field experiences.

Taylor, a preservice teacher in the GPU English education program, used the Notebook to link a practicum experience teaching *To Kill a Mockingbird* (Lee, 1960) to ninth graders with the array of ideas presented in the Methods II course, in tandem with concepts from educational psychology.

> "Can a jury ever be totally unbiased?" My question hung crisp in the air, feather-fluttering a few seconds to thud in my anxiety chest. Rephrase. A few meager nibbles. "There are no right answers," I clarified to wide, black-and-white, expectant eyes. "We are just discussing; I am asking for your opinions." The structure of a dialogic classroom and the modeling I perform in front of 24 young teenagers becomes apparent in the responses I receive; it is also wildly obvious how adolescent development and the conditioning of a traditional banking model (Freire, 1987) or "frontal" model (McCann, Johannessen, Kahn, & Flanagan, 2006) play into my need to expand and disrupt what came before my classroom. Through watching the thinking moves of my cooperating teacher, Paul, and my current educational psychology class, I've been able to glean specifics on how to foster a community of inquiry (Lipman, 2003)—important to my overall goals of fostering the growth of my students into prepared and engaged democratic citizens.

In Taylor's words, there is evidence of a budding criticality, as accented in the stated desire to educate and engage democratic citizens through actively disrupting the banking model of education. In these ways, Notebooks not only promote the habit of reflective practice but also provide the raw material for productive dialogue toward critical pragmatism.

Fostering Preservice and In-Service Teacher Dialogue in Methods I and II

Finally, the shared vision of the GPU English education instructors requires that preservice teachers understand their primary professional role is to act in the best interest of students. Though as future teachers they will necessarily be required to "manage the plural politics of schools" (see Siebert, Dowding, Quigley, Bills, & Brooke, 1997), they must do so with the needs of their students always in mind. This point is underscored throughout the methods sequence by including the perspectives of recent program graduates in activities and projects.

These recent graduates, often in their first or second year of teaching, are invited back to methods classes to discuss their own transition into the role of teacher. In past years, program graduates have shared the Crestview School District curriculum binders they were issued as new teachers with the preservice teachers in Methods I, and have discussed their own approaches to making curricular and pedagogical adjustments with their students.

The value of this practice was highlighted by Jeanette, a GPU preservice teacher, who remarked on the insight she gleaned with regard to the concept of backward design (Wiggins & McTighe, 2005) when Mara, a recent GPU graduate and current middle school teacher, visited the Methods I class.

> While having [essential] questions to frame the entire year is useful, there is also value in having students generate their own questions with our guidance and scaffolding. When Mara from Central Middle School visited our class, she mentioned that after the literature circles with the nonfiction texts, her class will transition to a unit about being an "upstander" rather than a bystander. In order to transition to that unit, she says that she wants to plant the seeds from now until then.... Mara explained, "When the students see an idea that I have, it's sort of interesting, but when they come to the idea on their own, it's fascinating for them." Her strategy is an interesting example of experiences that "naturally" transition from accumulation of experiences and questions.

In addition to offering a window into how theoretical concepts can be actualized in practice, other graduates have provided critical feedback on preservice teachers' unit plans in Methods II, and still others have been involved in an array of small partnerships wherein GPU preservice teachers hone skills such as providing substantive feedback on students' writing and workshopping instructional strategies. Offering students access to models of current Crestview teachers that are actively navigating district requirements in creative ways prepares students to think of themselves as critical pragmatists.

Mentor teachers in the Crestview district are recruited and selected through coordination efforts made by the professor of practice in the English education program. Through the selection process each term, the professor of practice confers with her or his tenure-lined English education colleague to finalize the field experiences. As a former high school English teacher within the district, the professor of practice draws from funds of knowledge and continued professional ties with the district to enable thoughtful, intentional matches of preservice and in-service colleagues. Contextualized knowledge and nuanced relationships built over time, informing practicum, and student teaching placements are crucial factors toward ensuring a conceptual home base is reinforced and extended into the field.

Three lines of inquiry are considered with each preservice and in-service teacher pairing: (1) Does the mentor teacher enact a critical praxis—the melding of theory and practice—in approaching instructional leadership and decision making in the classroom? (2) Do the mentor teacher's pedagogical practices align with asset-based views of students and communities? And (3) does the mentor teacher embrace the creative process in teaching and learning while affording sufficient room, oversight, and effective coaching abilities to guide a novice teacher? With these conditions accounted for, the stage is set for an educative experience for both mentors and preservice teachers alike.

EDUCATING CRITICALLY PRAGMATIC EDUCATORS

Underlying these commitments at GPU to educating critical, creative, ethical, and caring educators through their varied experiences in methods classes is the firm belief that if preservice teachers are familiar with the disconnect between what they have learned through their GPU coursework and what they may be asked to do in their future roles—and have had ample space to practice balancing these at times conflicting messages—they are likely to be more effective educators on the whole.

The English language arts (ELA) classroom is, currently, a contested site in which a particular view of ELA and literacy learning—one that is sometimes antithetical to widely accepted scholarship on best practices—has taken hold. For English teacher educators, the English methods class might be productively envisioned not only as a place where preservice teachers are encouraged to consider what is *possible* in secondary English classrooms but also as a place to observe, interrogate, and critique what is currently happening in schools.

Through the lens of critical pragmatism, which provides the "conceptual home base" of the GPU English education program, we seek to educate English teachers to maneuver the educational landscape with the ultimate aim of ensuring enriching, equity-minded learning experiences for secondary English students.

REFERENCES

Applebee, A. (1996). *Curriculum as conversation: Transforming traditions of teaching and learning.* Chicago: University of Chicago Press.

Appleman, D. (2015). *Critical encounters in high school English: Teaching literary theory to adolescents.* New York: Teachers College Press.

Beers, K. (2003). *When kids can't read: What teachers can do.* Portsmouth, NH: Heinemann.

Beers, K., & Probst, R. (2012). *Notice and Note: Strategies for Close Reading.*

Biesta, G. J. (2004). Education, accountability, and the ethical demand: Can the democratic potential of accountability be regained? *Educational Theory, 54*(3), 233–250.

Fay, J. & Funk, D. (1995). *Teaching with love and logic: Taking control of the classroom.* Golden, CO: Love & Logic Press.

Freire, P. (1970). *Pedagogy of the oppressed.* London: Bloomsbury.

Gallagher, C., & Lee, A. (2008). *Teaching writing that matters: Tools and projects that motivate adolescent writers.* New York: Scholastic Press.

Hillocks, G. (1995). *Teaching writing as reflective practice.* New York: Teachers College Press.

hooks, b. (1994). *Teaching to transgress: Education as the practice of freedom.* New York: Routledge.

hooks, b. (2009). *Teaching critical thinking: Practical wisdom.* New York: Routledge.

Kim, J. (2018). School accountability and standard-based education reform: The recall of the social efficiency movement and scientific management. *International Journal of Educational Development, 60*, 80–87.

Lee, H. (1960/1988). *To kill a mockingbird.* New York: Harper Collins.

Lipman, M. (2003). *Thinking in education.* Cambridge: University of Cambridge Press.

McCallum, A. (2012). *Creativity and learning in secondary English: Teaching for a creative classroom.* New York: Routledge.

McCann, T. M., Johannessen, L., Kahn, E., & Flanagan, J. (2006). *Talking in class: Using discussion to enhance teaching.* Urbana, IL: NCTE.

Noddings, N. (2003/2013). *Caring: A relational approach to ethics and moral education.* Berkeley: University of California Press.

Noddings, N. (2005). *The challenge to care in schools.* New York: Teachers College Press.

Robinson, K. (2001/2011). *Out of our minds: Learning to be creative.* Chichester, UK: Capstone.

Serafini, F. (2013). *Reading the visual: An introduction to teaching multimodal literacy.* New York: Teachers College Press.

Siebert, S., Dowding, R., Quigley, S., Bills, M., & Brooke, R. (1997). Between student and teacher roles: Negotiating curricula during teacher training. In G. Tayko & J. P. Tassoni (Eds.), *Sharing pedagogies: Students and teachers write about dialogic practices.* Portsmouth, NH: Boynton/Cook.

Smagorinsky, P. (2002). *Teaching English through principled practice.* Upper Saddle River, NJ: Merrill/Prentice Hall.

Smagorinsky, P., Cook, L. S., & Johnson, T. S. (2003). The twisting path of concept development in learning to teach. *Teachers College Record, 105*(8), 1399–1436.

Vygotsky, L. S. (1987). Thinking and speech. In R. Rieber & A. Carton (Eds.) and N. Minick (Trans.), *Collected works.* New York: Plenum.

West, C. (1989). *The American evasion of philosophy: A genealogy of pragmatism.* New York: Springer.

West, C. (2004). *Democracy matters: Winning the fight against imperialism.* New York: Penguin.

Wiggins, G. P., & McTighe, J. (2005). *Understanding by design.* Alexandria, VA: ASCD.

Zeichner, K. M., & Gore, J. M. (1990). Teacher socialization. In W. R. Houston (Ed.), *Handbook of Research on Teacher Education* (pp. 329–348). New York: MacMillan.

A Response to Chapter 1

Melissa Schieble

With the publication of this edited volume, it suffices to say teacher education exists in hard times. With multiple and competing pathways to certification, rank-and-file approaches to determining the quality of teacher education programs, and a general devaluing of the practice and scholarship in university-based teacher education, our roles as teacher educators require some redefining. We no longer (if ever) just educate teachers for the classroom; we prepare them to navigate a challenging neoliberal landscape as they begin or continue the journey of a professional educator.

One source of solace amid these tensions continues to bring me comfort: We do the direct work with the teachers of today and tomorrow in our programs. They are inspired (and inspire us) about their futures. They crave intellectual challenge. They are dedicated and enthusiastic about building caring relationships with young people to help them succeed in school and beyond.

The tensions that Gatti and colleagues' chapter raises resonate deeply for teachers, both novice and experienced, and teacher educators. Yet I read their work with growing enthusiasm for what the concept of critical pragmatism might offer us to productively exist within this tension. Thus, their response is organized around the concept of critical pragmatism as a "conceptual home base," giving us a generative way of thinking about spaces in educational institutions of which we at times feel confined. I conclude with two resources to support English educators in further contextualizing this work within their own contexts.

The problem of practice that opens this chapter is the central tension of the English methods class, that "teacher educators tend to educate preservice teachers for an idealized educational landscape—one in which they enjoy hearty amounts of both professional autonomy and institutional support" (p.

1). Gatti and colleagues' goal for preparing "critical, creative, and pedagogically flexible teachers" is the crux of the work we strive to do, yet I assume many others (like me) wonder what exactly our new teachers face as they graduate from our programs. I have increasingly come to redefine my role as preparing teachers to be advocates—for themselves, for students, and for families—and for the project of public education.

The concept of critical pragmatism gives us a way to understand the English methods course—and our programs—as the conceptual epicenter of supporting and preparing teachers to adopt an advocacy stance. As Gatti and colleagues state, "The critically pragmatic teacher . . . works to strike a democratic balance between complying with district demands and actively interrogating the assumptions from which they emanate" (p. 7).

As professional educators, meeting competing curricular demands while maintaining an ethical grounding to practice a pedagogy that is just for students and families is the crux of what makes teaching such a complex endeavor. Addressing the concept of critical pragmatism in the English methods class lays the epistemic groundwork for navigating these complex decisions with thoughtfulness and care for the communities with which we work.

Gatti and colleagues' chapter provides us with theoretical guidance about the construct of critical pragmatism and helpful ways the authors have integrated and implemented this work in their program. Therefore, in the remainder of this response, I offer two resources to extend their useful approach to help teachers notice, analyze, and problem-solve the pragmatic, philosophical, and ethical conundrums the examples from their chapter raise.

The first resource is local to my context in New York State, where English teachers are pressured to implement EngageNY curriculum (www.engageny.org) to adhere to the Common Core standards, a curriculum that demonstrates a supposed higher level of rigor for college and career readiness. My concerns with EngageNY are too extensive to develop in this response (namely, the devaluing of aesthetic response and overreliance on technocratic approaches to "close reading," among other issues).

Aside from these other issues, I have found one book chapter helpful in navigating "the compliant subject and inquisitive agent" positionality that teachers find themselves in when contemplating district or school leadership demands to follow this curriculum, for example. In the English methods course I teach, I ask students to read the chapter "Differentiating Literacy Instruction for Adolescents," by Zaline Roy-Campbell and Kelly Chandler-Olcott, and to use this chapter to analyze a module from EngageNY focused on *The Autobiography of Malcolm X*. The chapter provides teachers with support for differentiating an EngageNY unit for localized contexts—meeting the dual goals of a critically pragmatic approach to balance school-level curricular demands with students' needs and interests. A few sample questions to focus their analysis include the following:

- Read the first lesson for the unit. Identify and explain in your own words one pedagogical method or idea that you find helpful and interesting. Support your selection with evidence from course readings about why this method would motivate students and support their literacy growth.
- What might students struggle with if you were asked to teach this unit "by the book"?
- In the chapter, the fictional teacher Ms. Taylor differentiated a unit from EngageNY to meet the needs of her students. Consider the modifications that she made to the unit as a model for how you might revise this unit for your own future classroom. What is one change you would make to the unit based on suggestions from the chapter for differentiating literacy instruction for adolescents? Cite evidence from the chapter for support.

These questions help teacher candidates navigate the tensions that Gatti and colleagues describe and strike a balance regarding what is generative from the curriculum unit and how the teacher candidates might modify the unit based on principles from their program that focus on differentiation and culturally sustaining pedagogies. Building the knowledge and skills to navigate these tensions, as Gatti and colleagues remind me, must occur more often across our programs both in coursework and in the field.

A second resource was brought to my attention on a recent visit to a TESOL program at Kanda University in Tokyo, Japan. In a chapter describing their work with the practicum in a Japanese schooling context, students in this program complete what the authors call a Teaching Innovation Plan (TIP). This assignment requires students who are working full time in schools to "1) propose a large or small-scale change in their teaching contexts, 2) to make explicit or 'expose' the contextual factors that may inhibit their ability to carry out their change and 3) describe how they are going to address these obstacles" (Snyder, Hale, & Myskow, forthcoming, p. 10).

Like the EngageNY assignment described above, the TIP assignment helps teachers to identify, analyze, and problem-solve challenging policies or structures in the schools where they teach. This assignment supports an approach of critical pragmatism and helps us as teacher educators envision new opportunities to see ourselves and our teacher candidates as agents of change in educational contexts. Rather than cast aside confining policies or structures because we either disagree with them or assume they will change over time, these methods give us what we need to exist within these tensions in constructive and positive ways and develop the advocacy stance we need to be professional educators.

REFERENCES

Roy-Campbell, Z., & Chandler-Olcott, K. (2014). Differentiating literacy instruction for adolescents. In K. A. Hinchmann & H. K. Sheridan-Thomas (Eds.), *Best practices in adolescent literacy instruction* (pp. 330–347). New York: Guilford Press.

Snyder, B., Hale, C. C., & Myskow, G. (forthcoming). An in-service TESOL practicum in Japan. In A. Cirocki, I. Madyarov, & L. Baecher (Eds.), *Global perspectives on the practicum in TESOL* (pp. 1–18). Dordrecht, Netherlands: Springer.

Chapter Two

Enduring Assignments in the Methods Course

Lesson Planning and Microteaching as Trigger Points for Stimulating Social Justice Teaching

Terri L. Rodriguez

English teacher educators understand the urgency of teaching and assessing social justice dispositions and performances in teacher education, especially in light of the current political climate. However, they also continue to question what social justice teaching is, what it looks like in practice, and how to best educate teacher candidates for this goal.

The field of English teacher education has a strong history of attention to social justice teaching (see Alsup & Miller, 2014). This chapter extends the conversation and engages with several tensions in social justice–oriented English teacher education. These include the urgency of teaching and assessing dispositions and performances of preservice teachers; tensions related to how they are educated, especially at the program and course levels (Caughlan, Pasternak, Hallman, Renzi, Rush, & Frisby, 2017; Pasternak, Caughlan, Hallman, Renzi, & Rush, 2014); and questions about how typical "pedagog[ies] of assignments" (McDonald, 2008) within teacher education programs actually foster socially just dispositions and performances.

The chapter expands the findings of a study of one social justice–oriented English language arts (ELA) methods course and how opportunities to develop and practice social justice teaching were both afforded and missed (Rodriguez, Bohn-Gettler, & Israelson, in press). Discussion focuses on the design of two key assignments (microteaching and lesson planning), the dissonant teaching models that undergird them, and how these enable and constrain candidates' enactments of social justice teaching.

WHAT IS SOCIAL JUSTICE TEACHING?

Social justice teaching draws from theories and practices of critical multicultural education (Grant & Sleeter, 2006), culturally relevant teaching (Ladson-Billings, 2005; 2006), and equity literacy (Gorski, 2013; Gorski & Swalwell, 2015; Swalwell, 2013). Although distinct, these approaches are complementary. Taken together, they offer insights into social justice teachers' ways of *doing* and *being* (Ladson-Billings, 2006, p. 41).

Swalwell (2014) outlines a framework for teachers working with privileged K–12 students that fosters an "activist ally" identity, or that of "justice-oriented citizens with a deep understanding of systemic injustices, a sense of agency that is empowered and critically self-reflective, and the ability to mobilize their resources in order to act in concert with others" (p. 108). Swalwell's framework was employed in the study that undergirds this chapter because campus demographics here mirror those of many U.S. teacher education programs—a majority experience privileged identities along a multitude of dimensions (e.g., race, class, socioeconomic status, ability, sexuality, religion, and language). Further, many English teacher candidates who participated in the study attended suburban or private schools and expressed a desire to teach in similar schools (usually near their hometowns).

An important aim of this study is to open dialogue about social justice education goals, given the visible privilege of the teacher education program and the private college campus where the study took place. The activist ally framework is organized around three categories that extend what Swalwell calls "conventional" social justice pedagogy: content, classroom practice, and community connections. In comparing curricula along these lines, she illuminates how some practices (more than others) led students toward developing the hoped-for knowledge, skills, and dispositions rather than "backfiring" and supporting "thin conceptions of social justice and weak social obligations" (p. 111).

With Gorski (2013), Swalwell maintains that traditional conceptions of social justice education are unable to effect change because they do not go far enough in addressing how social class and economic structures impede justice. They propose an emerging framework that moves beyond a focus on culture (cultural competence or culturally relevant teaching) to a renewed focus on *equity* through "equity literacy," or the "skills and dispositions that enable us to recognize, respond to, and redress conditions that deny some students access to the educational opportunities enjoyed by their peers" (p. 6).

INSTITUTIONAL VALUES AND SOCIAL JUSTICE

The study took place at a liberal arts college of approximately 3,700 students in the upper Midwest. The institutional mission statement strives for justice, common good, and respect for persons. The liberal arts tradition embraces a values-centered education that also focuses on, among other things, dignity of work, listening, truthful living, and community living. The values of justice and service are reflected in the integration of social justice topics into coursework.

In the education program, this institutional commitment to service and justice is evident in experiential learning that accompanies the introductory course in the education major/minor, as well as in statements such as the following taken from the Education Department website:

> From our perspective, exemplary teachers embrace . . . values of commitment to service, concern for community, social justice . . . and the integration of a commitment to the common good with respect for the individual. . . . Teachers, therefore, should not only be knowledgeable and caring, but must have a passion for teaching and improving the lives of their students.

These particular political and institutional conceptions of social justice inform teacher candidates' experiences in their coursework across the college and in the teacher education program.

The Education Department conceptual framework places decision making at the heart of the teaching process. Drawing from Cooper (1999, as cited on the Education Department website) and Smith (1992, as cited on the Education Department website), teaching decisions are categorized into three domains: planning, interacting or implementing, and evaluating. Smith's rational decision-making model is employed as a way to structure this process.

Although the website explicates a belief in holistic, collaborative, and constructivist pedagogies that promote active and self-directed learning, it acknowledges that traditional approaches, including direct instruction, may be the most effective way to teach "some content and some learners" (Education Department website). In this way, the program is influenced by elements of behaviorism and aligns with Hunter's (1979) model of teachers as decision makers.

The Education Department offers an elementary education major and a variety of K–12 and secondary minors, all leading to state licensure. Students who wish to earn a 5–12 communication arts/literature license complete an English major and an education minor. The education minor requires foundational coursework in teaching and learning, human development, educational psychology, and young adult literature, as well as a midlevel pedagogy course, a secondary (9–12) pedagogy course, and student teaching.

SOCIAL JUSTICE IN THE SECONDARY METHODS COURSE

Socially just pedagogical practices are positioned centrally in the curriculum for the two pedagogy classes required by the preservice teachers, which include concurrent field experiences. The sequence of courses and field experiences are designed to explicitly connect the teaching of reading, language arts, and literature to social justice and to foster the development of an "activist ally" (Swalwell, 2013) identity in preservice teachers.

The course syllabus describes the following tenets of social justice teaching as central to the course:

> This course will address topics related to a social justice–oriented philosophy and curriculum for teaching English Language Arts (ELA) in the high school classroom. It provides information and experiences in using effective methods in secondary level language arts instruction with an emphasis on the development of socially just ELA pedagogies that seek to create and develop awareness, agency, and action in teacher candidates. We focus on theories of teaching reading, literature, writing, language, media, and speech through a critical lens that views teaching and literacy as social and political acts as we consider issues of inequity from an activist-ally ethic of care. The focus of the class always will be to facilitate the group as stronger, more insightful, more creative, and more compassionate teachers. (course syllabus)

The following social justice–oriented essential questions, among others, frame the course. They are aligned with the Standards of Effective Practice (SEPs) endorsed by the program and assessed by the state licensing board:

- What is effective and socially just secondary English language arts pedagogy? How will I embody and enact these practices in my instruction for diverse students?
- How will I create a community of learners in my ELA classroom?
- What is culturally relevant pedagogy, and how can I design a responsive curriculum within the institutional, economic, and political structures that frame my teaching?
- What does it mean to teach English from a social justice perspective? How can I be an activist-ally?
- What are the English language arts skills needed for the 21st century?
- How do I support adolescents as readers of challenging texts?
- How will I use a variety of communication methods, for example, verbal, nonverbal, multimedia, and technology, to enrich diverse students' learning opportunities?

In addition to the social justice–oriented course description and essential questions, course texts provide theoretical and practical strategies for developing social justice teaching methods. Examples include books and articles by Carey-Webb (2001); Christensen (2009; 2015; 2017); Oakes, Lipton, Anderson, and Stillman (2012); Smagorinsky (2007); and Wolk (2009). Each semester, a different issue-oriented young adult novel is also selected by the course instructor for a whole-class literature circle. Recent titles have included *Bifocal* (Ellis & Walters, 2008); *La Linea* (Jaramillo, 2006); *Luna* (Peters, 2006); and *Accidents of Nature* (McBryde Johnson, 2006).

ENDURING ASSIGNMENTS AS TRIGGER POINTS

Through progressive focusing (Stake, 1995), lesson planning and microteaching assignments were identified as *trigger points* in the case study of this methods course. The term is borrowed from the field of clinical physical therapy and refers to a sensitive area in the body that when stimulated lends itself to a specific effect in another area. This metaphor was employed as attention shifted from social justice teaching outcomes during the methods course in general (e.g., participants' performances in relation to course goals, texts, activities, discussions, or connections to field experience) to the particular outcomes of the two key assignments. This analysis makes visible how dissonant teaching models, which will be further discussed later in the chapter, are embedded within the methods course and key assignments.

Because of their omnipresence in methods coursework, lesson planning and microteaching are cornerstones of course design (Caughlan et al., 2017; Portes & Smagorinsky, 2010; Spelman & St. John-Brooks, 1972). Microteaching entails writing and performing a lesson plan designed for K–12 students but practiced in the contexts of a methods classroom with peers and the teacher educator as the audience. These enduring assignments, however, have been found to limit opportunities for teacher candidates to develop social justice–oriented pedagogies (Rodriguez et al., in press).

Much attention is given to how teacher candidates' dispositions, identities, and sense of agency inform how they take up or resist the social justice practice tools afforded by the methods course (see Bender-Slack, 2010; Davila, 2011; Johnson, 2012). Initially, it was assumed that if the course was theoretically oriented toward social justice (i.e., teacher candidates read about and discuss social justice teaching), they would automatically employ these concepts in the practice assignments. However, through analysis of performance outcomes, it became apparent that design elements of the assignments themselves led to missed opportunities.

Further, attention to these design elements made explicit the ways that dissonant teaching models undergirded them. Identifying these previously taken-for-granted and enduring assignments as trigger points and naming the teaching models upon which they are built provides hope for better alignment of complementary models and strengthening the development and practice of social justice teaching.

Teacher candidates in the secondary methods course described here write and microteach a literature-based reading lesson and a structured-process writing lesson. The literature-based reading lesson requires candidates to select a complex text for whole-class instruction and design before, during, or after reading comprehension instruction along with actively engaging students in interpretation and discussion. The structured-process writing lesson follows Smagorinsky, Johannessen, Kahn, and McCann's (2010) model for writing instruction. Although not specifically focused on social justice pedagogy, Smagorinsky and colleagues' text provides a clear framework for conceptualizing process-oriented writing instruction.

As noted above, the microteaching assignment asks teacher candidates to practice teaching the lesson to their peers in the methods course. Although discrete assignments with distinct processes, products, and assessments, lesson planning and microteaching are uniquely interrelated. It is this interrelatedness that creates a tension in the course design for the instructor. To what extent is the lesson plan its own product? How might the "steps" of planning and organizing instruction be assessed? How is the microteaching performance, then, assessed in relation to the written plan?

In earlier iterations of the course, the written lesson plans were collected and assessed prior to the microteaching demonstrations. The lesson plan rubric included the following National Council of Teachers of English (NCTE) standards-aligned criteria: previous lesson concerns addressed; instructional goals; state standards; resources, materials, and technology; lesson components; consideration of contexts: students, school, and community; instructional language; assessment; and presentation.

These criteria, however, did not align well with the current program-required, SEPs-aligned lesson plan template, which asks teacher candidates to write instructional plans addressing the following areas: state standards, central focus, academic language, learning target, rationale, materials and supplies, instructional content and procedure, accommodations, assessment, reflection, and applied learning theories.

Further complicating assessment was that microteaching demonstrations were then assessed in three broad areas: lesson design, organization of materials, and teaching of the lesson. For example, within the area of lesson design, the evaluation form specifies, "Is the selected reading/writing task appropriate for the intended grade level? Does the planned lesson encourage the full participation of class members? Is the reading/writing task modeled, practiced, and applied using adolescent literature or other engaging and relevant texts students will access both in and outside of school?"

In the area of teaching the lesson, the evaluation form asks, "Does the lesson contain a hook to engage students? Is the lesson interactive? Does the lesson draw upon the sociocultural experiences of students? (Are connections made to past knowledge and experiences and life beyond the classroom?)"

Given this confusing array of criteria and assessment instruments, the lesson plan rubric was dropped in favor of focusing teacher candidates' attention on the enactment of the plan and reflection on its outcomes. Teacher candidates who participated in the study submitted written plans using the program-required lesson plan template; however, submission occurred after the microteaching demonstrations and included reflection and revisions.

Consequently, course instructors are often found straddling many different standards and criteria (e.g., national content-specific standards like those written by NCTE; national accreditation standards like those written by the Council for the Accreditation of Teacher Preparation [CAEP]; state licensing standards; and program-specific standards) across all teacher education programs. This might be because there are multiple stakeholders with competing voices, distinct politics, and diverse views invested in teacher education and licensure.

Thus, written plans were collected after whole-class analysis and discussion of the microteaching performances in light of the evaluation criteria outlined above and in relation to fellow candidates' experience of the enactment. The course instructor facilitated the post-teaching discussion and guided teacher candidates toward making explicit connections between practice and social justice theory. This revised assignment and assessment design allowed teacher candidates to fine-tune their written plans in more authentic, practice-based, and social justice–oriented ways.

DISSONANT TEACHING MODELS

The trigger point analysis employed here makes visible how dissonant teaching models are embedded within the methods course and key assignments. Teaching models, or the ways in which learning environments and instructional experiences are constructed, sequenced, or delivered, are shaped by particular teaching beliefs, theories, or philosophies. Owen Wilson (2018) explains that teaching models (or systems) fit loosely into one of five families of education psychology: social, information processing, personal, behavioral, and constructivist. Behaviorist theory, for example, is evident in the program's "teacher as reflective practitioner" conceptual framework described above (Education Department website).

Conversely, the program-required lesson plan template (described above) is based on the Hunter (1980) model of mastery learning or direct instruction. It includes a wide array of possibilities for teacher candidates to consider as they design instruction but is often viewed as a set of required components that must be present in every lesson. The course instructor of the methods class described in this chapter was urged to provide multiple opportunities for teacher candidates to develop and practice these instructional design skills in preparation for assessment in the final phase of the program—student teaching.

During student teaching, a common program-wide observation instrument evaluates teacher candidates' abilities to plan and enact lessons with the following components: anticipatory set, objective and purpose, input, modeling, checking for understanding, guided practice, independent practice, and closure. Although Hunter (1985) and others (Wolfe, 1987) discourage educators from applying this "seven step lesson plan" model without considering teachers' in-the-moment reflective decision-making processes (Schön, 1983) and claim it has been misunderstood, the lesson plan template and student teaching observation instrument function as rigid checklists that constrain teacher candidates' development of alternate pedagogies in their methods coursework.

ALTERNATIVE MODELS FOR SUPPORTING SOCIAL JUSTICE TEACHING

Other, more humanistic possibilities for lesson planning and microteaching exist. For excellent examples of countermodels to the behaviorist lesson plan format, the website CRISPA (an acronym for Connections, Risk-Taking, Imagination, and Active Engagement) (2017) offers constructivist model lesson plans. These lesson plans are compared to behaviorist plans so that teachers can practice critically analyzing their own lesson plans using the same design elements.

Grant and Sleeter (2011) also offer numerous examples of "before and after" multicultural lesson plans across grade levels and content areas. Another example of an alternative teaching model widely adopted in science and math is the 5E instructional model (Bybee, 2014). The model employs the elements of engagement, exploration, explanation, elaboration, and evaluation and is rooted in constructivism.

One promising model for culturally relevant pedagogy in ELA is described in detail by Hefflin (2002). In her article, she documents how a framework that focused on the cultural patterns of the students' lives helped guide the planning process for a lesson using African American children's literature. The lesson components included a prereading activity followed by a read-aloud, group discussion, journal writing, and a follow-up activity. Hefflin envisions the pedagogical instruments of methods and materials through a framework that considers students' textual, social, cultural, and personal lives.

An exemplary model featuring alignment between methods courses and program design can be found in Poplin and Rivera's (2005) description of a program-wide renovation that provided teacher candidates with an "expansive repertoire of approaches to designing effective instruction" (p. 34). According to these authors, in order for teacher candidates to develop social justice teaching competencies, they need to be skilled in recognizing and using multiple teaching models. For example, they should be able to explain and apply theories from critical pedagogy, constructivism, feminism, relational pedagogy, and behaviorism in their teaching (Poplin & Rivera, 2005).

BEYOND A SINGLE MODEL

Critical pedagogies are important because they highlight the role of power in selecting curricular materials. Constructivism promotes the construction of new knowledge through experimentation and exploration. Feminist and relational pedagogies tend to place an emphasis on developing good relationships with students and attending to aesthetic dimensions of learning and teaching. They often highlight student voice (Poplin & Rivera, 2005).

Behavioral objectivism as a teaching model may be necessary for emphasizing the acquisition of specific skills but by itself is not sufficient for ensuring access to rigorous and high-quality instruction for all learners. Hunter's model has been critiqued as nonintellectual and overly technical. In fact, Gibboney (1987) writes that the "science" invoked by the model gives him a "vague sense of uneasiness. Terms such as *task analysis*, *specific objectives*, and *cause and effect* have a mechanistic ring" (p. 47).

Here Gibboney (1987) recalls Dewey's admonition (1916, as cited in Gibboney) on technique: "Mechanical . . . woodenness is an inevitable corollary of any theory which separates mind from activity motivated by a purpose" (p. 49). As Gibboney asserts, purpose is more than a behavioral objective. If teaching is reduced to a technical model of cause and effect decision making, what is lost in the discussion of ideas in a novel? For example, how might students and teachers engage in thoughtful conceptual analysis of ideas like racism, friendship, and social criticism in *The Adventures of Huckleberry Finn* (p. 49)?

Gibboney (1987) aptly declares that "fundamental reform [in teacher education] must begin with ideas, not techniques" (p. 50). The teacher-as-decision-maker model may have been an innovation in its time, and the field of educational psychology has surely advanced teaching as a science; however, where might alternative and evolving teaching models lead in the quest toward social justice teaching? What about models such as teacher as cultural navigator? Teaching as an ethic of care? Or teacher as transformative pedagogue?

Social justice–oriented teachers are able to employ appropriate teaching models for diverse students across the various contexts of classrooms situations in a rapidly changing world. They enact reflective decision-making processes. But they also need to see themselves as activist-allies (Swalwell, 2014). They must be provided with opportunities to question, challenge, and select the teaching models and instructional designs that best serve them and their students. While enduring assignments like lesson planning and microteaching may have value in the methods course, we need to question the models that undergird them, provide alternatives, and recognize the many possible pathways to realizing the goals of social justice teaching.

REFERENCES

Alsup, J., & Miller, S. J. (2014). Reclaiming English education: Rooting social justice in dispositions. *English Education 46*(3), 195–215.

Bender-Slack, D. (2010). Text, talk . . . and fear? English language arts teachers negotiate social justice teaching. *English Education, 42*(2), 181–203.

Bybee, R. (2014). The BSCS 5E instructional model: Personal reflections and contemporary implications. *Science and Children, 51*(8), 10–13.

Carey-Webb, A. (2001). *Literature and lives: A response-based, cultural studies approach to teaching English*. Urbana, IL: National Council of Teachers of English.

Caughlan, S., Pasternak, D., Hallman, H. L., Renzi, L., Rush, L., & Frisby, M. (2017). How English language arts teachers are prepared for 21st century classrooms: Results of a national survey. *English Education, 49*(3), 265–297.

Christensen, L. (2009). *Teaching for joy and justice: Re-imagining the language arts classroom*. Milwaukee, WI: Rethinking Schools.

Christensen, L. (2015). *Rhythm and resistance: Teaching poetry for social justice*. Milwaukee, WI: Rethinking Schools.

Christensen, L. (2017). *Reading, writing, and rising up: Teaching about social justice and the power of the written word* (2nd ed.). Milwaukee, WI: Rethinking Schools.

CRISPA: Perceptual Teaching and Learning. (2017). Lesson plan comparisons. Retrieved from http://www.crispateaching.org.

Davila, D. (2011). "White people don't work at McDonald's" and other shadow stories from the field: Analyzing preservice teachers' use of Obama's race speech to teach for social justice. *English Education, 44*(1), 13–50.

Ellis, D., & Walters, E. (2008). *Bifocal*. Brighton, MA: Fitzhenry & Whiteside.

Gibboney, R. A. (1987). A critique of Madeline Hunter's teaching model from Dewey's perspective. *Educational Leadership, 44*(5), 46–50.

Gorski, P. C. (2013). *Reaching and teaching students in poverty: Strategies for erasing the opportunity gap*. New York: Teachers College Press.

Gorski, P. C., & Swalwell, K. (2015). Equity literacy for all. *Educational Leadership, 72*(6), 34–40.

Grant, C. A., & Sleeter, C. E. (2006). *Turning on learning: Five approaches for multicultural teaching plans for race, class, gender and disability* (4th ed.). San Francisco: Jossey-Bass.

Grant, C. A., & Sleeter, C. E. (2011). *Doing multicultural education for achievement and equity* (2nd ed.). New York: Routledge/Taylor & Francis.

Hefflin, B. R. (2002). Learning to develop culturally relevant pedagogy: A lesson about cornrowed lives. *Urban Review, 34*(3), 231–250.

Hunter, M. (1979). Teaching is decision making. *Educational Leadership, 37*(1), 62–64, 67.

Hunter, M. (1980). *Teach more—faster*. El Segundo, CA: TIP.

Hunter, M. (1985). What's wrong with Madeline Hunter? *Educational Leadership, 42*(5), 57–60.

Jaramillo, A. (2006). *La linea*. New York: MacMillan.
Johnson, J. D. (2012). "A rainforest in front of a bulldozer": The literacy practices of teacher candidates committed to social justice. *English Education, 44*(2), 147–179.
Ladson-Billings, G. (2005). Reading, writing, and race: Literacy practices of teachers in diverse classrooms. In T. L. McCarty (Ed.), *Language, literacy, and power in schooling* (pp. 133–150). London: Lawrence Erlbaum.
Ladson-Billings, G. (2006). It's not the culture of poverty, it's the poverty of culture: The problem with teacher education. *Anthropology and Education Quarterly, 37*(2), 104–109. doi:10.1525/aeq.2006.37.2.104.
McBryde Johnson, H. (2006). *Accidents of nature*. New York: Henry Holt.
McDonald, M. A. (2008). The pedagogy of assignments in social justice teacher education. *Equity and Excellence in Education, 41*(2), 151–167. doi:10.1080/10665680801943949.
Oakes, J., Lipton, M., Anderson, L., & Stillman, J. (2012). *Teaching to change the world* (4th ed.). Boulder, CO: Paradigm.
Owen Wilson, L. (2018). Models of teaching. Second Principle. Retrieved from https://thesecondprinciple.com.
Pasternak, D. L., Caughlan, S., Hallman, H., Renzi, L., & Rush, L. (2014). Teaching English language arts methods in the United States: A review of the research. *Review of Education, 2*(2), 146–185. doi:10.1002/rev3.3031.
Peters, J. A. (2006). *Luna*. London: Little, Brown.
Poplin, M., & Rivera, J. (2005). Merging social justice and accountability: Educating highly qualified, responsible and effective teachers. *Theory Into Practice, 44*(1), 27–37.
Portes, P., & Smagorinsky, P. (2010). Static structures, changing demographics: Educating teachers for shifting populations in stable schools. *English Education, 42*(3), 236–247.
Rodriguez, T. L., Bohn-Gettler, C. M., & Israelson, M. H. (in press). Missed opportunities: Troubling the waters of social justice teaching in an English methods course. *English Education*.
Schön, D. A. (1983). *The reflective practitioner: How professionals think in action*. New York: Basic Books.
Smagorinsky, P. (2007). *Teaching English by design: How to create and carry out instructional units*. Portsmouth, NH: Heinemann.
Smagorinsky, P., Johannessen, L. R., Kahn, E., & McCann, T. (2010). *The dynamics of writing instruction: A structured process approach for middle and high school*. Portsmouth, NH: Heinemann.
Spelman, B. J., & St. John-Brooks, C. (1972). Microteaching and teacher education: A critical reappraisal. *Irish Journal of Education, 6*(2), 73–92.
Stake, R. E. (1995). *The art of case study research*. Thousand Oaks, CA: Sage.
Swalwell, K. (2013). "With great power comes great responsibility": Privileged students' conceptions of justice-oriented citizenship. *Democracy and Education, 21*(1).
Swalwell, K. (2014). *Educating activist allies: Social justice pedagogy with the suburban and urban elite*. New York: Routledge.
Wolfe, P. (1987). What the seven-step lesson plan isn't! *Educational Leadership, 44*(5), 70–71.
Wolk, S. (2009). Reading for a better world: With for social responsibility with young adult literature. *Journal of Adolescent and Adult Literacy, 52*(8), 664–673.

A Response to Chapter 2

Allison Wynhoff Olsen

In Chapter 2, Terri Rodriguez uses her agency as an English teacher educator to give us a call to action: We need to examine our teaching practices, programs, and ways of assessing teacher candidates. Specifically, we need to examine dissonances in how we explore social justice pedagogies with teacher candidates and how we provide opportunities (or not) for them to enact such pedagogies within our program's assignments and assessments.

As an English education professor teaching at a public, land-grant university in the West, I experience similar tensions to those Rodriguez narrates from her own Midwestern, liberal arts college; the concerns she raises are felt elsewhere. My teacher candidates and I regularly dialogue about their perceptions that professors teach them about how social justice should inform their ways of being in the classroom, as well as inform their epistemologies and assessments; yet some of these professors do not enact these practices themselves (Ladson-Billings, 1995; 2017; Sleeter, 2000).

Their frustration is compounded when the teacher candidates feel constrained when writing high-stakes portfolios for licensure requirements, claiming they are being asked to compromise what they have learned as effective and just in order to achieve proficiency. Teacher candidates also express confusion with a mismatch between what we teach at our universities and what occurs in K–12 systems (Feiman-Nemser & Buchman, 1985).

While it is normal to feel annoyance within bureaucratic systems (both for our candidates and ourselves), Rodriguez takes what can sit as emotional conflict and moves us into generative examination. Rodriguez asserts that the "rigid checklists" (p. 26) used within lesson planning and assessments of our teacher candidates as feedback to their microteaching might constrain our candidates from taking risks in applying social justice pedagogies. Emphasizing social justice, it is necessary to voice that our candidates are vulnerable and lack power. They seek information and licensure, and rely on accredited agencies to provide them with a repertoire of entry points to become effective and responsive teachers. When such agencies use unexamined approaches, teacher candidates are held to standards that teacher educators may not support, in theory, yet activate in assessment.

Throughout the chapter, Rodriguez provides us with the opportunity to examine our own roles in promulgating enduring assignments that may lead to missed opportunities; these assignments may be actively constraining our teacher candidates' development. As such, she asks us to use the power we have, as teacher educators, to find the dissonances, locate the rub, and engage in ways that irritate it. We cannot just continue to remark on the dissonances and anticipate frustrations; rather, we need to push for change.

I liken Rodriguez's request to Garcia and O'Donnell-Allen's (2015) pose *teacher as hacker*. The *teacher as hacker* pose necessitates a willingness to be vulnerable, examine practices, and change, thus opening up space for teachers and students to be "makers" in the classroom. In these positions, both teacher and students must be vulnerable and lean into the wobble (Fecho, 2011) of discomfort, making visible that changes need to be made within our programs in hopes of achieving growth and more fitting models (such as CRISPA, as Rodriguez notes on p. 26).

In a conversation about this chapter, Terri and I discussed how much her teacher candidates knew about the "activist ally" stance (Swalwell, 2014), and together we wondered about quantity and timing: (1) How much meta conversation with teacher candidates is necessary? And (2) when are teacher candidates the most capable of holding such conversations in generative ways?

The teacher candidates I work with sometimes worry about how they will be perceived if they center their practices on social justice approaches, particularly in remote, rural areas. With a goal of offering "the right instruction, right on time," Terri pushes me to consider ways I can examine my own use of an activist ally stance (Swalwell, 2014) with teacher candidates in articulated ways. It also strikes me that adding in deliberate meta conversations with teacher candidates—both about the activity ally stance and ways of shifting programmatic requirements to be more humanistic and responsive—might help teacher educators create and sustain a mutually vulnerable space with our own teacher candidates.

We cannot just be informed by social justice pedagogies; rather, we need to embolden ourselves to shift our systems and our requirements. Given that our teacher candidates become our colleagues upon entering the teaching realm, we need to involve them in conversations of examination so they have access to not just planning and teaching but also conversing and thinking about the rationale and theories underlying them.

Continually inviting our teacher candidates into the conversation can also help us model and enact how to build more humanistic approaches to planning and performing teaching in methods classes, a model that should serve them well as they shift into their own teaching spaces. Examining and dialoguing with our candidates can also help us stay fluid with our requirements, checking in together to determine fit instead of getting stuck in a new, normalized format.

REFERENCES

Fecho, B. (2011). *Teaching for the students: Habits of heart, mind, and practice in the engaged classroom*. New York: Teachers' College.

Feiman-Nemser, S., & Buchman, M. (1985). Pitfalls of experience in teacher preparation. *Teachers College Record, 87*(1), 53–65.

Garcia, A., & O'Donnell-Allen, C. (2015). *Pose, wobble, flow: A culturally proactive approach to literacy instruction*. New York: Teachers College Press.

Ladson-Billings, G. (1995). Toward a theory of culturally relevant pedagogy. *American Educational Research Journal, 32*(3), 465–491. Retrieved from https://ezproxy.lib.uwm.edu.

Ladson-Billings, G. (2017). The (r)evolution will not be standardized: Teacher education, hip hop pedagogy, and culturally relevant pedagogy 2.0. In D. Paris & H. Alim (Eds.), *Culturally sustaining pedagogies: Teaching and learning for justice in a changing world*. New York: Teachers College Press.

Sleeter, C. (2000). Epistemological diversity in research on preservice teacher preparation for historically underserved children. *Review of Research in Education,* 25, 209–250.

Swalwell, K. (2014). *Educating activist allies: Social justice pedagogy with the suburban and urban elite*. New York: Routledge.

Chapter Three

Exploring Tensions During Critical Conversations About Race in English Education

Amy Vetter and Melissa Schieble

During an English methods class, preservice teachers sat in pairs reviewing video-recorded lessons they taught. Students came prepared with a 30–60-minute recorded lesson, a 10–15-minute transcribed section of that lesson, and a written reflection (see Vetter & Schieble, 2016, for the assignment). One of the questions candidates were expected to discuss was how race, class, gender, and sexual orientation shaped how they positioned themselves and their students during the transcribed interaction. After the small groups discussed, the whole class debriefed. Toward the end of the discussion, Adam (all names are pseudonyms), a self-identified biracial (Latinx and white) student, asked, "All right, so I am curious for y'all—I mean, some of you might be dealing with completely white classrooms, some of you might not be, but I'm curious; how do y'all honestly deal with race? How does race affect your classrooms? Your race, your students' race, both?" Here, Adam pushed his white peers to talk more about how issues related to race surfaced in their classrooms. This comment, from Adam, is an example of a critical conversation because he pressed his peers to deconstruct how racial inequities played out in their classroom interactions. At this point, he challenged candidates who might have preferred to remain silent to really talk about their experience in authentic ways. As a result, Adam's peers responded by sharing dilemmas and possible solutions related to issues of race in their classrooms.

Although several dilemmas were discussed in class, the focus of this chapter is about responding to racialized jokes and name-calling in and out of the classroom. Two English educators closely examine how preservice teachers discussed the tension of responding to such comments and the possible solutions they created based on that dialogue.

This kind of conversation is especially important in English methods courses because it opens spaces for preservice teachers, most of whom are white (Taie & Goldring, 2017), to critically examine how racial identities shape curricular choices (Grant & Sleeter, 2006), teaching methods (Ladson-Billings, 2014; Paris & Alim, 2014), and classroom interactions (Rex & Schiller, 2009). The goal of the chapter is to highlight components of this critical conversation with the possibility of informing similar dialogue in other English methods courses.

WHAT IS A CRITICAL CONVERSATION?

Critical conversations are a pedagogical strategy that is theoretically informed by practices related to critical literacy and racial literacy. This chapter draws from Lewison and colleagues (2015) who define critical literacy as having the following four dimensions of critical social practice:

1. disrupting the commonplace;
2. considering multiple viewpoints;
3. focusing on the sociopolitical; and
4. taking action to promote social justice.

According to this model, as teachers and students engage in critical social practices they draw on personal and cultural resources to make meaning that at times challenges the authority of another's perspective.

This research also draws from racial literacy to define how participants in critical conversations examine the ways racism pervades our social, cultural, material, and political worlds (Guinier, 2004; Rogers & Mosley, 2006; Sealy-Ruiz, 2011; Skerrett, 2011). Racial literacy practices include viewing racism as structural rather than individual, seeing everyday forms of racism, and challenging undemocratic practices (Bolgatz, 2005; Twine, 2004).

A critical conversation is occurring when classroom discussion enacts and envisions these dimensions of critical social practice and elements of racial literacy. Engaging in these dimensions of critical social practice fosters teachers and students' *critical language awareness* (Fairclough, 2013), which gives students tools to notice, analyze, and reflect on how harmful discourses about race or gender, for example, circulate in everyday life to privilege dominant culture and oppress marginalized identities.

Developing critical language awareness also gives students tools to use language to speak back to injustices. In doing so, teachers and students develop and enact a critical stance toward a given situation. Engaging a critical stance becomes a way of reading and being in the world (Freire, 1970), is a necessary literacy practice for democratic participation, and sustains marginalized students' cultural and linguistic identities (Paris & Alim, 2014).

In an English methods classroom, preservice teachers often enter critical conversations by describing a tension in their teaching practice. For English educators facilitating such conversations, it is important to use those tensions as a resource for challenging undemocratic practices and disrupting commonplace notions about how identity markers, such as race, shape the educational experiences of students. Facilitation often means listening to students as they discuss these tensions and knowing when to ask questions that provide another perspective that is not being shared. To illustrate those nuances, we share an example of a critical conversation with preservice teachers about how race shaped their classroom interactions.

Tensions in Critical Conversations

Scholarship has illustrated several tensions that participants experience when attempting to engage in critical conversations about race (Brown et al., 2017; Solomona, Portelli, Daniel, & Campbell, 2005). For example, Hytten and Warren (2003) found that white students in an education course about the political and social power of whiteness drew upon a variety of discourses that actually served to protect and secure a dominant position. Other research shows how white students often remain silent about issues of race, take a colorblind approach, or express beliefs that racial prejudice is a thing of the past (Anagnostopoulos, Everett, & Carey, 2013; Copenhaver-Johnson, 2000).

Students of color, however, have been shown to discuss and name race in ways that demonstrate a level of critical understanding (Anagnostopoulos et al., 2013; Copenhaver-Johnson, 2000; Schaffer & Skinner, 2009). Research also shows that students of color oftentimes stay silent during critical conversations about race because they do not feel safe to publically contest certain conceptions of race (Carter, 2007).

With that said, preservice teachers from all backgrounds come with different experiences and abilities in regard to talking about race. The English methods class is an important context for such work, as it gives preservice teachers practice with engaging in conversations about race with knowledgeable others (Michael, 2015) as a way to support this work in schools. English educators, then, need to help preservice teachers think critically about their own identities.

For example, teacher educators can help white teachers see how they view the world through whiteness so they are prepared to help their students unpack issues of race in classrooms (Pixley & VanDerPloeg, 2000). Without that critical examination, teachers are likely to reify stereotypes and maintain structural forms of privilege and oppression (Hollingworth, 2009; Schieble, 2012). English educators can also help students enter and maintain critical conversations by becoming more comfortable with the messiness of open-ended discussions rather than searching for "neat" conclusions (Bolgatz, 2005).

Overall, English methods courses can be a space that encourages critical reflection and asks educators to unpack how personal backgrounds shape the assumptions they make about learning and instruction in order to improve English language arts (ELA) education for students (Gay & Kirkland, 2003; Haddix, 2015; Mosley, 2010). In the context of this work, educators would benefit from more scholarship about how to prepare preservice and in-service teachers for engaging in critical conversations.

METHODS

This research was guided by the following question: In what ways did preservice teachers discuss tensions related to race during critical conversations in an English methods course? The researchers conducted a qualitative study with 11 English preservice teachers enrolled in a university-based teacher education undergraduate program in the southeast United States. Students attended two courses over one year related to English methods. The first involved a 50-hour internship completed during an English methods course (Teaching Practices and Curriculum in English Education). The second involved a 10-week student teaching component completed during an English education seminar (Student Teaching in English Education Seminar).

Ten of those preservice teachers were white and one was biracial; six were female and five were male. All preservice teachers in the course agreed to be part of the study even though everyone is not represented in the conversation for this chapter. Students were placed in urban, rural, and suburban schools with students from diverse backgrounds (see Table 3.1). Most came from a middle-class background, based on the information they shared during discussions. Most preservice teachers grew up in the surrounding area, and approximately 80% remained in the area after graduation.

In the first course, Amy set up critical conversations by asking students to engage in several readings related to critical and racial literacy (see box below). In addition, Amy shared a few examples of transcripts from critical conversations in her past classes (Vetter & Schieble, 2016). As a whole group, preservice teachers had the opportunity to explore how other preservice teachers talked about the ways in which identity markers (e.g., race, class, gender, and sexual orientation) shaped classroom interactions. Finally, Amy shared a transcript from her teaching and modeled making herself vul-

Table 3.1. Demographics for Student Teaching Placements

Preservice teacher	School context	Demographic of students
Adam multiracial male	Greenland High School urban	41% White; 27% Black; 26% Latinx; 4% multiracial; 2% Asian; 1% American Indian
Richard White male	William High School urban	41% Black; 35% White; 14% Latinx; 5% multiracial; 4% Asian; 1% American Indian
Sydney White female	Sandelwood High School rural	63% White; 28% Black; 5% Latinx; 3% multiracial; 1% Asian; 1% American Indian
Dan White male	Round Mountain High School urban	39% White; 37% Black; 11% Asian; 9% Latinx; 4% multiracial; 1% American Indian
Bryan White male	Newbury High School suburban	78% White; 7% Black; 6% Latinx; 5% Asian; 3% multiracial; 1% American Indian
Amanda White female	Sandelwood High School rural	63% White; 28% Black; 5% Latinx; 3% multiracial; 1% Asian; 1% American Indian
Julie White female	Round Mountain High School urban	39% White; 37% Black; 11% Asian; 9% Latinx; 4% multiracial; 1% American Indian
Chad White male	Nandina High School suburban	71% White; 18% Black; 6% Latinx; 3% multiracial; 1% Asian; 1% American Indian; 1% Pacific Islander
Christy White female	Azalea High School rural	41% White; 40% Latinx; 14% African American; 3% multiracial; 2% Asian; >1% American Indian; >1% Pacific Islander
Harper White female	Azalea High School rural	41% White; 40% Latinx; 14% African American; 3% multiracial; 2% Asian; >1% American Indian; >1% Pacific Islander

Preservice teacher	School context	Demographic of students
Tanya White female	Round Mountain High School urban	39% White; 37% Black; 11% Asian; 9% Latinx; 4% multiracial; 1% American Indian

nerable as the teacher to demonstrate what a critical conversation might look like in the methods course.

Readings for Critical Conversations about Race in English Methods

Bolgatz, J. (2005). Teachers initiating conversations about race and racism in a high school class. *Multicultural Perspectives, 7*(3), 28–35.

Copenhaver-Johnson, J. F. (2000). Silence in the classroom: Learning to talk about issues of race. *Dragon Lode, 18*(2), 8–16.

Hollingworth, L. (2009). Complicated conversations: Exploring race and ideology in an elementary classroom. *Urban Education, 44*(1), 30–58.

Kohli, R. (2014). Unpacking internalized racism: Teachers of color striving for racially just classrooms. *Race Ethnicity and Education, 17*(3), 367–387.

Lester, N. A. (2014). The n-word: Lessons taught and lessons learned. *Journal of Praxis in Multicultural Education, 8*(2), 3.

McIntosh, P. (1988). White privilege: Unpacking the invisible knapsack. *Race, class, and gender in the United States: An integrated study, 4*, 165–169.

Pixley, M. F., & VanDerPloeg, L. S. (2000). Learning to see: White. *English Education, 32*, 278–289.

Roberts, R. A., Bell, L. A., & Murphy, B. (2008). Flipping the script: Analyzing youth talk about race and racism. *Anthropology and Education Quarterly, 39*(3), 334–354.

Sassi, K., & Thomas, E. E. (2008). Walking the talk: Examining privilege and race in a ninth-grade classroom. *English Journal*, 25–31.

Thein, A. H., Guise, M., & Sloan, D. L. (2011). Problematizing literature circles as forums for discussion of multicultural and political texts. *Journal of Adolescent and Adult Literacy, 55*(1), 15–24.

During the second course, when data was collected, preservice teachers were asked to complete a video analysis assignment (see Vetter & Schieble, 2016, for the assignment). Students came prepared to discuss their video analysis in small and whole groups. Before those discussions, Amy and her preservice teachers created a list of discussion expectations that included behaviors such as "give constructive feedback and respect multiple perspectives." The class also used Singleton's (2014) four agreements for talking about race: stay engaged, speak your truth, experience discomfort, and expect and accept nonclosure.

Data sources for the study, collected by Amy, were culled from one weekly meeting during the second course and the collection of aforementioned assignments. Data sources included (a) four audio-recorded small-group conversations (45 minutes each); (b) one audio-recorded whole-group conversation (60 minutes); and (c) nine video assignments with transcripts that asked preservice teachers to engage in discourse analysis about identity positions (video, reflection, and transcript).

After data were collected, Amy collaborated with Melissa for qualitative data analysis (Merriam & Tisdell, 2016). Together, we used collaborative coding (Smagorinsky, 2008) with codes developed from our framework to analyze the transcripts. During the analysis phase, the researchers coded for possible areas of tension. The authors defined tensions as moments that placed participants in opposition to something within or outside their classrooms, or anything that appeared to cause candidates' discomfort. Next, the researchers reviewed those tensions and assigned codes related to the described characteristics of critical conversations. Those tensions are described below.

FINDINGS

The findings focus on one important tension that arose for the preservice teachers when race was a salient factor in students' interactions in the classroom. Specifically, preservice teachers were uncertain about ways to respond to instances of when youth of color used racialized jokes and name-calling in and outside of the classroom. Throughout the writing of this chapter, we thought carefully about how to describe the language that teacher candidates were noticing and naming when youth used language in schools related to race.

We took the lead from Roberts, Bell, and Murphy (2008), who investigated how storytelling and the arts were used with youth to engage in inquiry about race and racism in society. Their study complicated instances when youth of color used what they term "racialized jokes and name-calling," citing Rose (1994) to explain it as a strategy "that although filled with contradictions, also reflects, comments on, and attempts to challenge the persistent racial, social, economic, and political injustices that permeate their lives" (p. 337).

Throughout the chapter, we acknowledge the tensions and contradictions in racialized jokes and name-calling when used by youth of color in schools. As a result of these tensions, teacher candidates, who were mostly white, often remained silent despite their desire to disrupt such language use. To change that, they brainstormed possible solutions for talking with students about racialized jokes and name-calling.

Below, two important components of the critical conversation are discussed: (1) sharing teaching experiences to make sense of how race shapes teaching practices and interactions, and (2) strategizing how to make changes toward equity based on the discussed tensions. It is important to note that the conversation discussed in this chapter focuses on responses preservice teachers gave to a question that their peer asked about how race shaped classroom interactions.

Although Amy had opened up this topic earlier in the discussion, preservice teachers did not provide in-depth comments until Adam asked the question. Reasons for their hesitancy are unknown, but it was evident that they felt more comfortable talking about race in the classroom with their peers. As a result, Amy took a facilitator approach and listened to responses. She only commented to clarify or add another perspective, as seen at the end of the "Findings" section in regard to Dan's comment about who had permission to engage in racialized jokes and name-calling.

We recognize that Adam, the only preservice teacher of color, took the main role of asking questions and giving advice about how to handle racialized jokes and name-calling. At this point, he posed questions and shared perspectives to support his white peers' learning about how race shapes classroom interactions. Such work by students of color is typical when engaging in critical conversations with white peers and often requires vulnerability, risk, and exhaustion (Welton et al., 2015).

We are not advocating for English educators to position students of color as the spokespersons for topics about race. This critical conversation, however, shows an excerpt in which Adam positions himself as a knowledgeable advocate for talking to students about race. At that moment, he was able to foster the critical conversation in a way that Amy was not. If this positioning were to happen consistently throughout the course, Amy would need to talk with Adam and develop alternative strategies that worked for him and the group (e.g., small-group conversations, written critical self-reflection, etc.).

Sharing Teaching Experiences Related to Race

As a whole group, students debriefed about their small-group discussion related to video-recorded segments of student teaching. After Adam asked the opening question about how race shapes his peers' classroom interactions, candidates began by sharing specific teaching experiences that related to their uncertainty about addressing students' use of racialized jokes and name-calling. For example, Sydney, a white female, explained,

> A lot of my students joke about their race. For instance, on the first day of school, we went around and had them introduce themselves, and tell their name, and something about them. This one student who's from Laos, was like, "And a fun fact about me, I do not eat dogs." He constantly makes those comments of his race. I didn't know what to do at first because like, "Whoa." But everyone else laughs, and he laughs. And then other students are like . . .

> Latino students they say, "Hey, Papa. Hey, Pedro." And I look at them like, "What are you doing?" He's like, "No, it's okay, they like that. You like that, right? You told me to call you that, right?" I feel uncomfortable I don't know what to do because I don't know what relationships they have outside the class.

Here Sydney shared a story from her classroom related to students joking about race. She knew this was not a constructive way to interact, but she was unsure how to proceed. By doing nothing, though, Sydney risked sending the message to students that racialized jokes are humorous, despite her belief that they are harmful.

In addition, these comments ("I do not eat dogs") could also reflect internalized racism, a concept used to describe moments when individuals of color consciously or unconsciously accept a racial hierarchy (Kohli, 2014). Such beliefs can affect youth's confidence and performance in school (Kohli, 2014). As a teacher, it is important to recognize when such instances are occurring in order to disrupt them by supporting students to interrogate why and "who benefited most from them holding this belief" (Malo-Juvera, 2017, p. 41).

Dan also described the racialized jokes and name-calling that he heard kids use in the hallway.

> They are absolutely terrible to each other, and there's a whole push for bullying. Friends bully each other more than anything. You hear racial slurs up and down the halls, people screaming it. So I mean, I don't know at what point . . . I think that sort of conversation and education has to happen way sooner than high school. Because by the time they get there, it is funny. They find it funny. And it's so funny to the point that it's lost any significant meaning to them. They drop the n-bomb like it's their name.

Here, Dan highlighted two important patterns associated with this tension. He noticed that friends, in this instance students of color, addressed each other in less official school spaces such as the hallway by repeatedly using the n-word. He also noted that students have not thought critically about the words they use ("they find it funny" and "it's lost any significant meaning"). He suggested that students would benefit from unpacking this language at an earlier age.

Dan's discomfort with this language and characterization of it as a form of bullying among youth of color demonstrates a place for further critical discussion. Neal Lester, a professor of English at Arizona State University who has taught a course on the history of the n-word, describes how there are conflicting views on the use of this word but that it will "always be tainted with social negativity, no matter the spelling or nuanced pronunciation or the illusion of those who believe that this word can be appropriated as 'a term of endearment' to take away its negative sting" (p. 19).

Dan's inclination that students would benefit from "unpacking this language" shows not only his thoughtfulness about the issue but also the need for greater knowledge about the perspectives of its use in context. We also note that for Dan, as a white, male teacher, unpacking the n-word with youth of color may be met with "political and critical suspicion from some students" (Lester, 2013, p. 10). Following Dan, two other preservice teachers shared similar stories and expressed their lack of knowledge about how to help students unpack this language. We recommend Teaching Tolerance's interview with Neal Lester and Chapter 4 from *Raising Race Questions* by Price, 2011 as further readings for preservice teachers about this work.

Strategizing

Following these teaching experiences, Adam offered some specific solutions for the group.

> Go to your Laotian student and be like, "Okay, why do you make these jokes? Why is that funny?" And kind of try and get him to unpack it, like, "Well, it's funny because it's racist?" Try and get them to figure out why that's funny, and then go to your Hispanic students, "Okay, why is calling you Paco and all this, why is that funny?" Because when you get right down to it, if you can get them to unpack that and kind of figure out it's like, "Okay, well why am I laughing at this?" It might be like, "Oh, it's a joke and it's funny." It's like, "Okay." And some of them might go, "Oh, yeah. I guess I'm kind of being racist to me, huh? I'm probably not helping myself here. Ugh." Like, we had a discussion about that in my class. Someone made a joke about a serious topic and I was like, "Okay, why is that funny?" They were like, "Because it is." I was like, "Why is it funny?" And they were like, "I don't know?" And I was like, "Then why are you laughing?" You have to think about this y'all, you have to critically analyze, if you just help them do that it'll probably pay off a lot.

Adam did several things in this response to help his peers think through this tension. First, he advised that they help their students critically unpack the language they are using. Second, he gave specific questions and statements for how Sydney, in particular, could address the situations she described. Third, he brought up how he addressed a similar issue in his classroom.

Here, Adam recognizes that sometimes students do not understand how using racial stereotypes can harm themselves and those around them. He also hints at issues of internalized oppression that manifest in many ways, such as unconsciously allowing hegemonic ideations of inferiority and believing that power comes from oppressing others (Rodriguez & Gonzalez, 2005). He challenged his peers to take up this tension as a teaching moment and to help their students think about other, more productive ways to interact.

Dan also strategized by suggesting that teachers could take a no tolerance approach. He explained, "I was just going to say, because I have similar instances. . . . Not necessarily in my classroom, because I squash that conversation immediately. You don't use derogatory terms for another human being. That just doesn't happen in this room, and if you don't like it you can get out." Dan addressed the racialized jokes and name-calling in his classroom by explicitly stating his expectations (no derogatory terms) and consequences (get out). While it is important to make sure that there are consequences for those who are disrespectful in the classroom, we also know that such language will continue unless students are taught to critically examine the language used in pop culture, including youth culture, and to question it. Although he is not staying silent about the racialized jokes and name-calling being said, he is not helping students think critically about the words they use. Despite this critique of his strategy, we believe that multiple perspectives are important and oftentimes inspire others to share, as we see below.

As the conversation progressed, Bryan drew on his own experiences of prejudice to explain why students might use jokes: "Not to get too personal but, maybe in defense of these kids and a different perspective. Sometimes, speaking from experience, I knew it was easier to make the joke first before somebody else could. Again, not that any of this is right, and you shouldn't do that, but that might be what some of these kids are doing." Here, Bryan, who had a physical disability, drew on his own experience to say that perhaps making the first joke or claiming the racialized (in his case, a disability-related) jokes and name-calling was a way to survive socially.

Adam agreed. He also talked more about the importance of helping students, even those that are using slurs to each other, break down what racism looks like and how those racialized jokes and name-calling might affect other students.

> One more thing . . . and obviously I need to write a paper with this title because I really like it, but get ready for a slur. . . . Basically, I've never been called "beaner" by a stranger. . . . That should absolutely still come into your unpacking. If you call them on it, you know, "We're friends, we're friends." Just be like, "Okay. Why are you being like that to your friend?" You still need to have them analyze it. Like, "Listen. What you're doing is racist." And they're like, "Well, it's not racist because it's my friend, I'm not like that." It's like, "Of course you're not. So why are you doing it?" Because like I said, never been called "beaner," "wetback," any of that by a stranger. You've got to have them unpack that too. Because friendship or no, it's still racist. It's still something we have to learn to say, "Wait a minute, why are you doing it?"

Here, Adam strategized ways that his peers could address this tension by taking them through an imagined scenario. He attempted to offer potential language they could use to help students unpack these dilemmas. He also validated his peers' beliefs that this language is hurtful and that teachers need to consistently address these dilemmas both in and outside the classroom.

Oftentimes, a critical conversation will end with more questions to explore in the future. With that said, it is clear that other strategies are missing. Although Adam hints at notions of internalized racism, he does not use that phrase and does not articulate the impact it has on youth's behaviors and discourses. For teacher educators, this is a teaching opportunity for the next class: to read and discuss what internalized racism is and how it is connected to youth's use of language. We also think it would be generative in this context to research and discuss the history of racialized jokes and name-calling so that teachers have an in-depth understanding of this language when it is used in schools and how to approach from a stance of critical self-reflection and inquiry (Roberts et al., 2008).

With that in mind, the class ended with discussion about the possibility for more exploration in relation to that concept:

> Amy: But then sometimes people can reclaim words and make them their own, and it can be an empowering.
>
> Dan: But where is the line?
>
> Amy: Every situation is different. . . . But I think teaching kids how to talk to each other in ways that is empowering rather than disempowering is the issue here.

For teacher educators, the end of this discussion might mean taking away a portion of planned lesson for next class with readings and discussion related to the question above.

USING TENSION AS A RESOURCE

Lewison and colleagues' (2015) four dimensions of a critical stance argue for the importance of using tension as a resource. For teacher educators, this is especially important to do during critical conversations. The data from this chapter illustrate how preservice teachers not only shared teaching experiences about a specific tension related to race but also strategized for specific ways to address those tensions.

Preservice teachers come to class with various entry points and personal experiences for talking about race. For example, some students have engaged in critical self-reflection about how their race shapes teaching and learning in a classroom. For other students, such critical self-reflection has just begun. Teacher educators need to help preservice teachers learn how to engage in critical conversations that challenge undemocratic practices and disrupt commonplace notions about race. They also need to do this work themselves. Below are two ways that teacher educators help preservice teachers do just that.

Sharing Teaching Experiences Related to Race

Engaging in critical conversations is a process that occurs over time. Thus, it is helpful to provide multiple opportunities for candidates to share teaching experiences related to race. Before preservice teachers engage in conversations about their own teaching practices, as discussed in sections above, preservice teachers benefit from talking about race in low-stakes ways. This might mean a chalkboard discussion (asking preservice teachers to write down initial words/phrases that come to mind) related to how they might define racism in schools and classrooms, what racialized jokes and name-calling sounds like, and what educators are doing to address the issues they observe.

For example, preservice teachers might have benefited from reading literature about how to handle racialized jokes and name-calling in and outside of the classroom. From here, candidates benefit from writing autobiographical narratives about high school experiences related to race. As seen above, preservice teachers learned from telling stories about tensions related to racialized jokes and name-calling. It can be helpful to ask teachers to write about a time when they experienced something similar in their own school. How was it handled?

Next, we recommend candidates read articles about critical conversations about race in ELA classrooms (see box above). After discussing these articles throughout the semester, candidates can do an equity audit for their clinical or student teaching experience, which includes answering questions about multicultural and culturally responsive pedagogy, curricula and materials in the classroom, the variety of instructional strategies that meet differing learning styles and backgrounds, and using students' funds of knowledge (MAEC, 2016).

Finally, we also recommend candidates engage in the video analysis described in this chapter. As seen in the findings, having a transcript and recorded lesson allows individuals and small groups to closely examine classroom interactions and refine their critical language awareness.

Strategizing

While it is helpful to share teaching experiences related to tensions, preservice teachers need some strategies to think critically about the dilemmas that arise in the context of classroom practice. Teacher educators can facilitate that process by asking candidates if they know of any possible solutions. When solutions are shared, teacher educators can push candidates to take the class through a possible scenario, as Adam did.

Finally, candidates benefit from resources that help them think more about the tensions they experience. In this instance, Amy could have shared *Speak Up at School* by Teaching Tolerance (Willoughby, 2012), which lays out ways to deal with racialized jokes and name-calling in school, such as speaking up against biased talk with colleagues and responding to hate speech by making personal connections.

Overall, this study illustrates how analysis of video-recorded classroom interactions can be used as an entry point into critical conversations about race, specifically related to improvised responses during daily interactions. Educators would benefit from more research on how English teachers enter and sustain critical conversations in their high school classrooms in relation to literature.

REFERENCES

Anagnostopoulos, D., Everett, S., & Carey, C. (2013). "Of course we're supposed to move on, but then you still got people who are not over those historical wounds": Cultural memory and US youth's race talk. *Discourse and Society, 24*(2), 163–185.

Bloome, D., Carter, S. P., Christian, B. M., Otto, S., & Shuart-Faris, N. (2004). *Discourse analysis and the study of classroom language and literacy events: A microethnographic perspective.* New York: Routledge.

Bolgatz, J. (2005). *Talking race in the classroom.* New York: Teachers College Press.

Brontsema, R. (2004). A queer revolution: Reconceptualizing the debate over linguistic reclamation. *Colorado Research in Linguistics, 17*(1), 1–17.

Brown, A. F. (2010). "Just because I am black and male doesn't mean I am a rapper!" Sociocultural dilemmas in using "rap" music as an educational tool in classrooms. In D. P. Alridge, J. B. Stewart, & V. P. Franklin (Eds.), *Message in the music: Hip hop, history, and pedagogy* (pp. 281–300). Washington, DC: ASALH Press.

Brown, A. F., Bloome, D., Morris, J. E., Power-Carter, S., & Willis, A. I. (2017). Classroom conversations in the study of race and the disruption of social and educational inequalities: A review of research. *Review of Research in Education, 41*(1), 453–476.

Carter, S. P. (2007). "Reading all that white crazy stuff": Black young women unpacking whiteness in a high school British literature classroom. *Journal of Classroom Interaction,* 42–54.

Copenhaver-Johnson, J. F. (2000). Silence in the classroom: Learning to talk about issues of race. *Dragon Lode, 18*(2), 8–16.

Copenhaver-Johnson, J. F. (2006). Talking to children about race: The importance of inviting difficult conversations. *Childhood Education, 83*(1), 12–22.

Fairclough, N. (2013). *Critical discourse analysis: The critical study of language.* New York: Routledge.

Fecho, B., Collier, N. D., Friese, E. E., & Wilson, A. A. (2010). Critical conversations: Tensions and opportunities of the dialogical classroom. *English Education, 42*(4), 427–447.
Freire, P. (1970). *Pedagogy of the oppressed*. London: Bloomsbury.
Gay, G., & Kirkland, K. (2003). Developing cultural critical consciousness and self-reflection in preservice teacher education. *Theory into practice, 42*(3), 181-187.
Grant, C. A., & Sleeter, C. E. (2006). *Turning on learning: Five approaches for multicultural teaching plans for race, class, gender and disability* (4th ed.). San Francisco: Jossey-Bass.
Guinier, L. (2004). From racial liberalism to racial literacy: Brown v. Board of Education and the interest-divergence dilemma. *Journal of American History, 91*(1), 92-118.
Haddix, M. M. (2015). *Cultivating racial and linguistic diversity in literacy teacher education: Teachers like me*. Routledge.
Hollingworth, L. (2009). Complicated conversations: Exploring race and ideology in an elementary classroom. *Urban Education, 44*(1), 30–58.
Hytten, K., & Warren, J. (2003). Engaging whiteness: How racial power gets reified in education. *International Journal of Qualitative Studies in Education, 16*(1), 65–89.
Juzwik, M., Borsheim-Black, C., Caughlan, S., & Heintz, S. (2013). *Inspiring dialogue: Talking to learn in the English classroom*. New York: Teachers College Press.
Kendi, I. X. (2016). *Stamped from the beginning: The definitive history of racist ideas in America*. London: Hachette UK.
Kohli, R. (2014). Unpacking internalized racism: Teachers of color striving for racially just classrooms. *Race Ethnicity and Education, 17*(3), 367–387.
Ladson-Billings, G. (2014). Culturally relevant pedagogy 2.0: A.k.a. the Remix. *Harvard Educational Review, 84*(1), 74–84.
Lester, N. A. (2013). The n-word: Lessons taught and lessons learned. *Journal of Praxis in Multicultural Education, 8*(2), 3; 1–40.
Lewison, M., Leland, C., & Harste, J. (2015). *Creating critical classrooms: Reading and writing with an edge* (2nd ed.). New York: Routledge.
Malo-Juvera, V. (2017). A Postcolonial Primer with Multicultural YA Literature. *English Journal, 107*(1), 41.
Merriam, S. B., & Tisdell, E. J. (2016). *Qualitative research: A guide to design and implementation*. San Francisco: Jossey-Bass.
Michael, A. (2014). *Raising race questions: Whiteness and inquiry in education*. Teachers College Press.
Mid-Atlantic Equity Consortium (MAEC). (2016). Criteria for an equitable classroom: An equity audit. Retrieved from https://maec.org.
Mosley, M. (2010). 'That really hit me hard': moving beyond passive anti-racism to engage with critical race literacy pedagogy. *Race Ethnicity and Education, 13*(4), 449-471.
National Council for Teachers of English. (2010). Resolution on social justice in education. Retrieved from http://www2.ncte.org.
Paris, D., & Alim, H. S. (Eds.). (2017). *Culturally sustaining pedagogies: Teaching and learning for justice in a changing world*. Teachers College Press.
Pixley, M. F., & VanDerPloeg, L. S. (2000). Learning to see: White. *English Education, 32*, 278–289.
Price, S. (2011). Straight Talk about the N-Word. Teaching Tolerance. https://www.tolerance.org/magazine/fall-2011/straight-talk-about-the-nword
Rex, L. A., & Schiller, L. (2009). *Using discourse analysis to improve classroom interaction*. New York: Routledge.
Roberts, R. A., Bell, L. A., & Murphy, B. (2008). Flipping the script: Analyzing youth talk about race and racism. *Anthropology and Education Quarterly, 39*(3), 334–354.
Rodriguez, R., & Gonzalez, P. (2005). Column of the Americas: Diagnosing internalized oppression.
Rogers, R. (2003). *A critical discourse analysis of family literacy practices: Power in and out of print*. Abingdon, UK: Routledge.
Rogers, R., & Mosley, M. (2006). Racial literacy in a second-grade classroom: Critical race theory, whiteness studies, and literacy research. *Reading Research Quarterly, 41*(4), 462-495.

Rose, T. (1994). *Black noise: Rap music and black culture in contemporary America* (Vol. 6). Middletown, CT: Wesleyan University Press.

Sassi, K., & Thomas, E. E. (2008). Walking the talk: Examining privilege and race in a ninth-grade classroom. *English Journal*, 25–31.

Schaffer, R., & Skinner, D. G. (2009). Performing race in four culturally diverse fourth grade classrooms: Silence, race talk, and the negotiation of social boundaries. *Anthropology and Education Quarterly, 40*(3), 277–296.

Schieble, M. (2012). Critical conversations on whiteness with young adult literature. *Journal of Adolescent and Adult Literacy, 56*(3), 212–221.

Sealy-Ruiz, Y. (2011). Learning to talk and write about race: Developing racial literacy in a college English classroom. *English Quarterly, 42*(1), 24–42.

Singleton, G. E. (2014). *Courageous conversations about race: A field guide for achieving equity in schools*. Thousand Oaks, CA: Corwin Press.

Skerrett, A. (2011). English teachers' racial literacy knowledge and practice. *Race Ethnicity and Education, 14*(3), 313-330.

Smagorinsky, P. (2008). The method section as conceptual epicenter in constructing social science research reports. *Written Communication, 25*(3), 389–411.

Solomona, R. P., Portelli, J. P., Daniel, B. J., & Campbell, A. (2005). The discourse of denial: How white teacher candidates construct race, racism and "white privilege." *Race Ethnicity and Education, 8*(2), 147–169.

Taie, S., & Goldring, R. (2017). Characteristics of public elementary and secondary school teachers in the United States: Results from the 2015–16 National Teacher and Principal Survey. First Look. NCES 2017-072. National Center for Education Statistics.

Thein, A. H. (2013). Language arts teachers' resistance to teaching LGBT literature and issues. *Language Arts, 90*(3), 169–180.

Twine, F. W. (2004). A white side of black Britain: The concept of racial literacy. *Ethnic and racial studies, 27*(6), 878-907.

Vetter, A., & Schieble, M. (2016). *Observing teacher identities through video analysis: Practice and implications*. New York: Routledge.

Welton, A. D., Diem, S., & Holme, J. J. (2015). Color conscious, cultural blindness: Suburban school districts and demographic change. *Education and Urban Society, 47*(6), 695-722.

Willoughby, B. (2012). *Speak up at school*. Montgomery, AL: Teaching Tolerance.

A Response to Chapter 3

Lauren Gatti

In the winter of 2018, a two-hour video of a white supremacist student at the university where I teach in the Midwest began circulating around campus and, eventually, the country. In the video, the student—a neo-Nazi and member of the Vanguard America group that violently beat a man at the Unite the Right rally in Charlottesville, Virginia, in August of 2017—explained to his Google Hangout audience, "I want to be violent. Trust me. Really violent. It's just not the right time. We need to build ourselves up. We need to be disciplined. We need to train ourselves and make ourselves hard . . . so that when the time comes, we can do what needs to be done." The university community reacted immediately and loudly, demanding conversations with university leadership about whether this student should be kicked out of the university. He was not.

The week of this incident, my English language arts methods students shuffled into class more subdued than usual. I surveyed the room, noting the quiet. I reflected on my graduate students' reaction to the incident the night before when we spent more than an hour discussing the video, debating the university leadership's responsibility to its students—especially our students of color—and linking the racist ideologies of the student's rants to the historical texts we had been reading related to education in the Reconstruction Era.

Shelving my lesson plan for the first part of class, I told my class that in light of the video we had all seen or heard of, we were going to take time to talk about white supremacy and racism on our campus. I wrote two sentences on the board: "How are we feeling right now?" and "What are we thinking/wondering about?"

How are we feeling? *Unsure. Demoralized. Confused. Mad as hell. Powerless. Anxious. Unsafe. Worried. Passive.* What are we thinking/wondering about? *Why is my university not acting? How do white allies help but not overshadow? What do you do when school leaders are legally right but morally wrong? How am I supposed to respond when hate ideologies surface (unapologetically) in my classroom?* In keeping with the four agreements from Singleton (2014) that Vetter and Schieble cite (p. 40), we understood that the point of the conversation was not to generate consensus or answers but rather to expect and accept nonclosure.

Vetter and Schieble's work on critical conversations comes at a crucial time as racist language, policies, platforms, and ideologies become increasingly normalized in public discourse and, unsurprisingly, in schools. In their informal survey distributed to 2,000 K–12 teachers immediately following the 2016 election, the Southern Poverty Law Center (SPLC) found that the 2016 primary season "produc[ed] an alarming level of fear and anxiety among children of color" (Costello, 2016, p. 4), something they call the "Trump Effect." (See also Sondel, Baggett, & Hadley Dunn [2018] for an analysis of postelection political trauma.)

Although they are not making a causal argument related to the "Trump Effect," Vetter and Schieble's chapter illustrates how larger tensions and conflicts regarding race and racism do seep into classroom interactions, in this case the problem of navigating the terrain of responding to racialized jokes in the classroom. Their research invites us to consider how preservice teachers who are learning to teach in public schools face a multilayered dilemma: They must learn to confront and untangle their own histories and experiences with race and racism; they must learn to notice and responsibly respond to incidents of racism and racial tension; and they must work to help the students in their classrooms identify, analyze, and critically interrogate those incidents.

By naming the problem of racialized jokes in the secondary English classroom, Vetter and Schieble help bridge the broader realities of racism that students experience and witness (both on the ground and in the media) to the day-to-day work of helping novice English teachers identify and respond to the myriad expressions of racism that surface in K–12 classrooms.

There were two aspects of this chapter that were particularly interesting to me. The first was Adam's role in the work of critical conversations in Amy's classroom. As the only preservice student of color in the class, the authors explain that "Adam positions himself as a knowledgeable advocate for talking to students about race . . . [and] was able to foster the critical conversation in a way that Amy was not" (p. 42). Even though Adam is able to pose questions and facilitate critical conversations about racialized jokes—using detailed examples from his own life to highlight how fraught classroom dilemmas around humor are—the authors carefully explain that they are "not advocating for English educators to position students of color as the spokespersons for topics about race" (p. 42).

Adam's role in the classroom made me think about how this specific classroom moment in a methods class is inextricably linked to the larger ethical mandates we have as a field to diversify our English education programs. Arguments for the recruitment, retention, and support of students of color often stall at the level of programmatic concern. They can become circular arguments—*we need more diverse teacher candidates because we value diversity*—or, worse, these arguments for the recruitment, retention, and support of students of color can become slogans that suggest a program is committed to justice simply because it discursively foregrounds diversity as a guiding principle.

But what I think this chapter illustrates so clearly is that having more diverse students in our English education programs is an ethical imperative because only when we have more diverse perspectives and voices in our classrooms—like Adam's voice—can we support our teacher candidates' learning to teach processes in more holistic and justice-oriented ways. Adam was able to powerfully question and beautifully challenge his classmates' thinking by sharing his own experiences with racialized jokes. But while his experiential resources as a person of color allow him to push his classmates' thinking, he himself is still a student who needs to be supported and challenged and validated by *other* diverse students whose experiences might be similar to or different from his. Creating cohorts where Adam is not alone as a student of color is one way to ensure he is not unintentionally positioned as the spokesperson for all people of color.

In addition to provoking my thinking around the ethical mandates we have to diversify the pool of teacher candidates in teacher education, this chapter made me think about the ways in which the structures and sequences of our programs must also reflect our commitments to learn with and from local communities of color. One powerful example I see of this work is Guillén and Zeichner's (2018) research on the role of community partnerships in teacher education and, specifically, the way that these partnerships can affirm the learning experiences of teachers of color.

In their research, Guillén and Zeichner describe the Community Teaching Strand (CTS) at Pineridge University in the Pacific Northwest. Primarily housed in the field experiences seminar for elementary and secondary students, the CTS was a partnership between the university and community organizations. University teacher educators worked with a group of community leaders who had formed the Family and Community Mentor Network (FCMN), and together these leaders worked collectively as teacher educators to engage preservice teachers in panel discussion with community leaders, community forums, community guided walks, home visits, professional development, and mini-conferences based on issues in education (i.e., school-to-prison pipeline; see Zeichner, Bowman, Guillén, & Napolitan, 2016). Guillén and Zeichner (2018) describe the ways in which this kind of community partnership had particularly powerful effects for teachers of color. They write,

> Another positive and initially unexpected impact on preservice teachers was the impact of the CTS in supporting preservice teachers of color in the cohort. Exit tickets indicated that preservice teachers of color reported feeling supported and affirmed in their visions of teaching because of the CTS and their relationships with community mentors. Community mentors of color took great pride in seeing preservice teachers of color, often connecting on different levels and in different types of conversations about what it means to be community teachers. (p. 151)

There are many ways we can and should respond to the kinds of challenges that Vetter and Schieble's work illustrates. For me, this chapter helps me remember that our commitments to justice in English education can be operationalized at different levels. We can express our commitments to justice when we craft and model assignments that invite students to critically analyze their words and interactions with students, as the authors do with their video assignment. We can live our commitments when we approach our admissions in a way that explicitly values diverse perspectives and experiences. And we can demonstrate humility and asset-based pedagogies when we leave our university classrooms to learn with and from local families and communities of color.

REFERENCES

Costello, M. (2016). *The Trump effect: The impact of the presidential campaign on our nation's schools*. Montgomery, AL: Southern Poverty Law Center. Retrieved from https://www.splcenter.org.

Guillén, L., & Zeichner, K. (2018). A university-community partnership in teacher education from the perspectives of community-based teacher educators. *Journal of Teacher Education, 69*(2), 140–153.

Singleton, G. E. (2014). *Courageous conversations about race: A field guide for achieving equity in schools*. Thousand Oaks, CA: Corwin Press.

Sondel, B., Baggett, H., & Hadley Dunn, A. (2018). "For millions of people, this is real trauma": A pedagogy of political trauma in the wake of the 2016 U.S. presidential election. *Teaching and Teacher Education, 70*, 175–185.

Zeichner, K., Bowman, M., Guillén, L., & Napolitan, K. (2016). Engaging and working in solidarity with local communities in preparing teachers of their children. *Journal of Teacher Education, 67*(4), 277–290.

Part II

Practices in English Education

Chapter Four

Writing in and for the 21st Century

Crossing Digital and Multimodal Thresholds in ELA Methods Courses

Amber Jensen

"What kinds of writing are important for students to value and have fluency with in their English classes?" This question, posed to preservice teachers during the first week of their first graduate-level English teaching methods course, generated a set of responses reflecting beginning preservice teachers' conceptions and values of writing pedagogy. The responses raised concerns about the extent to which preservice teachers' notions of what counts—or what might count—as writing in their future classrooms reflects 21st-century approaches. Moreover, the responses furthered the course instructors' examination of how their English language arts (ELA) methods course challenges and expands preservice teachers' mindsets about 21st-century writing instruction.

This chapter describes course modifications made in an English teaching methods course. These modifications intended to foster preservice teachers' 21st-century mindsets about writing instruction. This chapter explores how the course succeeded and struggled to move preservice teachers' through "thresholds" (Adler-Kassner & Wardle, 2015) that included understanding 21st-century writing and enacting pedagogy that honors that knowledge. Based on preservice teachers' writing and reflections from the course as well as the instructors' observations, the chapter offers four approaches likely to support preservice teachers in crossing these thresholds.

Data was collected from one semester of an English Teaching Methods I course, the first subject-specific course taken by preservice teachers in secondary English education enrolled in the graduate teacher licensure and master of education program at Eastern Southern University, a large, public university located in the eastern United States. The students in the program—and in this course, specifically—reflect a broad range of academic backgrounds, professional work experiences, and ages. Some have recently completed their undergraduate degrees, while others are returning to graduate school after stretches of time devoted to schooling, careers, and families.

Despite their varied backgrounds, the preservice teachers' responses to the question about the kinds of writing experiences students should have in English class were fairly consistent and not altogether surprising. Susan (all names of people and places are pseudonyms) wrote, for example, "Students should be able to write well-crafted responses, essays, and letters." Kaitlin focused on narrative, descriptive, and persuasive modes. Carlos discussed grammar, sentence structure, and form.

What lacked in the preservice teachers' responses prompted the two instructors of the course to reconsider their assumptions about how 21st-century preservice teachers think about writing in and for school. None of the preservice teachers in the class, regardless of age or previous professional or academic backgrounds, explicitly mentioned digital genres, visual modes, writing with technology, public audiences, or collaboration—many of the aspects that characterize writing in the 21st century.

Not until preservice teachers responded to further questions about writing in personal and professional contexts and about the role of technology in writing did any of them explicitly name any of these kinds of characteristics of 21st-century writing. The responses to this simple question raise two important questions for English educators who think about preparing the next generation of English teachers:

1. What do we know about the way incoming teachers to the profession conceive of writing instruction?
2. How should that understanding frame the way we approach teaching English methods courses in the 21st century?

English educators can design their methods courses to position preservice teachers as either facilitators or gatekeepers of writing pedagogies that truly embody the affordances and possibilities of the 21st century. One way to replace entrenched academic patterns is by practicing strategies and fostering dispositions required to teach and advocate for evolving 21st-century literacies (Curwood, Lammers, & Magnifico, 2017) in methods courses. Doing so helps preservice teachers become more aware of the conceptions, values, and practices they bring with them—or do not—as they cross the threshold into becoming a 21st-century English teacher.

THRESHOLD CONCEPTS AND 21ST-CENTURY WRITING

Nearly twenty years into the 21st century, it might be tempting to assume that preservice teachers are proficient digital and multimodal writers, and that their writing pedagogies will thus reflect these proficiencies. However, English educators must be careful not to make these assumptions. Current research calls attention to the ways that even so-called digital natives (Prensky, 2001) are often unaware of the influence of digital technologies and multimodality on their writing practices, even when they are active composers in social and digital platforms (Boche, 2014; Howard, 2014; Kew, Given, & Brass, 2011; Schieble, 2010).

Even proficient digital and multimodal writers need to evolve their teaching mindsets to adopt pedagogies that acknowledge these shifts, particularly as they move into academic settings, where attention to digital and multimodal, collaborative and public, forms of writing may take a backseat to more familiar and traditional writing practices of their own schooling experiences.

While many writing teachers do embrace new methods and approaches to teaching writing (DeVoss & Hicks, 2010; Hicks & Turner, 2013), current research still shows that when it comes to digital and multimodal writing, old mindsets, old content, and old pedagogies still persist (Caprino, 2015), particularly when it comes to classroom practices. This disposition is also true of preservice English teachers before they enter the classroom full time (Hundley & Holbrook, 2013).

Composition theorists Adler-Kassner and Wardle (2015) used "threshold concepts" as a framework to highlight how making knowledge about writing explicit is a first step to changing teaching practices. Naming theories and principles is an important step; however, transcending a threshold also requires that practitioners work with these concepts "in their fullness" (Anson, 2015). Though digital and multimodal writing may be *happening* in methods classes (for example, students may compose in Google Drive or create PowerPoint presentations or submit writing via Blackboard), unless it is, in Anson's words, "fully articulated, active" (p. 216) and plentifully explained, these multimodal happenings may be simply that—happenings—and not transformative experiences likely to frame future writing pedagogies.

As preservice teachers cross the threshold from writer and student of writing to teacher of writing, their personal theories, grown from their experiences and the "apprenticeship of observation" (Lortie, 1975), shape their expectations for writing and learning in their classrooms (Smagorinsky & Barnes, 2014; Yancey, Robertson, & Taczak, 2014). Thus, uncovering deeply held and often unexamined beliefs about writing and challenging habituated practices must be a key goal of teaching methods courses. This is especially important to helping preservice teachers shift their paradigms about writing pedagogy toward a 21st-century mindset.

What would a 21st-century mindset for teaching writing entail? Writing in the 21st century includes composing with technology and using digital platforms, of course. But it need not be limited to technological and digital forms; 21st-century writing also features the ways different modes—text, image, video, and sound—interact in any medium.

In *Literacy Theories for the Digital Age*, Mills (2015) discussed how digital text production, collaborative writing, multimodality, and virtual communities change the way writers think about and experience writing. Often, writing in the 21st century is public, collaborative, and responsive, shifting students' roles from passive consumers to critical composers of the kinds of texts they interact with daily. To make possible writing pedagogies that reflect these ways of thinking, preservice teachers must fully understand the rhetorical and transformative principles and possibilities of 21st-century writing.

ENGLISH TEACHING METHODS I COURSE

Because the teacher licensure and master of education program does not include a requirement for students to take a course dedicated to 21st-century teaching and learning theories (though some students do take an elective course on educational technology), these theories and perspectives must be integrated into the program's core courses, particularly the subject-area teaching methods courses. In order to more explicitly address implications of teaching writing in the 21st century, the English Teaching Methods I instructors modified core learning and writing experiences within this course to cultivate opportunities for preservice teachers to practice new forms of digital and multimodal writing, reflect on their evolving beliefs about writing, and articulate their goals and strategies for teaching 21st-century composition in their future classrooms.

Recognizing the ways teachers' own writing experiences shape their teaching beliefs and practices, the course provided preservice teachers many low-stakes opportunities to compose as 21st-century writers. Table 4.1 outlines the core course activities, featuring their digital, multimodal, and collaborative components. These activities ranged from informal, end-of-class writing reflections in a range of multimodal genres (e.g., memes, infographics, and blogs) to digital peer collaboration on an extended multigenre research project and a literacy autobiography and student interview synthesized and remixed from poster to narrative and to digital video.

In addition to the major course assignments listed in Table 4.1, regular reflective responses and in-class activities invited students to interrogate their

Table 4.1. English Teaching Methods Course Assignments

Major course assignment	Digital, multimodal, and/or collaborative writing component
Demonstration lesson and digital teaching tool	Students chose unfamiliar digital platforms appropriate for presenting information and generating/guiding class discussion; in groups, students demonstrated use of the platform to discuss course readings.
Remixed literacy autobiography	Students composed using their choice of digital product that combined images, text, and voice/video recording to tell their own literacy autobiography alongside that of an adolescent they interviewed for the project.
Multigenre research project	Students selected genres through which they depicted their chosen research topics; digital genres were optional, though all students were required to conduct a digital peer review (via Google Docs, Skype, FaceTime, etc.) and complete a reflection on their experiences.
Daily genre study write-outs	Students wrote low-stakes, end-of-class reflections in a variety of new and familiar "real world" genres, including digital and multimodal genres such as infographics, memes, tweets, and Google Form surveys, etc.
Lesson plan and analysis	Students selected lesson plan topics, learning activities, and assessments that related to their multigenre research projects. Digital, multimodal, and/or collaborative writing components were not a requirement of this assignment, though many students included them.

own assumptions about teaching writing from a 21st-century perspective. Students completed open-ended surveys at the beginning and at the end of the course to articulate their beliefs about writing instruction and examine how their views changed throughout the course. Class discussions about these topics and individual writing conferences also provided ongoing reflection and intervention opportunities.

The intention of these activities was to push preservice teachers to consider the kinds of texts—visual, multimodal, and digital—and experiences that that could count as writing in a 21st-century classroom, to make explicit the ways that their own experiences shape these conceptions, and to prepare them to articulate their stances in new contexts.

CONSIDERATIONS FOR DEVELOPING A 21ST-CENTURY MINDSET

Preservice teachers' reflective responses on the pre- and postcourse surveys suggested that their conceptions of school-based writing pedagogy in the 21st century evolved over the course of the semester. At the beginning of the course, students only named traditional academic modes (e.g., expressive, expository, and persuasive) and genres (e.g., research paper, personal narrative, and poetry) as important to writing instruction, but in the postcourse surveys, nearly every student's response also identified multimodal, multimedia, digital, public, or collaborative writing experiences as important.

At the end of the course, students were more likely to describe writing tasks and experiences within their rhetorical contexts: They acknowledged professional or public audiences beyond the teacher (e.g., workplace correspondence, social media, and blogs) and emphasized the importance of flexible and context-based, rather than teacher-driven, forms of writing. On the whole, their responses reflected a much more varied and flexible approach to writing. This attention to 21st-century concepts in their frameworks about writing instruction was a likely result of explicit attention to these kinds of writing in the course learning activities.

Based on their experiences and reflections, it could be logical to conclude that the course had, indeed, transformed the preservice teachers' conceptions toward a more comprehensive view of writing in the 21st century. Perhaps it did. However, the more important question about how and if these conceptions would sustain beyond the methods course itself persisted: Would the preservice teachers apply their knowledge to enact 21st-century writing pedagogies in their classrooms? Would they successfully advocate for these practices and push back against curricular norms and traditions that reflected a more limiting view? Were there ways in which the methods course had—or could have—given them the framework and experiences to truly cross the threshold toward 21st-century writing pedagogy in practice?

Reflecting on both the successes and the challenges of the course, particularly the moments when disconnects emerged and tensions arose, four important considerations arose for how English teaching methods courses might more intentionally support preservice teachers in crossing the threshold. It seems that developing a 21st-century mindset requires the following four key moves:

1. Interrogating familiar practices,
2. Moving toward a "parallel pedagogy,"
3. Transcending surface approaches, and
4. Advocating for 21st-century writing practices.

Interrogating Familiar Practices

One challenge that arose in the course is when the preservice teachers questioned the notion that 21st-century writing could be valid and valued in academic spaces. This assumption, often implicit, became most evident when they shifted from thinking of themselves as writers to thinking of themselves as teachers of writing. For example, for a first draft of her writing-based lesson plan, Kaitlin designed a teacher-delivered PowerPoint presentation on the "hamburger method" of writing a five-paragraph essay, including directions on crafting an introduction, a thesis statement, three supporting reasons with evidence, and a conclusion. In her lesson, students would take notes on the presentation and then compose a structured writing assignment.

Despite the instructors' intention to problematize such standardized, decontextualized, and inauthentic approaches to writing in the methods course, Kaitlin's lesson plan draft reflected a troubling disconnect: When she imagined herself in a teaching role, she reverted to familiar forms and familiar pedagogies. In a writing conference with her instructor, she was asked to explain where the idea for the PowerPoint presentation came from. She noted that it mirrored how she had learned to write in high school. Her response pointed to how deeply ingrained her own schooling experiences were and how profoundly they influenced her view of academic writing instruction.

This prompted a discussion about what other ways of learning and forms of writing could be more relevant in accomplishing the learning goals Kaitlin set for her students. Reflecting on the multimodal literacy autobiography she had composed earlier in the course, she considered how that project—and the remixing process she used to compose it in visual, textual, digital, and multimodal layers—could be a new model for what teaching writing could look like.

Kaitlin's revised lesson plan included gestures toward her developing 21st-century mindset: Students would write for a public audience and consider the form best suited for that. Her end-of-semester reflection also indicated her evolving thinking. She wrote, "I didn't consider that things such as tweets, memes, and statuses could be considered as 'writing.' This opens up . . . the way our students engage with texts."

Likewise, "opening up" Kaitlin's way of thinking about teaching writing was a necessary intervention to shifting her mindset. When preservice teachers' conceptions are limited to what they remember from their own writing classes, they are likely to exclude the kinds of texts that more fully represent 21st-century genres, forms, and purposes. We may counteract this by reframing the learning and writing experiences of methods courses as academic—and exploring how and if they are truly valid—as a first step to supporting preservice teachers in crossing these important thresholds.

Moving Toward a "Parallel Pedagogy"

Introducing a different way of thinking about writing can have the unintended consequence of pitting *new* and *old* against each other. This is made more challenging because even the terms *21st-century writing* and *New Li-*

teracies imply a break from the old and a replacement with something new. However, the notion that digital and multimodal writing could be considered anything other than a constitutive component of composition reflects limited—and limiting—views of writing and writing education writ large. This perception may lead teachers to falsely believe they must choose one or the other, that teaching web-based writing, for example, comes at the expense of teaching the argument essay.

Turner and Hicks (2012) explain that a binary mindset is particularly troublesome for preservice teachers who are developing their teaching frameworks: When they "[see] digital writing as additional, rather than as an essential component of holistic instruction," it causes them "to draw on a time/cost framework to defend their views that multimodal writing could not, and perhaps should not, be incorporated into their teaching" (p. 70). This can be exacerbated in practice, as time constraints and institutional pressures reiterate such a time/cost framework.

The methods course featured here adopted what Leander (2009) called a "parallel pedagogy" approach, in which print and digital compositions exist side by side, where one is not privileged at the expense of the other. Parallel pedagogy encourages writers to consider the full range of semiotic resources available, technological or not, enabling them "to discover—to choose—the modalities that best help them convey what they want to communicate" (Palmeri, 2012, p. 37) rather than limit them by artificial and predetermined boundaries. All writing experiences, then, become essentially 21st century in nature.

The first assignment of the methods course, a remixed literacy autobiography, was designed to honor writing in a range of modes. It required preservice teachers to evaluate the affordances and possibilities of each. First, the preservice teachers composed written reflections of their own past writing experiences. They adapted these reflections into visual representations to share in peer groups. Then, they conducted interviews with youth about their literacy lives, and finally, they remixed their written reflections, visual interpretations, and interview audio recordings into a digital, multimodal product integrating all of the components of the process.

Tensions arose at various points along the way, as the preservice teachers wondered if their compositions "looked right," struggled to use new digital tools, and worried about how their final products would be assessed. When Rachel brought in her visual draft—a children's book that she had written and illustrated, rather than the stand-alone posters that most of her peers brought—she started to hide it, wondering if she had done it wrong. This opened the way for a critical conversation about visual genres and rhetorical possibilities of various approaches.

Rachel's final multimodal video product did not end up using the storyline approach that her earlier visual draft did, but her understanding of how various kinds of writing interact evoked a mindset inclusive of visual and digital forms. In her reflection, Rachel wrote that multimodal remixing "transforms the material and texts provided to students in a new way. This transformation offers a new perspective, therefore offering a unique understanding of the content." Another preservice teacher, Dan, indicated his understanding of parallel pedagogy when he wrote, "Playing with modes and media can help destabilize approaches and make [students] reconsider how they go about certain tasks" to create "more meaningful applications."

Rather than valuing written over visual or digital over print, working toward a parallel pedagogy means integrating both *old* and *new* kinds of writing in meaningful ways, and being explicit about those decisions. The redesigned methods course modeled parallel pedagogy in the range of writing tasks and experiences the preservice teachers encountered. Just as importantly, the conversations held alongside these writing experiences made explicit the parallel pedagogy framework to avoid theorizing digital and multimodal writing as replacements for—or worse, threats to—traditional school-based writing.

Transcending Surface Approaches

A related challenge to integrating new writing experiences with preservice teachers is the tendency to subordinate writing's rhetorical and contextual purposes to focus on the digital or technological medium through which it is mediated. It is accepted that literacy and technology have shaped and will continually shape one another (New London Group, 1996; Ong, 1986), but the way writers or teachers approach the digital aspects of writing may belie that understanding.

Some teachers may believe that their writing instruction reflects a 21st-century approach when they collect student writing via Google Classroom rather than in print copy, for example. They may think that assigning a visual component to a research paper fulfills the expectations of multimodal literacy. However, in these examples, the genres, audiences, and modes of writing do not fully engage the rhetorical contexts or semiotic affordances of 21st-century writing; they simply use digital technology and images to replicate existing practices. Integrating multimodal and digital texts to the writing curriculum in meaningful ways demands teachers who value both the technical requirements and the rhetorical possibilities of digital and visual literacies (Brooke, 2013; Grabill & Hicks, 2005).

For the "Story of Injustice" assignment, an original narrative that would anchor the preservice teachers' multigenre lesson plans, preservice teachers were encouraged to write using the genres or mediums that best represented their stories. Still, most of the preservice teachers' first drafts were text only. In a writing conference with Amira about how she might revise her story about a Middle Eastern girl facing Islamophobia at school, a discussion ensued about how visual modes might change the way a reader experiences the story. She surprised even herself when she decided that, while she did not consider herself an artist, she wanted to compose the next version of her story as a graphic novel. It was a risk worth taking, in her mind, as she realized how a visual representation of the main character might elicit more connection and empathy through the reader's interpretation of the story.

Amira's drawing skills may have dissuaded her from composing with pictures, but prioritizing the rhetorical thinking behind such choices encouraged her to see beyond the possibilities of a text-only version of her story. Amira's experience composing a graphic novel influenced her end-of-course lesson plan design, in which she planned for her future students to read and evaluate the graphic novel *Persepolis*, considering why the story was told in visual form and how the images conveyed the meaning. They would then compose their own graphic novels.

It is important to remember that the mere existence of digital or multimodal composition in methods courses does not serve as evidence of transformed and threshold-crossing teaching practices (Cervetti, Damico, & Pearson, 2006). Brooke (2013) challenges teachers to avoid an "instrumentalist attitude" that just moving writing into digital spaces will change the way writers compose. Similarly, Grabill and Hicks (2005) encourage teachers to extend beyond this *fundamental* or *simple* use of technology in the composition classroom to think about *how* these technologies—and any range of modalities—can be used to help writers reframe and rethink what and why they write.

Without considering why digital or multimodal writing is included in a methods course and making those reasons explicit to preservice teachers, for example, English educators will miss an opportunity to help them cross the 21st-century threshold.

Advocating for 21st-Century Writing Practices

Finally, preservice teachers must be prepared to become advocates for the threshold-crossing practices and values they are developing. This means helping them learn to assess infrastructures and institutional expectations, anticipate barriers, identify allies, and take appropriate risks. It is one thing for preservice teachers to practice 21st-century writing in a university course, but successfully implementing these teaching practices requires preservice teachers to know how and why these practices matter.

To simulate the experience of anticipating opposition and naming and defending 21st-century writing pedagogies, one course session included a structured debate in which preservice teachers assumed the roles of various stakeholders: teacher colleagues, students, parents, and administrators. They discussed how these stakeholders might question or support digital or multimodal writing approaches, and they prepared rationale to address the anticipated concerns using theory- and practice-based language they had learned and practiced so far in the course.

This classroom debate raised the aforementioned tensions between perceived *old* and *new* literacies in schools; however, many of preservice teachers used words like "motivating," "engaging," "fun," and "creative" as they practiced explaining to potential skeptics their reasons for integrating 21st-century writing in their hypothetical classrooms. For example, in response to an imagined administrator who expressed concerns about student performance on standardized tests, Fiona said, "At the end of the day, don't we want our students to be super engaged and super excited about learning? If we can do that by adding in different kinds of activities and projects where they can collaborate, what more do you need?"

Of course it is important to consider what kinds of texts and learning activities will engage students, but framing a teaching rationale in these terms alone raises concern as it carries the risk of sidelining the inherent and necessary rhetorical view of digital and multimodal writing. These kinds of responses may deprioritize attention and commitment to newer ways of teaching writing in contrast to the so-called real stuff of the traditional writing classroom: grammar, thesis statements, and other concepts likely to appear on high-stakes exams.

Preservice teachers need to be able to articulate rhetorical, cognitive, and methodological reasons for integrating multiple modes in any writing task. The simulated debate revealed that the preservice teachers were still learning to articulate their understanding in ways that would persuade possible future critics. This reflective practice opportunity was an important start.

When teachers ground their pedagogical choices within their knowledge of writing and learning theories, they become powerful in claiming the authority to teach in these ways. In helping preservice teachers recognize their biases and assumptions, develop integrated theories of learning and writing, and articulate their rationale to various audiences, they will become empowered with tools that nudge them closer to the threshold of 21st-century writing.

FURTHER CONSIDERATIONS

For preservice teachers, crossing the threshold of 21st-century writing instruction means reflecting on and reconfiguring their beliefs and experiences as writers. It means becoming aware of and articulating the social, cognitive, and communicative possibilities made available through new literacies. It means being willing and empowered to challenge existing (often powerful and imposing) institutions and structures that resist such changes. Shifting paradigms—crossing thresholds—is what English educators ask of preservice teachers, and not only that but also we ask them to pioneer writing instruction in contexts that may be set up to resist these changes.

Teaching this redesigned methods course prompted further questions as to how and to what extent methods courses position preservice teachers to be open to new ways of thinking, writing, and teaching as new genres emerge, as digital technologies change, and as they prepare to move within and between institutions. What would it look like to integrate the four considerations outlined above as a more explicit part of an English methods curriculum, rather than as responsive interventions to the misconceptions and tensions that arose? What happens with these conceptions once preservice teachers enter their own classrooms?

English methods instructors are limited to mapping how preservice teachers' beliefs develop within the contexts of the courses they teach, though they know that the real test comes when preservice teachers go into classrooms and find their voices in enacting these principles. Johnson's (2016) recent study of 21st-century teaching and writing calls for examining preservice teachers' transitions from university-based learning to classroom teaching more closely in context. This chapter echoes Johnson's call: Further research examining how teachers' mindsets develop and shift as they move between different sites of teaching and learning will help English educators understand how and to what extent teachers' enacted practices reflect their learning experiences as preservice teachers in English methods courses.

Ultimately, the lessons learned from this English methods course reiterate Graban and colleagues' (2013) admonition that it is the job of English methods instructors not to "enculturate preservice teachers to a particular style of teaching (or writing)" (p. 249) but rather to help them develop habits of mind and a theoretical and experiential foundation that will inform their choices in the classroom. With an eye to their future teaching lives, methods courses must engage emerging and evolving notions of writing in the 21st century to best support preservice teachers in likewise embracing and enacting these flexible and changing principles.

REFERENCES

Adler-Kassner, L., & Wardle, E. (2015). *Naming what we know: Threshold concepts of writing studies*. Boulder, CO: University Press of Colorado.

Anson, C. M. (2015). Crossing thresholds: What's to know about writing across the curriculum. In L. Adler-Kassner & E. Wardle (Eds.), *Naming what we know: Threshold concepts of writing studies*. Boulder, CO: University Press of Colorado.

Boche, B. (2014). Multiliteracies in the classroom: Emerging conceptions of first-year teachers. *Journal of Language and Literacy Education, 10*(1), 114–135.

Brooke, C. G. (2013). New media. In G. Tate, A. R. Taggart, K. Schick, & H. B. Hessler (Eds.), *A guide to composition pedagogies* (2nd ed.). New York: Oxford University Press.

Caprino, K. A. J. (2015). *Investigating an online study group as a path to critical digital writing for four middle grades English teachers: A qualitative study* (doctoral dissertation). University of North Carolina at Chapel Hill, Chapel Hill, NC.

Cervetti, G., Damico, J., & Pearson, P. D. (2006). Multiple literacies, new literacies, and teacher education. *Theory Into Practice, 45*(4), 378–386.

Curwood, J. S., Lammers, J. C., & Magnifico, A. M. (2017). From research to practice: Writing, technology, and English teacher education. In H. Hallman (Ed.), *Innovations in English language arts teacher education* (Vol. 27, pp. 121–141). Bingley, UK: Emerald.

DeVoss, D. N., & Hicks, T. (2010). *Because digital writing matters: Improving student writing in online and multimedia environments* (1st ed.). San Francisco: Jossey-Bass.

Grabill, J. T., & Hicks, T. (2005). Multiliteracies meet methods: The case for digital writing in English education. *English Education, 37*(4), 301–311.

Graban, T. S., Charlton, C., & Charlton, J. (2013). Multivalent composition and the reinvention of expertise. In T. Bowen & C. Whithaus (Eds.), *Multimodal literacies and emerging genres* (1st ed., pp. 248–281). Pittsburgh, PA: University of Pittsburgh Press.

Hicks, T., & Turner, K. H. (2013). No longer a luxury: Digital literacy can't wait. *English Journal, 102*(6), 58.

Howard, P. (2014). Affinity spaces and ecologies of practice: Digital composing processes of preservice English teachers. *Language and Literacy, 16*(1).

Hundley, M., & Holbrook, T. (2013). Set in stone or set in motion? Multimodal and digital writing with preservice English teachers. *Journal of Adolescent and Adult Literacy, 56*(6), 500–509.

Johnson, L. L. (2016). Writing 2.0: How English teachers conceptualize writing with digital technologies. *English Education, 49*(1), 28.

Kew, B., Given, K., & Brass, J. (2011). Teachers as researchers of new literacies: Reflections on qualitative self-study. *Journal of Language and Literacy Education*, 67–84.

Leander, K. (2009). Composing with old and new media: Toward a parallel pedagogy. In V. Carrington & M. Robinson (Eds.), *Digital literacies: Social learning and classroom practices*. Los Angeles: Sage.

Lortie, D. C. (1975). *Schoolteacher: A sociological study*. Chicago: University of Chicago Press.

Mills, K. A. (2015). *Literacy theories for the digital age: Social, critical, multimodal, spatial, material and sensory lenses*. Bristol, UK: Multilingual Matters.

New London Group. (1996). A pedagogy of multiliteracies: Designing social futures. *Harvard Educational Review, 66*(1), 60–92.

Ong, W. (1986). Writing is a technology that restructures thought. In G. Baumann (Ed.), *The written word: Literacy in transition* (pp. 23–48). Oxford, UK: Clarendon.

Palmeri, J. (2012). *Remixing composition: A history of multimodal writing pedagogy*. Carbondale: Southern Illinois University Press.

Prensky, M. (2001). Digital natives, digital immigrants: Part 1. *On the Horizon, 9*(5), 1–6.

Schieble, M. (2010). The not so digital divide: Bringing preservice English teachers' media literacies into practice. *Journal of Media Literacy Education, 2*(2), 102–112.

Smagorinsky, P., & Barnes, M. E. (2014). Revisiting and revising the apprenticeship of observation. *Teacher Education Quarterly, 41*(4), 29–52.

Turner, K. H., & Hicks, T. (2012). "That's not writing": Exploring the intersection of digital writing, community literacy, and social justice. *Community Literacy Journal, 6*(1), 55–78.

Yancey, K., Robertson, L., & Taczak, K. (2014). *Writing across contexts: Transfer, composition, and sites of writing* (1st ed.). Logan: Utah State University Press.

A Response to Chapter 4

Mike Metz

I remember when I first began teaching in 1995. The internet was just taking off, computers were still large and clunky, and I ended each day covered in a fine dusting of chalk from writing on . . . chalkboards. In those days, talk of 21st-century skills was talk of an imagined future. We dreamed of what students might need to know and be able to do in order to be successful in a world we were just catching glimpses of. We couldn't conceive of Snapchat, video blogs, and multimedia-infused student-created remixes of literacy autobiographies posted to curated YouTube channels.

Fast-forward to 2018 and we can't imagine a world where students *don't* compose multimedia mash-ups with computers they carry around in their pockets.

The challenge this poses to English teacher educators is twofold. First, English teacher educators need to grapple with the shifting terrain of the discipline. English has always been contested terrain (Scholes, 1998; 2011), and that contestation continues to take new forms as we rapidly move from a discipline based in printed word to a discipline on the forefront of the consumption, composition, and interpretation of multimodal texts (Miller, 2015). The second challenge, if English teacher educators choose to embrace—rather than resist—the move toward digital and multimodal texts, is how we educate English teachers to work with texts that didn't exist when we taught at the grade school ourselves. Chalkboards, remember? Amber Jensen's treatment of 21st-century writing teacher education helps us consider how to support teachers entering a space of new and evolving text forms.

Most of the undergraduate students entering my university this fall were born in the 21st century (one of the first entering classes for whom this is true); thus, for them, 21st-century writing is simply writing. Still, the schools they teach in, and the systems they interact with, have been dragged into this century kicking and screaming (Kress, 2008; Scholes, 2011). For this reason, the traditional literacy practices these future teachers experienced in school were drastically different than the contemporary literacy practices they were immersed in out of school. This divide exacerbates the inertia toward stasis in schooling, as preservice teachers continue to rely on the *apprenticeship of observation* (Lortie, 1975) as a primary source of knowledge for teaching.

To counter the apprenticeship of observation (Grossman, 1991; Lortie, 1975), Jensen highlights the development of metacognition about writing processes. The importance of metacognition stems from a long tradition in writing studies (Flower & Hayes, 1981; Goodman, 1986). Expanding this metacognition to include consideration of 21st-century writing practices is an important extension of this work. By prompting teacher candidates to articulate the literacy practices they use every day, and the digital and multimodal skills interwoven in those literacy practices, the approach Jensen describes helps future teachers move past teaching the way they were taught.

By including the concept of a *parallel pedagogy* (Leander, 2009), Jensen ties 21st-century writing to a larger postmodern and poststructural movement. Breaking down binaries and thinking holistically about communication arts echoes the repertoire approach advocated in poststructural approaches to grammar and language teaching (Garcia, Flores, & Spotti, 2017; Metz, 2017). Rather than pitting one writing tradition against another, the goal is to give students an extensive repertoire of approaches—so they can meet the needs of 21st-century communication. The development of this multimodal writing repertoire goes hand in hand with the promotion of new rhetorical contexts and opportunities.

Jensen touches on the structural constraints English teachers will need to contend with. In an era when explicit rubrics and concrete exemplars form the basis of a tight-knit standards-based curriculum, it is hard to make space for the generative and creative potential of multimodal, collaborative, and responsive composing. Jensen begins to unpack the development of new rhetorical traditions that accompany these multimodal genres. But the potential conflict with a high-stakes testing and standards-based school culture will be a continuing challenge.

When English teachers assign students to construct a video of a spoken word poem in response to a text, they cannot use a traditional argumentative essay rubric to assess the rhetorical structure. The types of multimodal composing Jensen encourages teachers to adopt are situated in multifaceted contexts with layered audiences and purposes. These forms of writing require adaptive thinking about what constitutes criteria of quality in emergent genres.

With these challenges in mind, it is important that Jensen also supports teachers to advocate for the value of this type of composing. If English teacher educators educate teachers to break with long-standing traditions, we must also prepare them for the resistance they may encounter. Jensen describes what this preparation looks like and how it might be organized. There is an implicit stance here that positions new teachers as change agents in schools, a stance that aligns 21st-century writing with 21st-century teacher education (Darling-Hammond, 2006). Anchoring larger educational change within core content is a key element of transformative teacher education.

Overall, Jensen's chapter calls to mind the prescriptive tendency in English education that privileges a backward-looking, historical lens. Jensen's chapter makes the case for shifting that lens, not fully toward the future, but at least into the present. The tradition of English educators holding on to romantic visions of the past is a staple of the discipline, but one English educators can no longer afford to promote. The rapid pace of technological advancement, and with it the evolving and generative nature of textual production, requires teachers who can adapt on the fly (Kress, 2008).

By helping future teachers of writing embrace a descriptive, rather than prescriptive, stance, Jensen acknowledges the value of the writing processes our newest teachers are already immersed in. Developing their metacognition, a poststructural repertoire approach, and the ability to articulate the value of this approach will support these writing teachers to better serve their students.

REFERENCES

Darling-Hammond, L. (2006). Constructing 21st-century teacher education. *Journal of Teacher Education, 57*(3), 300–314. https://doi.org/10.1177/0022487105285962.

Flower, L., & Hayes, J. R. (1981). A cognitive process theory of writing. *College Composition and Communication, 32*(4), 365–387. https://doi.org/10.2307/356600.

Garcia, O., Flores, N., & Spotti, M. (2017). A critical poststructural perspective. In *Oxford handbook of language and society* (pp. 1–16). New York: Oxford University Press.

Goodman, Y. M. (1986). Children coming to know literacy. In W. H. Teale & E. Sulzby (Eds.), *Emergent literacy: Writing and reading* (pp. 1–14). Norwood, NJ: Ablex.

Grossman, P. L. (1991). Overcoming the apprenticeship of observation in teacher education coursework. *Teaching and Teacher Education, 7*(4), 345–357. https://doi.org/10.1016/0742-051X(91)90004-9.

Kress, G. (2008). A curriculum for the future. In N. Norris (Ed.), *Curriculum and the teacher: 35 years of the Cambridge Journal of Education* (pp. 211–222). New York: Routledge.

Leander, K. (2009). Composing with old and new media: Toward a parallel pedagogy. In V. Carrington & M. Robinson (Eds.), *Digital literacies: Social learning and classroom practices*. Los Angeles: Sage.

Lortie, D. C. (1975). *Schoolteacher: A sociological study*. Chicago: University of Chicago Press.

Metz, M. (2017). Addressing English teachers' concerns about decentering standard English. *English Teaching: Practice and Critique, 16*(3), 363–374. https://doi.org/10.1108/ETPC-05-2017-0062.

Miller, S. (2015). Teacher learning for new times: Repurposing new multimodal literacies and digital video-composing for schools. In J. Flood, S. B. Heath, & D. Lapp (Eds.), *Handbook of research on teaching literacy through the communicative and visual arts* (pp. 441–453). A project of the International Reading Association. New York: Routledge.

Scholes, R. (1998). *The rise and fall of English: Reconstructing English as a discipline*. New Haven, CT: Yale University Press.

Scholes, R. (2011). *English after the fall: From literature to textuality*. Iowa City: University of Iowa Press.

Chapter Five

Moving Preservice English Teachers From Egocentric to Sociocentric Readings

Crag Hill

Reader response has been a fruitful critical lens from which to read a text for more than a generation (Beach, 1993; Probst, 1992; Probst, 2004). Preservice English teachers today have grown up in a culture that values their role in reading transactions in and out of the classroom. In fact, many English majors find it difficult to give up the primacy of their perspectives, finding it discomfiting to interrogate a text, especially literary narratives, from perspectives other than their own—a skill they very well may have learned from their own secondary education.

In secondary classrooms, teachers value the readings their students produce—that valuation is one of the primary ways teachers motivate their students to read—but to prepare these students to read the variety of texts they will encounter in their lifetimes and to read their worlds, teachers need to provide students the means to develop the ability to read critically from more than their own point of view.

In reading a novel such as *The Hunger Games*, many readers identify with the protagonist, Katniss; while rooting for her, they also imagine what they would do in similar circumstances. But there are many more possible readings of *The Hunger Games* when readers reach beyond their own responses. The ability to read text in multiple ways is especially critical for teachers as they prepare to teach the novel to their students.

Once preservice teachers see the benefit of reading from different points of view, they can then transfer these kinds of readings to their own classrooms. If we, as teachers, expect students to read from multiple perspectives, we need to make sure we provide ample opportunities to practice these kinds of readings in teacher education programs.

We, as teacher educators, need to ask preservice teachers to read from

1. Their own egocentric perspective, reader-as-self;
2. The perspective of one of the characters, reader-as-character, reading the character's world, not imposing one's own parameters on it;
3. The point of view of a teacher, reading from the point of view of the spectrum of readers they will soon be working with, from avid, independent readers to readers who have not yet been engaged by print narrative;
4. The point of view of a writer producing these kinds of texts, thinking about the decisions the writer has made; and
5. The perspective of a literary critic, evaluating the text through lenses that reveal how these texts speak to sociocultural issues and practicing sociocentric readings in ways that expand critical skills.

These readings are transacted not discreetly but rather simultaneously, synergistically. But when we devote instructional time to studying and practicing each of the different perspectives in a young adult (YA) literature course or another literature course open to a variety of genres and texts that engage contemporary issues, preservice teachers will be able to gain the level of understanding necessary to teach their prospective students to read from multiple perspectives as well, to ensure their reading world expands.

ENGLISH MAJORS IN YOUNG ADULT LITERATURE CLASSES

A shift occurs each semester in undergraduate YA literature classes after students have read and discussed the kinds of novels instructors use to introduce that genre. Students have been surprised and pushed by the novels at the beginning of these courses, even as many now come to these classes in the wake of the *Harry Potter* wave having read more YA literature than college students did a generation ago.

Laurie Halse Anderson's *Winter Girls*, M. T. Anderson's *Feed*, and David Levithan and John Green's *Will Grayson, Will Grayson* have been particularly effective in transforming students' mis/conceptions of what constitutes YA literature, surprising them with their literary quality and gut-wrenching depictions of the lives of adolescents.

But oftentimes, these English majors invariably declare how other novels, such as Pam Munoz Ryan's *Becoming Naomi Leon*, Deborah Meadow's *No Ordinary Day*, or Jacqueline Woodson's *Miracle's Boys*, have not met their literary standards. Despite having their misconceptions scrambled by the introductory novels, they still measure other novels against the standards they have been formulating since they first became avid readers and that have been reinforced by literature instruction in schools.

For many of our students, literary quality is measured by not only the complexity of the prose (syntax and vocabulary, in particular) but also the complexity of character and plot development. These readers believe that the prose of writers such as Munoz, Meadow, and Woodson is simplistic; as readers, they have no difficulties with syntax and vocabulary and in comprehending characters and plot elements. Comparing these novels to those they have read in their other English classes, they question why only the protagonist is fully developed and why the plot commonly has only one major layer.

Yet, if these preservice teachers fail to consider that the novels selected for YA literature courses are written to engage the 14–18-year-old readers they will be teaching in the near future, some who may have different (but not lower) standards, some who may or may not have read much fiction, and some who may not have read much of anything at all, they may not have the mindset to help their students become better readers. The rest of each semester, then, must be spent setting up opportunities for preservice teachers to practice reading from the five different perspectives, those perspectives enumerated above.

READER-AS-SELF

For English majors to read-as-self means they are able to tap into reading skills acquired over years of reading, layers and layers of preference and rejection, readings and rereadings of favorite authors and genres, encounters with clarifying or befuddling criticism, and conversations with characters and other readers. To read-as-self means to revel in intra/interpersonal connection with a text world that is as vivid, and as vital, as the world outside the pages. It means an incessant intertextuality, a community of books as lively as a group of friends, old and new. It means vulnerability, self-protectiveness—these texts are one's own. It is a perspective many of the grade 6–12 students these preservice teachers will soon be teaching cannot fathom.

As the majority of teachers are White, female, and middle class (*Education Week*, 2017), many may have not encountered someone like Tyrell in Coe Booth's *Tyrell* (2010). Tyrell is a young African American man trying to hold his family together. Yet, in reading novels such as these, preservice teachers find it difficult to make the kinds of personal connections they have with other characters.

Tyrell frequently breaks the law to earn money to pay the rent and to feed his mother and younger brother. Though he bucks the stereotype of African Americans in urban areas by refusing to sell drugs, many of the preservice teachers with whom the author works read from within their own systems of values and recoil at his behavior. That he also has a sexual relationship with a young woman living in the same temporary housing with his family, even though he has a girlfriend, pushes him beyond the pale for many of these same readers. They are incapable of seeing the world through his eyes.

Here, reading only from one's point of view narrows the interpretations readers can take away from the novel. For readers who know a Tyrell, however, his lived experience may ring true. They may identify with Tyrell's struggle, and they may be cheering for him to find a way to keep his younger brother out of the foster care system. They may not agree with his actions, but they will understand their roots. They will see his strengths and not his weaknesses.

For every novel that students read in YA literature classes, then, we must first open space for them to voice their own points of view. We must continue to model that their readings are valued. But we cannot stop there. We must move the readings of each novel to other points of view, including a consideration of how the world of characters like Tyrell may be very different from their own world.

READER-AS-CHARACTER

A common reading perspective for emerging readers, one that students typically exercise in and out of school from an early age, is identification with one or more characters. The reading process includes begging characters to make the decisions they themselves would make, becoming emotionally engaged in what is happening to characters, and sharing successes and failures with the protagonist. As readers read more literary fiction, identification is enhanced by increased empathy (Oatley, 2016).

But whether one identifies with or empathizes with a character, preservice teachers need to read from the character's points of view, to judge them according to the values present within the character's world, not according to their own system of values, which may not even be present to the characters at this point in their lives.

For example, some preservice teachers severely judge Sticky in Matt de la Pena's *Ball Don't Lie* (2007). As they do with Tyrell, they hold Sticky to standards he has no sustained exposure to, few compelling models of, and no lifetime of practice with. They fail to view the world of the novel through Sticky's eyes. Though physically scarred by abuse in his childhood, mistreated in the foster care system, and suffering from obsessive compulsive disorder, Sticky is determined to live up to what his group home director has said to him: He is a good person. Beginning with his basketball skills, Sticky is intent on making a better life for himself.

To critically appreciate this book, preservice teachers need to question the values Sticky lives by. How did he form these values? How have these values been reinforced in his lived experience? Are his standards moving toward or away from the norms these preservice teachers know? To more fully understand Sticky, it is incumbent upon preservice teachers to first explicate what they think are his lack of morals, but they also then need to look at his actions like his compulsive shoplifting and try to discern how they fit into *his* system of values.

Novels such as *Ball Don't Lie* are rarely mirrors for these preservice teachers, but many will teach in schools where the novel may be such a mirror for their 6–12 students. Novels such as *Ball Don't Lie* and *Tyrell* help preservice teachers empathize with students who are more like Tyrell and Sticky than perhaps anyone else they have known. Reading as character helps support preservice teachers to read with their future students in mind.

READER-AS-TEACHER

Some of the students in grades 6–12 that preservice teachers will meet will be readers who will read anything put in front of them; some will be those who have read extensively in genres not generally included in a classroom (fantasy, science fiction, romance, and comics). Some, though, will be individuals who have not met a book that interested them in their entire lives.

Some of the readers preservice students will engage with in the near future may not yet have the ability to sort out plot and character or to predict how characters will act in certain situations. Some may not yet have the ability to parse out detail from plot and setting, and some may not be able to use word attack skills or context clues to meet vocabulary needs. Some students may not be able to hold the first clause of a compound sentence in their minds long enough to make meaning after they have read the second clause.

Therefore, it is important that preservice teachers practice reading from a teacher's point of view. How might a mixed group of students in grades 6–12 approach the text assigned in class or as independent reading? What would teachers want students to take away from the reading? What prior knowledge does it require or activate? Will students see themselves in the text, or will they see others in unforeseen ways? What are the language demands? Foremost, how can we help 6–12 students acquire the critical reading skills many preservice teachers take for granted?

All American Boys (2015) by Jason Reynolds and Brendan Kiely may not be a difficult book to decode for many readers, but it has different challenges. Written from two perspectives in alternating chapters, Rashad, an African American student, and Quinn, a White student, some students may find the novel difficult to follow. At the beginning of the book, one preservice teacher recently suggested that the class could create a map of each chapter, marking where the characters live and where the school is, and locating where and when the events of the novel take place.

The most difficult challenge for preservice teachers, though, might be the topics of racism and police brutality. When a group of preservice teachers read the novel in a methods class, they commented that discussion of the book had to be framed so that students were respectful of their peers' opinions. Otherwise, the discussion of the book might become too heated and unproductive.

Teachers should make sure not only that students feel comfortable sharing their opinions but also that students in grades 6–12 not be attacked for their beliefs. The preservice teachers commented that teachers will have to make sure the class engages in discussion and not in argument. Diffusing tension will be an important action for teachers to prepare for in leading discussion of the novel.

What can teachers do so every student in grades 6–12 engages meaningfully with the text or texts they will be assigning or the texts that they will be self-selecting? Is this is a difficult text for students in grades 6–12? How will teachers scaffold the reading so that those students will acquire the skills that will help them grow into the independent readers we would like them to be? Preservice teachers must acknowledge that none of these are easy questions to answer.

READER-AS-WRITER

Another approach all future English teachers need to take toward texts is to read from the point of view of a writer producing these kinds of texts. One compelling reason to ask students to read literary fiction is to enhance one's own writing. This reading perspective then asks preservice teachers to analyze the text for the decisions the writer has made in order to expand the awareness of decisions one can make in one's own writing. What moves did the writer make? Why did the writer make these moves? Are they effective? If not, how could a text be revised to strengthen it? What can this writer teach students about writing and reading?

In English class at all levels we spend a great deal of time de/constructing characters. Constructing a character is analogous to constructing an argument. The development of a character is cumulative, with each element building on the previous element and each particle of information contributing to the whole. For an example, in reading *Tyrell* (2010), preservice teachers need to look closely at how author Coe Booth builds Tyrell.

Booth does not simply tell us that Tyrell wants a life in the future very different from the life he is currently living. Instead, she shows again and again that he is not mired in the present moment as is often the assumption made of youth in the inner city. In every action, readers can observe how Tyrell, unwilling to follow in the self-destructive footsteps of his parents, looks to the future, to finding safe and secure shelter for his brother and to acquire the means to control his own life. By the end of *Tyrell*, Booth has fashioned a character that embodies the argument that youth struggling in poverty are not without dignity, not without a sense of purpose.

In another semester, a different group of students read two novels written in verse, Kate Braverman's *Home of the Brave* (2008) and Dana Walrath's *Like Water on Stone* (2014). The first of many questions these preservice teachers asked was, why were these two books written in verse? They wondered what the novels would be like if they were written in prose, and what would be gained and what lost.

When these preservice teachers rewrote some of the poems into prose, they felt the narratives had lost their voice. For *Home of the Brave*, the narrative is told from the point of view of Kek, an 11-year-old refugee from Sudan. Students felt that the short lines helped capture the way Kek looks at the world—in small strokes—as he tries to make sense of his new home. They also felt the lines embodied Kek's at-first-hesitant use of English.

Like Water on Stone is told from five different points of view, including an eagle. Students felt the poems helped create distinguishing characters, each carrying a distinct voice. They felt the style of the poems helped convey a culture they knew nothing about—Armenian culture at the time of World War I. Walrath's choice to include poems from the point of view of the eagle, they thought, gave the novel a mythical, otherworldly feel. Preservice teachers learned that the choice of genre for a narrative can be critical and that that genre can enhance the characters and the tone of a story. These are writerly decisions not to be taken lightly.

READER-AS-LITERARY CRITIC

College English and English education faculty in the last 20 years have done significant work in exposing preservice teachers to literary criticism and paving the way for literary criticism to be a part of the high school curriculum. Appleman (2015), Eckert (2006), Gillespie (2010), Soter (1999), Moore (1997/2004), and others have published informative and practical guides that offer strategies to help preservice teachers incorporate a range of critical points of view into their future classes.

As English majors, preservice teachers have studied literature through feminist, deconstructionist, Marxist, new historicist, and other lenses. Yet reading YA literature through these lenses initially challenges skilled, college-level readers. As readers, preservice teachers are comfortable with and well practiced in reader response, and with historicizing a text. However, when they are asked to take up other layers and to unpack texts for what they say about sociocultural issues such as gender, race, and sexuality, preservice teachers may struggle to give up their personal reading for readings that raise difficult questions.

Two relatively new approaches—the youth lens and ecocriticism—provide the means to look at the novels from the outside, as it were, rather than demanding the readers to put their personal positions on controversial issues in today's world into play. The youth lens examines culture and how schools, literature, and other media reinforce or upend stereotypes about adolescents (Sarigianides, Petrone, & Lewis, 2017), while Glotfelty and Fromm (1996) define ecocriticism as "the study of the relationship between literature and the physical environment" (p. xviii).

In a fall semester of a YA literature class, preservice teachers read Angela Johnson's *The First Part Last* (2003) and Scott Westerfeld's *Uglies* (2005). To enhance the reading of the novels, they also read two chapters from Hill (2014) in which YA literature scholars examined the two novels from one of these two lenses. After learning about the youth lens, these preservice teachers agreed with Lewis and Durand (2014) that *The First Part Last* resisted prevalent stereotypes about youth.

The cover image of *The First Part Last* shows a young black boy with dreadlocks, holding a child dressed in a pink shirt. The image represents Bobby, the protagonist, and his infant daughter, Feather. The cover then foregrounds that *The First Part Last* is "a departure from stories about teen pregnancy that typically focus on girl's experiences" (Lewis and Durand, 2014, p. 48). Again, in agreement with Lewis and Durand, the preservice teachers in the course believed the novel countered the narrative about African American men as absentee fathers. Though Bobby makes mistakes like many new parents, preservice teachers recognized that he fully embraced a role he had no prior training for.

In *Uglies* (2005), Tally cannot conceive of living outside the self-contained city-state comprised of Uglytown and New Pretty Town, two highly domesticated spaces designed to provide for all the needs and security of its citizens. "It's wrong to live in nature," she tells her friend Shay, "unless you want to live like an animal" (p. 92). Tally's view of the natural world as something to be shunned by humans, however, evolves as she sees the cost of the town's separation from nature, especially when she discovers what the leaders do to keep the citizens content and passive. When she leaves the city to pursue her friend Shay to the Smoke, a community hidden in the forest far from the city, Tally's attitude begins to slowly shift. "As she travels, a sense of the sublimity of nature begins to strike her" (p. 118). She realizes that humans are a part of and not apart from the natural world.

MOVING READERS DEEPLY INTO THEIR WORLDS

In reading through these two lenses and from the other perspectives described above, preservice teachers can discover how literature not only tells stories to personally care about and offers characters to identify and or empathize with but also provides models for effective writing. Literature can be a vehicle that discloses thematic and artistic concepts to broach with preservice teachers' future students. Throughout the YA literature course, preservice teachers learned that literature can, when read as a critic, reveal how writers are speaking to and about the worlds in their novels. Not only should preservice teachers and their future students read for pleasure, but also they should read to think deeply into their world.

REFERENCES

Appleman, D. (2015). *Critical encounters in high school English: Teaching literary theory to adolescents*. New York: Teachers College Press.
Arigo, C. (2014). Creating an eco-warrior: Wilderness and identity in the dystopian world of Scott Westerfeld's *Uglies* series. In C. Hill (Ed.), *The critical merits of young adult literature: Coming of age* (pp. 115–129). New York: Routledge.
Beach, R. (1993). *A teacher's introduction to reader-response theories*. Urbana, IL: National Council of Teachers of English.
Booth, C. (2010). *Tyrell*. New York: Scholastic.
Braverman, K. (2008). *Home of the brave*. Reprint ed. New York: Square Fish.
de la Pena, M. (2007). *Ball don't lie*. New York: Penguin Random House.
Eckert, L. (2006). *How does it mean? Engaging reluctant readers through literary theory*. Portsmouth, NH: Heinemann.
Education Week. (2017). The nation's teaching force is still white and female. Retrieved from https://www.edweek.org.
Gillespie, T. (2010). *Doing literary criticism: Helping students engage with challenging texts*. Moorabbin, Australia: Hawker Brownlow Education.
Glotfelty, C., & Fromm, H. (Eds.). (1996). *The ecocriticism reader: Landmarks in literary ecology*. Athens: University of Georgia Press.
Hill, C. (2014). *The critical merits of young adult literature: Coming of age*. New York: Routledge.
Johnson, A. (2003). *The first part last*. New York: Simon & Schuster.
Lewis, M. A., & Durand, E. S. (2014). Sexuality as risk and resistance in young adult literature. In C. Hill (Ed.), *The critical merits of young adult literature: Coming of age* (pp. 38–54). New York: Routledge.
Moore, J. N. (1997/2004). *Interpreting young adult literature: Literary theory in the secondary classroom*. Portsmouth, NH: Boynton/Cook Publishers Heinemann.
Oatley, K. (2016). Imagination, inference, intimacy: The psychology of *Pride and Prejudice*. *Review of General Psychology, 20*(3), 236–244.
Probst, R. E. (1992). Reader response theory and the problem of meaning. *Publishing Research Quarterly, 8*(1), 64–73. https://doi.org/10.1007/BF02680522.
Probst, R. E. (2004). *Response and analysis: Teaching literature in secondary school*. Portsmouth, NH: Heinemann.

Reynolds, J., and Kiely, B. (2015). *All American boys*. New York: Simon & Schuster.
Sarigianides, S. T., Petrone, R., & Lewis, M. A. (2017). *Rethinking the "adolescent" in adolescent literacy*. Urbana, IL: National Council of Teachers of English.
Soter, A. O. (1999). *Young adult literature and the new literary theories: Developing critical readers in middle school*. New York: Teachers College Press.
Walrath, D. (2014). *Like water on stone*. New York: Ember.
Westerfeld, S. (2005). *Uglies*. New York: Simon Pulse.

A Response to Chapter 5

Christopher M. Parsons

Crag Hill's central question—In what ways might beginning English teachers be best developed as skilled, flexible interpreters of texts?—is an important one for English teacher educators. In particular, Hill engages with five ways of reading (i.e., egocentric reading, reading as a character, reading as a teacher, reading as a writer, and reading as a literary critic) that might develop teacher candidates' skills within a young adult literature class.

The title of the chapter (*from* egocentric *to* sociocentric readings) reflects Hill's argument that egocentric readings come more easily to a reader, while the sociocentric ways of reading need more cultivation. Hill also emphasizes that, through these various readings, "preservice teachers will be able to gain the level of understanding necessary to teach their prospective students to read from multiple perspectives as well" (Hill, p. 76).

Hill joins colleagues in English teacher education who are concerned about the ways in which English teachers read texts and guide their students' readings. As Hill points out, Probst (1994) has long focused on reader response theory in secondary English classrooms, and Appleman (2015) has engaged the affordances of using critical theories with adolescents. More recently, Alston and Barker (2014) developed a "reading for teaching" model, and Rejan (2017) attempted to recast the histories and pedagogical uses of reader response and New Critical approaches in English classes.

While these ways of reading are clearly a consistent concern for English teacher educators, Hill points to an intriguing direction for future work. He argues, "These readings are transacted not discreetly but rather simultaneously, synergistically" (Hill, p. 76). The five ways of reading that Hill outlines, then, do not happen in separate silos; they necessarily interact and react upon contact with each other. Hill's move to consider multiple ways of reading at once exchanges the analytic concerns of one reading for a more holistic "ways of reading" ecology to which teacher candidates are exposed.

I would be curious to hear more from Hill about how such an interpretive ecology might work in context. Specifically, if Hill is right—that these five ways of reading happen "simultaneously, synergistically" (and I believe he is right)—I wonder

1. How might these various readings be(come) synergistic? How might English teachers make multiple readings synergistic for their students?
2. Where do teacher candidates encounter various ways of reading? In what ways might we, as English teacher educators, foster spaces for candidates to manage various (and perhaps even contradictory) ways of reading?

I know, most concretely, that English teacher candidates educated at the college where I work are exposed to many ways of reading throughout their undergraduate years and within their teacher education program. All teacher candidates are English majors, and their English professors offer critical perspectives, from New Critical to critical race, reader response, and ecocriticism. In their college composition courses or creative writing courses, teacher candidates receive instruction on learning to read with a writer's eye, and in their pedagogical grammar course, they delve into rhetorical theory.

In their education courses, and especially in their methods of teaching English courses, the teacher candidates at my institution get a more diffuse exposure to different ways of reading. Candidates consider critical theory in terms of using such theories with students (Appleman, 2015). They also consider how one might read as a teacher (following Alston & Barker, 2014). We even occasionally afford them minutes to react to literature, as Hill puts it, egocentrically—but only out of base weakness.

I include this background in an attempt to illustrate the two questions posed above about Hill's synergistic readings. To take the second question first, I am struck by the many sites in which teacher candidates are exposed to different ways of reading (i.e., in English, education, and composition). Hill, of course, includes his five ways of reading in one young adult literature course where the course structure presumably places them in useful conversation. But taken more broadly, Hill's chapter forces me to consider how the interdisciplinary sites where candidates learn ways of reading are in conversation with each other—or not. Without bringing these ways of reading together in some tangible way, teacher educators risk missing the opportunity to connect them or to enrich them for teacher candidates.

In order to make these connections (interdisciplinary or otherwise), I would argue that teacher educators need more focus on how ways of reading might be "synergistic" in the first place. A quick gloss of critical theories, for example, often portrays these readings as opposed almost by definition (e.g., the New Critics vs. Rosenblatt). And the line "Professor X in English is such a Marxist/feminist/and so forth" is well worn. I would imagine that teacher candidates internalize the idea that not all ways of reading can live in the same head.

How and where can we concoct the right *ways of reading* brew for candidates headed into English classrooms? I am not exactly sure. Hill's article, though, pushes me to consider the affordances of including many ways of reading in one classroom space. Hill is right, I think, to push candidates from egocentric readings to sociocentric ones. My next question, though, asks, how do all these new ways of reading cohabitate in the new English teachers' pedagogical frameworks?

REFERENCES

Alston, C. L., & Barker, L. M. (2014). Reading for teaching: What we notice when we look at literature. *English Journal, 103*(4), 62–67.

Appleman, D. (2015). *Critical encounters in high school English: Teaching literary theory to adolescents*. New York: Teachers College Press.

Probst, R. E. (1994). Reader-response theory and the English curriculum. *English Journal, 83*(3), 37–44.

Rejan, A. (2017). Reconciling Rosenblatt and the New Critics: The quest for an "experienced understanding" of literature. *English Education, 50*(1), 10–41.

Chapter Six

Powerful Influence and Absurd Neglect

The Legacy of Louise M. Rosenblatt in Secondary English Language Arts Methods Courses

Sue Ringler Pet

Louise Rosenblatt (1904–2005) is considered a fountainhead in the fields of literature, literacy, and literacy education. She is widely recognized for introducing the transactional theory of reading, which she mapped out in two books: *Literature as Exploration* (five editions, 1938–1995) and *The Reader, the Text, the Poem: The Transactional Theory of the Literary Work* (1978). Her works appear regularly in English language arts (ELA) methods courses where instructors typically spotlight the central tenets of her work, particularly the transactional theory and the efferent-aesthetic continuum of literary response (1938; 1978).

However, while impactful and oft quoted, Rosenblatt's work has endured absurd neglect among literary critics and in ELA education (Booth, 1995) for various reasons stemming from misrepresentation of her theory and teaching practices (Appleman, 2000; Clifford, 1991) to accusations of "runaway subjectivity" and "anything goes" literary response that led Rosenblatt to defend misappropriation for decades (Rosenblatt, 2005). This chapter discusses Rosenblatt's misrepresentation, marginalization, and merit—ultimately celebrating her position among literary scholars and calling for perpetuating her legacy through ELA methods courses.

Transactional theory was largely viewed as a reaction to New Critical emphasis on meaning contained in the text (Clifford, 1991; Rejan, 2017). However, Rosenblatt (1995), in fact, insisted that meaning resides neither in the reader nor in the text but rather is constructed by a subconscious reciprocal process with both players essential. With recognition of this "give-and-take with the signs on the page" (p. 26), the traditionally marginalized reader became important, implications for teaching became exciting, and Rosenblatt's reputation became more controversial.

In combating schools of thought that saw a defined "right way" to teach a piece of literature, Rosenblatt's conception of meaning-making with literary text unsettled the teaching of English, tilting it in a progressive direction. It underscored that literature "lends little comfort to the teacher who seeks the security of a clearly defined body of information" (1995, p. 27). Rosenblatt implied the opposite—that transactional theory applied to ELA classrooms adds complexity—to both reading and teaching.

In teacher education, mainstay methods course texts integrate Rosenblatt's theory as support for rich teaching methods that value what individual readers bring to text (Burke, 2014; Smagorinsky, 2008). Alsup and Bush (2003) embrace meaning-making à la Rosenblatt as a process that moves beyond the personal—to build cross-cultural understandings and empathy (p. 10). Scholarship continues to acknowledge Rosenblatt's work while offering sophisticated critiques (Lewis, 2002; Rejan, 2017; Soter, Wilkinson, Connors, Murphy, & Shen, 2010).

However, today's prospective teachers are posed with a limited understanding of Rosenblatt as giant. Internet resources increasingly paraphrase her groundbreaking ideas almost as public domain. Texts that appropriately celebrate her legacy (Clifford, 1991; Karolides, 1992; Probst, 2004) are showing up on "free books" tables in teacher education departments, while they remain on Rosenblatt's loyalists' top shelves and syllabi.

Despite the uneven reverence of her work, including Rosenblatt's seminal texts (1938; 1978; 2005) and the work of Rosenblatt scholars on the syllabus has enriched methods classes and changed minds about teaching literature for decades (Clifford, 1991; Faust, 2000; Karolides, 1992; Probst, 2004). ELA teacher educators continue to spotlight Rosenblatt's hallmarks, particularly transactional theory and efferent-aesthetic stances (Rosenblatt, 1938; 1978).

The latest volumes to reach methods courses represent a long-awaited surge to teach for equity and social justice. Chapters address sociocultural imperatives, give voice to traditionally marginalized populations and perspectives, and disrupt stale teaching models (Brass & Webb, 2015; Morell & Scherff, 2015; Paris & Amon, 2017). However, within them, Rosenblatt's name is rarely mentioned. When it is, she is associated with a limited definition of reader response (Brass & Webb, 2015; Morell & Scherff, 2015), which is unfortunate, because transactional theory resonates with calls for critical literacy, widely embraced by teacher educators and K–12 practitioners.

Critical literacy views texts as social constructs calling for readings that seek bias, note marginalized voices, take multiple perspectives, and consider power and positioning (Dozier, Johnston, & Rogers, 2006; Ellis, 2013; Lewison, Flint, & Van Sluys, 2002; Luke, 2000; Vasquez, 2003; Wood & Jocius, 2013). Transactional reading can be seen as critical in that it recognizes "multiple viewpoints and cause[s] readers to further reconsider their own . . . belief structures." (Karolides, 1992, p. 185). Within this current dialogue surrounding the ELA methods courses, Rosenblatt resonates perfectly with the voices in new culturally responsive methods texts (Brass & Webb, 2015; Morrell & Scherff, 2015).

ROSENBLATT IN TODAY'S ENGLISH LANGUAGE ARTS METHODS CLASS

What, specifically, is important about Rosenblatt's legacy for English teachers? What are the best ways to communicate these ideas to prospective teachers? Should candidates read portions of her seminal works (1938; 1978) and collected essays (2005)? Should they read the literature about her (Clifford, 1991) and experiment with Rosenblatt's teaching practices (Probst, 2004)? Or should future teachers examine their own lived-through experience of reading (Buckley, 1992)?

Including Rosenblatt in today's methods courses might take any of these forms toward fruitful ends. Alongside and interspersed with culturally responsive/sustaining teaching methods (Brass & Webb, 2015; Morrell & Scherff, 2015; Paris & Alim, 2017), transactions with literature will be powerful. Rosenblatt's lifework essays in *Making Meaning With Texts* (2005) serves as an excellent anchor text alongside and interspersed with the work of Rosenblatt scholars (e.g., Clifford, 1991; Faust, 2000; and Probst, 2004). Her essays call for paying close attention to one's own reading process if one alleges to teach transactions with literature with integrity.

In "The Acid Test for Literature Teaching" (1956), Rosenblatt suggests that readers ask this crucial question: "What in this book, *and in me*, caused this response?" (p. 70; italics in original). This chapter purports that raising this single question provokes the reader/preservice teacher to engage in critical transactions with text. During and after their lived-through (aesthetic) experience with literature, readers consider not only the text but also the personal reservoir of linguistic and life experience they bring to the text (Rosenblatt, 1993) and how that affects meaning-making.

Additionally, this question urges preservice teachers to discover blind spots difficult to acknowledge, including privilege and positioning in society (Lensmire et al., 2013; Margolin, 2015) and "single stories" they may hold (Tschida, Ryan, & Ticknor, 2014)—that affect meaning-making with text and with life. As preservice teachers reflect on their reading processes, their positioning within those transactions and in society, and how they would go about ensuring that their future students are positioned as readers this way as well, Rosenblatt's legacy finds its place in contemporary teaching strategies.

Close reading of one's own reading in an ELA methods course can affect prospective teachers' assumptions about pedagogy. Buckley (1992) had teachers examine their own reading processes, asking not "how they *think* they should read or how they *would like* to read. . . . But how *does one* [actually] read?" (p. 50; emphasis added). Challenged to visualize and describe, think aloud and emote, write, draft, share, edit, and compare, teachers were amazed at the "incredible individuality of reading," and found themselves "never again . . . satisfied with the simplistic, fatuous, delusive explanations of reading proposed by educational technicians," and full out rejected prescriptive and rigid teaching methods (p. 55).

Teacher educators can offer opportunities for candidates in methods courses to come to similar revelations by participating in deliberate and metacognitive acts of lived-through experience with literature. One activity, "The Poetry Jar" (S. Voake, 1981, personal communication), highlights how personal associations with texts and objects vary significantly from person to person and thus affect the reading experience. Modeling with teacher candidates how the activity might play out in an ELA classroom, the methods instructor places an object (e.g., a mouselike toy) inside a large glass carafe. She then poses a series of questions/prompts as observers jot responses.

Prompts and jotted responses might include the following:

- What do you see in the poetry jar? (mouse, tail, rat, 2 ears, fur, shadow, beady eyes)
- What does it remind you of? (Adirondack bathtubs, mouse poops in the kitchen drawers at the lake house, rats, garbage, city sidewalks, dump, sewers, cartoons)
- What else do you see in the poetry jar? (reflection in his eyes, upward-pointing tail, shades of brown)
- What kinds of situations come to mind? (scurrying into mouse holes, mousetraps in cartoons, *CATS!*, 1950s housewives on tables swatting with brooms)
- What words or phrases do you associate with what you see in the poetry jar? (eek, squeak)
- Ask a question to what you see in the poetry jar. (Where would you rather be, mouse?)

Candidates then peruse poetry books scattered around the room, charged to search for a poem that *goes with* what they see in the poetry jar, share the poem aloud, give a reason for choosing the poem, and describe their search process—that is, metacognitively consider what they *did* to find their poem. This activity gets participants digging into poems, reading lines and stanzas aloud, naming poets, and most importantly noting the vast range of responses to what initially appears to be a simple exercise: "reading the text" inside the jar.

Discussion inevitably focuses on surprise about texts and associations with personal reservoirs, including the "incredible individuality of reading" and the conclusion that one-right-answer pedagogy in ELA classrooms is indeed "fatuous" (Buckley, 1992, p. 55). Candidates experience further delight when, removed from the jar, the toy mouse scurries across the table at the push of an on-off button. Talk about still deeper, unpredictable response, including implications for teaching about the effects of events that occur while one is reading, is literally brought to the table.

The activity wraps up beautifully when the methods instructor shares her own "association" poem as "Introduction to Poetry" by Billy Collins (1988), particularly the fifth and sixth lines. Class reading of the entire Collins poem typically lands on the last stanza as fuel for discussion about how to teach poetry à la Rosenblatt.

This activity paves the way toward fruitful reading and discussion of "What Facts Does this Poem Teach You?" (Rosenblatt, 1980), which generally cements the ridiculousness of the title in candidates' teaching minds, as they evolve to appreciate how Rosenblatt viewed the reader's role in the meaning-making process. Rosenblatt (1938/1995) wrote about the relationship among reader, text, and meaning: "No one else can read a literary work for us. The benefits of literature can emerge only from creative activity on the part of the reader himself. He responds to the little black marks on the page or to the sounds of the words in his ear and he makes something of them" (pp. 164–165). To further the exploration, the ELA methods course can unpack the significance of what Farrell (2005) noted as a "cunningly, deceptively simple" question that Rosenblatt regularly asked her students after they had read a text: "What do you make of it?" (p. 69). This question is empowering—especially in the way the words *you* and *make* reverberate and represent transactional theory. The significance can be evoked as lived-through experience of the children's book *The Man Who Walked Between the Towers* by Mordicai Gerstein.

To enact a three-part lived-through experience, the methods instructor supplies each candidate with an 11" × 7/8"-thick trifold paper strip to be used for quick-jot responses to "What are you thinking and/or feeling now?" at three, pre-chosen points during the read-aloud of this vibrantly illustrated, poignant picture book. After the reading, candidates are asked to review their three responses, turn over the paper strip, and respond in writing to "What do you make of it?"—that is, of the experience of hearing and responding to the text.

Shared and elaborated upon, responses will range from "At first I related to the tightrope walker's sense of freedom, high above Manhattan, then I was brought down suddenly at the end" to direct connection between text and life experience: "The fold-down vertical illustration of a dumbfounded crowd, in 1978, peering up at the man on the wire brought back my experience on 9/11/2001. *I was there*, looking up at the towers . . ." Depending on where and with whom this activity takes place, one or two candidates may be brought to tears by the abrupt ending "Now the towers are gone."

"What do you make of it?" fuels subsequent discussion, as the reader and the text in transaction become obvious main players, each affecting the other in the "live circuit set up between the reader and the text'" (Rosenblatt, 1978, p. 14). As Stanley Fish (1980), another theorist associated with reader response put it, "Interpretation is not the art of construing but the art of constructing. Interpreters do not decode poems; they *make* them" (p. 327; emphasis added). As teacher candidates review and share "what they made of" their lived-through experiences, transaction seems more visible.

For further tangibility, the instructor can offer another zinger of lived-through experience, by querying candidates about why they had to respond on a thin strip of cardstock while hearing the story read aloud. Future teacher/English scholars wonder about space constraint fostering creativity or concision; they suggest that attempts to evoke personal response are somehow amplified by smallness, and so on. Only returning to the text—the page where the tightrope wire is pictured close up in a person's hands—reveals that the 7/8" strip is precisely the stated thickness of the tightrope Phillipe Petit strung between the twin towers in 1978.

As this element of surprise impresses upon the group, no one is silent; somehow, the involuntary "Whoas" and "OMGs" become a significant aspect of the aesthetic experience altering the metacognitive replay for each individual. This aspect of the activity represents how Rosenblatt saw literary response as a progression from personal evocation, through negotiation (with others and with text), toward considered response—as a temporal, unfolding event (Faust, 2000, p. 27). For the community of readers as a whole, it offers a perfect segue into implication for teaching texts more typically taught in 7–12 grades.

What in This Book, *and in Me*, Caused This Response?

Consider William Stafford's "Traveling Through the Dark" (1962). Ostensibly, this poem is about a driver who stops late at night on the side of a back road and discovers that a pregnant doe has just been hit by a car and killed, while a fawn is still warm inside. The driver faces and handles an ethical-moral dilemma—with nobody but conscience present. From explicating the poem line by line to evoking free-write response, to intensely discussing punctuation, strategies for introducing this poem in secondary English classes (or deciding not to) vary across the spectrum of pedagogical philosophy.

With particular regard to framing a legacy for Rosenblatt as a literacy educator primarily concerned with teaching literature to "contribute to democratic education" (1995), teacher educators can begin to see that this poem has as much to teach about the text as it does about the self—and about the self in relation to others and society. The methods class can evoke individual reader response, open up discussion, and move toward individual and communal considered response.

When teacher candidates read and respond personally and discuss the text with others, then consider "What in this [text], *and in me*, caused this response?" they enact critical work about their own positioning in society and as readers with various and intersecting identities. In the case of Stafford's poem, candidates will review and may rethink their stances on the definition of life and what actions exemplify murder, finding themselves surprised by their own static or mutable viewpoints, and become aware of literature's potential to shape and change minds.

Rosenblatt has not been typically thought of as "critical" in this way, however. Her work has been criticized as individualist (Dressman & Webster, 2001; Lewis, 2002), which makes sense, if meaning-making as fostering "fruitful . . . transactions—between individual readers and individual literary texts" is understood only with regard to an individual reader transacting with a single text (Rosenblatt, 1995, pp. 25–26). However, attention to the temporal aspect of literary response brings out the full aesthetic and critical potential of the reading process. It emerges as dynamic, and its benefits stretch beyond the single reader to promote civil discourse.

According to Rosenblatt (1956), the reader's first steps are personal if not emotional: "The reader will be aglow with a particular response . . . register this response . . . and reflect on it," aware that it is "the result of the way the work fits into his own past experience of books and life" (p. 73). Importantly, the reader then "test[s] how their response stands up to revisiting the text and to other readers' responses" (p. 72), wondering, "What *in me* caused this response?" In this light, transaction is self-reflective and inclusive of the text and other readers; it may be seen (and celebrated) as a means to open minds.

Rosenblatt's legacy as proto-critical pedagogue is thus illuminated. She purported that important things happen when readers self-question: "Why did I care so much about what happened to a feeble, ignorant old man?" Or, "Why did I jump to such wrong conclusions?" (Rosenblatt, 1956, p. 74). From a teaching perspective, this questioning process can be viewed not as egocentric or individualistic but rather as critically literate moves to uncover "ideas and assumptions . . . sensitivities and . . . blind spots . . . that [one] brings to [one's] reading" (p. 73). Emphasized in ELA classes, these moves may be seen not only as *fruitful* but also as *critical* transactions.

CRITICAL TRANSACTIONS IN THE ELA CLASSROOM

In the context of the ELA classroom, fostering critical transactions offers opportunities for readers to notice and question their stations in life, including positioning and privilege, as they read and study literature. For example, when reading the young adult novel *The Hate U Give (THUG)*, by Angie Thomas, readers encounter Starr Carter, African American protagonist, who code-switches her identities to obtain respect from white peers and teachers: "Williamson Starr doesn't use slang—if a rapper would say it, she doesn't say it, even if her white friends do . . . [she] doesn't give anyone a reason to call her ghetto" (p. 71).

Critically transacting with text, the reader learns not only to respond to the character's actions but also to ask, regularly, "Why did I respond this way?" When a reader notices that the African American communities portrayed in *THUG* struggle with the emotional labor of charged relationships between black youth and law enforcement, white readers may begin to notice their own positioning and privilege in society. In methods classes, future teachers will realize that if each and every reader is bringing their own reservoir of experience to class, to bear, and to a text, all of that matters with regard to how literature is approached in ELA classes.

As young adult (YA) novels like *THUG* provide a "window" (Tschida, Ryan, & Ticknor, 2014) into black lives victimized by police violence, white readers may begin to engage in serious reflection on privilege (Carrasquillo, 2013; Lensmire et al., 2013) rather than conduct performative white privilege work (McIntosh, 1998). In line with the goal of #BlackLivesMatter, which was "not to show, shame, or to teach people how and why black lives matter, but . . . to create conditions for black lives to thrive" (Austin, Cardwell, Kennedy, & Spencer, 2016, para. 1), ELA teachers' work to create safe spaces that empower all students seems attainable.

Asking "What in this book, *and in me*, caused this response?" leads to surprising critical transactions with classic literature as well. When methods classes ask the question in the context of considering how to introduce *To Kill a Mockingbird* or *The Great Gatsby*, new answers emerge after each rereading—breathing new life into classic literature. In today's image-, injustice-, and information-filled society, it becomes clear that seeing a film adaptation, experiencing a hate crime, or discovering statistics about systemic racism or disparity of wealth in the United States affects one's transaction with any text—classic or otherwise.

Teaching English for democracy has always been at the heart of Rosenblatt's work, and amid this long-awaited surge to teach for equity and social justice, this proto-critical pedagogue deserves a seat at the table. Secondary ELA teacher educators can structure methods course opportunities with contemporary and classic literature as well as the literature by and about Louise

Rosenblatt such that prospective teachers embrace Rosenblatt's legacy as both literary critic and critical teacher. This legacy remains as relevant today as when she first developed her idea of reading as transaction.

REFERENCES

Alsup, J., & Bush, J. (2003). *But will it work with real students? Scenarios for teaching secondary English language arts*. Urbana, IL: NCTE.

Appleman, D. (2000). *Critical encounters in high school English: Teaching literary theory to adolescents*. New York: Teachers College Press.

Austin, P., Cardwell, E., Kennedy, C., & Spencer, R. (2016). Introduction: Teaching Black Lives Matter. *Radical Teacher: A Socialist, Feminist, and Anit-racist Journal on the Theory and Practice of Teaching, 106*, pp. 13–17.

Booth, W. (1995). Foreword. In L. M. Rosenblatt, *Literature as exploration* (pp. vii–xiv). New York: Modern Language Association.

Brass, J., & Webb, A. (Eds.). (2015). *Language arts methods courses: Critical issues and challenges for teacher educators in top-down times*. New York: Routledge.

Buckley, M. H. (1992). Falling into the white between the black lines: When teachers transact with texts. In N. Karolides (Ed.), *Reader response in the classroom: Evoking and interpreting meaning literature*. White Plains, NY: Longman.

Burke, J. (2014). *The English teacher's companion* (4th ed.). Portsmouth, NH: Heinemann.

Carrasquillo, A. (2013). *Teaching English as a Second Language: A Resource Guide*. New York: Routledge.

Clifford, J. (Ed.). (1991). *The Experience of reading: Louise Rosenblatt and reader-response theory*. Portsmouth, NH: Boynton/Cook.

Collins, B. (1988). *The apple that astonished Paris: Poems by Billy Collins*. Fayetteville: University of Arkansas Press.

Dozier, C., Johnston, P., & Rogers, R. (2006). *Critical Literacy/Critical Teaching: Tools for Preparing Responsive Teachers*. New York: Teacher College Press.

Dressman, M., & Webster, J. P. (2001). Retracing Rosenblatt: A textual archaeology. *Research in the Teaching of English, 36*, 110–145.

Ellis, A. (2013). Critical literacy, common core, and "close reading." *Colorado Reading Journal*, 45–50.

Farrell, E. (2005). Tribute to Louise Rosenblatt. *Voices from the Middle, 12*, 69.

Faust, M. (2000). Reconstructing familiar metaphors: John Dewey and Louise Rosenblatt on the literary work of art as experience. *Research in the Teaching of English, 35*(1), 9–34.

Fish, S. (1980). *Is there a text in this class? The authority of interpretive communities*. Cambridge, MA: Harvard University Press.

Gerstein, M. (2003). *The man who walked between the towers*. New York: Macmillan.

Karolides, N. (Ed.). (1992). *Reader response in the classroom: Evoking and interpreting meaning literature*. White Plains, NY: Longman.

Lensmire, T. J., McManimon, S. K., Tierney, J. D., Lee-Nichols, M. E., Casey, Z. A., Lensmire, A., & Davis, B. M. (2013). McIntosh as synecdoche: How teacher education's focus on white privilege undermines antiracism. *Harvard Educational Review, 83*, 410–431.

Lewis, C. (2002). Critical issues: Limits of identification; The personal, pleasurable, and critical in reader response. *Journal of Literacy Research, 3*, 253–266.

Lewison, M., Flint, A. S., & Van Sluys, K. (2002). Taking on critical literacy: The journey of newcomers and novices. *Language Arts, 79*, 382–292.

Luke, A. (2000). Critical literacy in Australia: A matter of context and standpoint. *Journal of Adolescent and Adult Literacy, 43*, 448–461.

Margolin, L. (2015). Unpacking the invisible knapsack: The invention of white privilege pedagogy. Retrieved from https://www.cogentoa.com.

McIntosh, P. (1998). White privilege: Unpacking the invisible knapsack. In M. McGoldrick (Ed.), *Revisioning family therapy: Race, culture, and gender in clinical practice* (pp. 147–152). New York: Guildford Press.

Morrell. E., & Scherff, L. (Eds.). (2015). *New directions in teaching English: Reimagining teaching, teacher education, and research*. Lanham, MD: Rowman & Littlefield.

Paris, D., & Alim, H. S. (2017). *Culturally sustaining pedagogies: Teaching and learning for justice in a changing world*. New York: Teachers College Press.

Probst, R. (2004). *Response and analysis: Teaching literature in secondary school* (2nd ed.). Portsmouth, NH: Heinemann.

Rejan, A. (2017). Reconciling Rosenblatt and the New Critics: The quest for an "experienced understanding" of literature. *English Education, 50*(1), 10–41.

Rosenblatt, L. (1938/1995). *Literature as exploration* (5th ed.). New York: Modern Language Association.

Rosenblatt, L. (1956). The acid test for literature teaching. *English Journal, 45*, 66–74.

Rosenblatt, L. (1978/1994). *The reader, the text, the poem: The transactional theory of the literary work*. Carbondale: Southern Illinois University Press.

Rosenblatt, L. (1980). "What facts does this poem teach you?" *Language Arts, 57*, 386–394.

Rosenblatt, L. (1993). The transactional theory: Against dualisms. *College English, 55*, 377–386.

Rosenblatt, L. (2005). *Making meaning with texts*. Portsmouth, NH: Heinemann.

Smagorinsky, P. (2008). *Teaching English by design: How to create and carry out instructional units*. Portsmouth, NH: Heinemann.

Soter, A. O., Wilkinson, I., Connors, S., Murphy, P. K., Shen, V. F. (2010). Deconstructing "aesthetic response" in small-group discussions about literature: A possible solution to the "aesthetic response" dilemma. *English Education, 42*, 204–225.

Stafford, W. (1962). *Traveling through the dark*. New York: Harper & Row.

Suleiman, S., & Crossman, I. (1980). *The reader in the text*. Princeton, NJ: Princeton University Press.

Tompkins, J. (Ed.). (1980). *Reader-response criticism: From formalism to post-structuralism*. Baltimore, MD: Johns Hopkins University Press.

Tschida, C., Ryan, C., & Ticknor, A. S. (2014). Building on windows and mirrors: Encouraging the disruption of "single stories" through children's literature. *Journal of Children's Literature, 40*, 28–39.

Vasquez, V. (2003). Getting Beyond "I like the Book": Creating Space for Critical Literacy in K–6 Classrooms. Newark, DE: International Reading Association.

Wood, S., & Jocius, R. (2013). Combating "I hate this stupid book!" Black males and critical literacy. *Reading Teacher, 66*, 661–669.

A Response to Chapter 6

Crag Hill

Sue Ringler Pet argues in "Powerful Influence and Absurd Neglect: The Legacy of Louise M. Rosenblatt in Secondary English Language Arts Methods Courses" that Louise Rosenblatt's transactional reading theory must be the foundation of English language arts (ELA) methods courses, especially those courses that prepare teachers to teach literature in pre-K–12 settings. She asserts Rosenblatt's work is relevant to the current focus in ELA methods courses on equity and social justice, writing that "Rosenblatt resonates perfectly with the voices in new culturally responsive methods texts" (p. 91).

I agree with Ringler Pet that few secondary teachers can identify by name Louise Rosenblatt, even if they studied transactional theory (perhaps more commonly known as reader response) in a preservice methods course. Many teachers might also not be able to list the tenets of New Criticism, though the practice of close reading, one of the primary tenets of New Criticism, may be painfully familiar to them.

In Ringler Pet's thorough literature review of Rosenblatt's transactional theory and its reception over the last 80 years, however, she points out that there are many factors contributing to the neglect of her influential theory, including that many recent methods textbooks that address sociocultural pedagogies (e.g., culturally responsive pedagogy) do not even mention Rosenblatt's work, though Ringler Pet demonstrates its relevance in those pedagogies.

That ELA teachers cannot name their literature teaching practices—whether they be reader-response, New Critical, or culturally responsive pedagogy—has serious implications. For one, these teachers may be conflicted as to which theories they implement. One hears the ringing of "Meet students where they are" and "Respect each student's reading of a text, while pushing them to support these readings." But in my role as a teacher educator, many of the teachers I observe privilege their own reading choices, even after generative exercises such as Socratic seminars and other strategies that provide students with the opportunities to co-construct readings with the text, their peers, and their own reading experiences/histories. Too often teachers still have the last word on what a text means.

There remains a disconnect between the practices teacher educators value and the practices enacted in secondary classrooms. Ringler Pet writes that "ELA teacher educators continue to spotlight Rosenblatt's hallmarks, particularly transactional theory and efferent-aesthetic stances" (p. 90), especially in light of the current emphasis on reading informational texts (efferent) alongside the movement in ELA to incorporate reading for pleasure into the curriculum, providing opportunities for students to choose what they read (Kittle, 2013; Miller, 2014). Despite these efforts, Ringler Pet argues "Rosenblatt's work has endured 'absurd neglect' among literary critics and in ELA education" (p. 89). How do we turn neglect into awareness? Ringler Pet suggests several strategies to incorporate Rosenblatt's theory into today's ELA methods courses.

For the remainder of my response, building off Ringler Pet's chapter as well as suggestions Rejan (2017) has offered, I outline a curriculum that could be integrated into a one-semester methods course.

To start, begin with a broad view by having teacher candidates visit websites such as Purdue Owl's "Literary Theory and Schools of Criticism" (https://owl.purdue.edu) to define transactional theory (or reader-response criticism) and New Criticism (or formalism, as it is called on some websites). Review or introduce the concept of close reading for literary analysis (see sample analysis on the University of Wisconsin's writing center website), a practice valued in transactional theory and in New Criticism. Ask teacher candidates to define the role of the reader and the text in the meaning-making process, debriefing as a class to arrive at a baseline understanding of the two positions. For each approach, what is the balance of reader and text?

Begin to zoom in by asking teacher candidates to read Rosenblatt and two critics associated with New Criticism, Brooks and Warren (1938/1976), whose book *Understanding Poetry* did much to shape the teaching of literature in the last seven decades, especially when textbook writers and test makers narrowed the vision of the New Critic's work into programmatic, testable dogma (Rejan, 2017).

One possible excerpt from Rosenblatt's work that could be illuminating for students is Chapter 2, "The Literary Experience," in *Literature as Exploration* (1938/1995). The introduction to *Understanding Poetry* provides an overview of the way Brooks and Warren conceived of the reading process, especially the confusions that arise in the way literature is taught in classrooms.

After reading, ask teacher candidates to refine their preliminary definitions of the role of the reader and of the text in making meaning for both schools of thought. Discuss where Rosenblatt's approach is similar to Brooks and Warren and where they are different. Create a Venn diagram to use as a template as students put into practice their emerging understandings of the two theories through reading poems, short stories, and if possible, a full-length novel or a play commonly taught in secondary classrooms. How would Rosenblatt read these texts? How would Brooks and Warren? If the readings diverge, where do they diverge? Why?

To cap this exploration, ask teacher candidates to create a lesson plan—or a series of lesson plans in a unit of study—that will guide their prospective students toward understanding the roles they play in reading texts, how their reading experiences play an important part, alongside the formal qualities—structure, language, and genre—the texts themselves carry. Both Rosenblatt and Brooks and Warren, I believe, would agree that the greatest realization we can give readers is that all texts deserve and demand a thoughtful negotiation between reader and text.

REFERENCES

Brooks, C., & Warren, R. P. (1938/1976). *Understanding poetry* (4th ed.). Boston: Wadsworth.

Kittle, P. (2013). *Book love: Developing depth, stamina, and passion in adolescent readers.* Portsmouth, NH: Heinemann.

Miller, D. (2014). The *book whisperer: Awakening the inner reader in every child*. Chichester, UK: Wiley.

Purdue Owl. (n.d.). Literary theory and schools of criticism. Purdue Owl. Retrieved from https://owl.purdue.edu.

Rejan, A. (2017). Reconciling Rosenblatt and the New Critics: The quest for an "experienced understanding" of literature. *English Education, 50*(1), 10–41.

Rosenblatt, L. (1938/1995). *Literature as exploration* (5th ed.). New York: Modern Language Association of America.

Writing Center. (n.d.). A short guide to close reading for literary analysis. University of Wisconsin Madison. Retrieved from https://writing.wisc.edu.

Chapter Seven

Teacher Candidates' Perspectives on Tensions Within the Methods-Based Field Experience

Christopher M. Parsons

Teacher candidates often have numerous, detailed questions about the where, when, what, and why of coursework and experiences in teacher education. They, quite understandably, want to learn everything possible to prepare for their future work, from how to write a lesson plan to how to manage a class and how to explain a nonrestrictive clause. This intensity, always present, usually reaches its (first) peak as an essential part of the methods course begins: the methods-based field experience.

At the time they occur, questions about field experiences can surprise teacher educators, in part, due to their urgency. Such questions can provoke teacher educators' practical and philosophical discomfort in answering them. Happily, with a little experience, though, teacher educators are often able to answer at least the practical questions. That said, candidates' urgency relative to the field experiences that take place in English methods courses continues to draw attention to the tensions arising at the intersection of "coursework" and "fieldwork."

Secondary English teacher preparation programs structure what are labeled in this chapter as methods-based field experiences (MBFEs) for candidates in various ways (Pasternak, Caughlan, Hallman, Renzi, & Rush, 2018; Smagorinsky & Whiting, 1995). For the purposes of this chapter, MBFEs for English teacher candidates are defined as required time at a secondary school site that takes place concurrently, and in connection with, a methods of teaching English course. This definition omits, for example, the student teaching experience as well as fieldwork that takes place in nonmethods courses (e.g., fieldwork as part of a behavior management course). Essentially, the MBFE is the fieldwork meant to complement discipline-specific instruction in the design, delivery, and assessment of secondary English content.

The exact work that goes on in an MBFE can depend on state licensure requirements, teacher preparation program guidelines, and methods instructor or teacher candidate preferences. Generally, though, candidates engage in a variety of secondary school-based work, from passive observation of cooperating teachers to the creation and delivery of sequenced lesson plans. Whatever the structure of a given MBFE, it frequently serves as an introduction to the intersections of the teacher education curriculum and actual secondary English classrooms—and the students in those classrooms.

Pasternak and colleagues' (2018) and Smagorinsky and Whiting's (1995) rich studies of field experiences helpfully examine large samples of syllabi from English methods classes throughout the United States. This chapter aims to begin a conversation that is situated as a complement to that work: examining the perspectives of teacher candidates engaged in professional preparation to become secondary English teachers.

This chapter examines tensions that can exist *for teacher candidates* within the MBFE, and interviews with seven teacher candidates surfaced two important tensions. First, teacher candidates reinterpreted the well-established theory/practice distinction as *hands-on* versus *hands-off* preparation. Importantly, both methods coursework and the MBFE could be hands-on— but so too could both be hands-off. Second, teacher candidates articulated a tension about the purpose of the MBFE as *exposure* across a diversity of placements versus *experience* in a placement similar to their desired/anticipated first teaching job. While candidates often preferred an exposure model, they complicated that model with another tension: *career decision* versus *career preparation*. This chapter touches briefly on work in English education around these tensions and analyzes how teacher candidates' voices might enrich that work.

INTERVIEW PARTICIPANTS' INSTITUTIONAL CONTEXT

This small sample of interviews and informal research design is meant to generate questions and ideas about tensions in the MBFE rather than to offer generalizable conclusions. Still, a brief gloss on both the interview process and the college and English education program in which the participants are trained may help to situate their perspectives.

This chapter draws on hour-long, qualitative interviews with seven undergraduate teacher candidates about their experiences in, and perceptions of, the MBFE and its connection (or not) to their methods courses.[1] At the time of the interviews, participants were all about a month removed from their

MBFE.[2] Though Institutional Review Board (IRB) approval was obtained for these interviews, one primary purpose for the project was an internal, programmatic review of how teacher educators connect English methods courses to the MBFE.

All seven candidates who are featured in this chapter are undergraduates enrolled full time at Keene State College (KSC). KSC is a small public liberal arts college located in Keene, New Hampshire, the largest city (20,000–25,000 residents) in rural southwestern New Hampshire. The vast majority of students at KSC identify as white (86%) and come from New England. Almost 40% of students are first-generation college students. The candidates in this chapter generally mirror these enrollment trends: Though this study did not ask about the first-generation designation, all identify as white and from New England. Four identify as male and three as female.

The secondary English education program at KSC is small, with between eight and 10 teacher candidates in each cohort. Candidates in the program are all dual English and secondary education majors and, upon graduation, can apply for licensure from the state of New Hampshire. Currently, their only field experiences prior to student teaching are in their two methods of teaching English courses. In these courses, candidates are required to complete at least 50 hours working with a cooperating English teacher in a local school (though some students complete more than 50 hours).

Both MBFEs include specific requirements for observation and work with students, but details differ based on factors like candidate readiness and cooperating teacher comfort level. Generally, candidates transition from observation to direct work with students and content delivery as their MBFEs progress. Since their methods instructor is also their field instructor in placements, their fieldwork often comes directly into the methods courses, and the methods coursework becomes a common reference point in postobservation conferences.

WHAT SHOULD THE MBFE DO IN A METHODS COURSE?

Before turning to teacher candidates' experiences of the MBFE, it is worth a moment to dwell on how the profession suggests grappling with and resolving these tensions. In the Conference on English Education (CEE; 2005) position statement, "What Do We Know and Believe about the Roles of Methods Courses and Field Experiences in English Education?" ELA teacher educators detail 16 "belief statements" about English education programs, methods coursework, and field experiences.

Of these, four are about the field experience,[3] and the beliefs expressed in the position statement often directly address the tensions that arose in my interviews with teacher candidates:

> Field experiences . . . provide a process through which candidates develop a new relationship to the classroom. They expose candidates to the widest possible variety of students, teachers, schools, and communities. They allow candidates to observe many different teaching styles, and to begin to develop their own teaching "voice" through active participation in the classrooms and other learning sites they visit ("What Do We Know").

Clearly, the CEE statement prefers that English education programs "expose candidates to the widest possible variety" of field experiences over engineering experiences to match the context of a school where the teacher candidate anticipates working upon graduation. Belief statement 13 goes into detail on the importance of variety: preparing candidates to teach in multiple contexts, offering candidates a broader picture of English teaching in the United States, and giving candidates the chance to work with diverse groups of students.

The CEE statement also comments on the "hands-on" versus "hands-off" tension, suggesting a purposeful process in which candidates move from more passive "obser[vation] of many teacher styles" to "active participation." Belief statement #4 especially articulates the way that field experiences should "build on and extend" each other.

As for the "career decision" versus "career preparation" tension, one might take from the "develop a new relationship to the classroom" point that the authors of the CEE statement imply that teacher candidates should use field experiences, in part, to make sure they feel capable of moving from a student role to a teacher role. That said, the statement focuses more on providing space where that teacher-becoming process *will* occur than on providing space where candidates consider if they *want* it to occur.

On the whole, the CEE statement, just like the methods syllabi surveys from Pasternak and colleagues (2018) and Smagorinsky and Whiting (1995), engages with many of the same tensions that the teacher candidates analyzed in this chapter do. As the analysis below will highlight, though, teacher candidates sometimes experience, and orient to, the tensions differently than what English teacher educators might envision.

Tension 1: "Hands-On" Versus "Hands-Off"

Instructors of English language arts (ELA) methods courses seem well aware of teacher candidates' longing for the "practical" (Orzulak, Lillge, Engel, & Haviland, 2014; Whitney, Olan, & Fredricksen, 2013), especially in reference to the well-worn practical/theoretical binary. Whitney, Olan, and Fredricksen (2013) further find that teacher candidates often associate the practical with experience in the field (p. 194). As their piece suggests, the navigation of teacher candidates' desire for the practical might be considered a "practical" (and ethical) problem of English teacher educators' own work.

That said, participants in this study, in considering the methods coursework and the MBFE, often resisted the theory/practice dichotomy. For example, Troy,[4] one of the participants in this study, collapses it: "I consider the work I do in the collegiate classroom to be teacher work because I think that teachers have to stay up to date on research. Teachers have to be doing behind-the-scenes work. I consider theory to be practice-ish, if that makes sense." Yes, that makes sense, and the sound you hear is a collective swoon from English teacher educators everywhere.

Even less ideally envisioned, though, one might push back against the description of methods coursework as "theoretical." That coursework, after all, is usually moored in English specifically (as a discipline) and covers meat-and-potatoes elements like designing unit/lesson plans and composing summative essay prompts. For example, Connor reflects, "I would say there was nothing in methods that we did that was just theory. I would say all of it was practical. If you want to talk about like [upper-level education class labeled 'Theories and Trends'], yeah, that was the highbrow type of theory thinking." Importantly, some coursework might get sorted into the theory bin, but for this set of teacher candidates, methods did not fit there.

Still, even if both methods and its concomitant field experience are *potentially* practical, that does not necessarily mean that it is *actually* practical. Teacher candidates in this study reinterpret the theory/practice binary in terms of what they consider a tension between *hands-on* and *hands-off* experiences. Without exception, they prefer the hands-on.

A hands-off experience is any experience in which a teacher candidate takes a passive role in an educational setting. Certainly, in these interviews, participants found some methods coursework passive and wondered how it would work with "real" students. But field experiences could be hands-off as well. For example, Gary considered his field experience to be impractical when it was passive—even if sited in a genuine secondary English classroom. He notes, "There wasn't any involvement in the observations, so it couldn't actually be practical." Gary's experience challenges any easy equation of fieldwork with the practical.

A hands-on experience is, in part, any in which a teacher candidate takes an active role in an educational setting. Again, both methods coursework and the MBFE can potentially be hands-on. Gary relates, "I think every education course so far has made me teach at least one class. . . . I feel like college [is] not only teaching you the theories of it but [is] forcing you to put that into action." As above, Gary's voice pushes back against a presumption that candidates believe their university coursework in education to be mere theory.

The purpose of the above discussion about hands-on and hands-off experiences is to disturb lingering assumptions about elements in the methods course and MBFE relationship. Or, as Gary puts it, "I don't think it's 'one is one' and 'one is the other.' I think that both of them could be both"; that is, neither the coursework nor the MBFE can be defined as hands-on or hands-off only by location in the university or secondary schools.

That suggestion leaves an important question in its wake: If not location, what makes an experience hands-on? What allows for an active stance? One answer, at least for these teacher candidates, is that an experience can become hands-on when candidates can actively embody the connections between the methods coursework and the MBFE.

Importantly, just *seeing* explicit connections between the two is often not enough. For example, discussing how to teach *Romeo and Juliet* in coursework and then observing the play taught in the field makes neither necessarily more hands-on (or practical). Hines explains, "My biggest thing is that lack of hands-on experience. So, while I got to see some of those things that we talked about in [methods] class at work in the [MBFE] classroom, I didn't feel I got the chance myself to maybe tinker with some of those ideas either working with some students or teaching a lesson."

Across the candidates, they emphasized active experimentation: "the chance myself to maybe tinker" (in the MBFE classroom) or "put that into action" (in college coursework). If this activeness seems obvious—of course candidates want an active role in their training—what is less obvious is that this hands-on work can happen (or not) at many sites in their professional preparation, not just ones with adolescent students. Candidates related active and inactive teaching work in their college courses *and* in field experiences.

What is also less obvious is that redefining "practical" as "hands-on" permits theory to be seen as potentially hands-on too. Hines recalls, "One of the better conversations that I had with [cooperating teacher (CT)] was when we were talking about her views on independent reading, we connected Atwell's book with the model that she was using." Hines brings the ideas from Nancie Atwell and Anne Atwell Merkel's (2016) *Reading Zone* into conversation with his CT's ideas and what they were *doing* in class. He considers this "hands-on" even though it involves a theory (Atwell's) and does *not* directly involve students (a conversation with his CT).

The process through which theory becomes hands-on is one in which coursework and the MBFE mutually reinforce each other. In Hines's example, the theory is introduced in methods and then made hands-on with a CT in a conversation about her classroom. When the candidates bring that activated theory back into methods seminar, the process continues.

Importantly, though, methods coursework can also be the catalyst for the beginning of a hands-off to hands-on process. Gary explains:

> I got into the classroom before we had really gotten into the meat of methods, so it was like "I'm in a classroom now, what am I looking for?" And then, as methods was going on, it allowed me to point out things. Like, "Oh, she [the

CT] starts every day with [described start of class routine], that ties in with what [methods instructor] was saying about the first five minutes of our lesson plan.

If the above MBFE is not exactly theoretical before "the meat of methods," it is hands-off, and Gary gets lost. In this case, the methods coursework allows a teacher candidate to say "oh" and begin to "point out things." Gary goes on to relate that this now-active observation leads him to use the MBFE as a resource for the lesson plans he wrote in his methods course, the sort of mutual reinforcement Hines shares above.

Put briefly, redefining the tension between the theoretical and the practical as a tension between hands-on and hands-off experiences has the potential to (1) afford teacher candidates the possibility of active engagement with both theory and practice; (2) place less pressure on fieldwork as the sole location of authentic English teacher preparation; and (3) emphasize the mutually reinforcing nature of methods coursework and the MBFE.

Tension 2: Exposure, Experience, and Career Decisions

As explored above, the CEE statement on the MBFE clearly advocates for "exposing candidates to the widest possible variety" of field experiences. This "exposure" model, however, is not the only possibility. For example, Goldhaber, Krieg, and Theobald's (2017) quantitative research on where teachers can most productively do their student teaching concludes, "Teachers appear to be more effective when the student demographics of their school are similar to the student demographics of the school in which they did their student teaching" (p. 351).

To be sure, the MBFE is designed differently than the immersion of student teaching—fewer hours, less direct instruction, and so forth. Still, it seems important to at least wonder aloud if Goldhaber, Krieg, and Theobald's (2017) finding—that placement schools are important to success in the first job—might extend to the MBFE.[5] Or, perhaps more relevant to this chapter is the question, What do teacher candidates think about exposure to a range of schools versus experience in their imagined first job school?

Teacher candidates' recognition of this tension does not prevent them from standing squarely with the CEE view. Almost unanimously, they want exposure to as much variety in their placements as possible. Even when prompted to react to a hypothetical teacher candidate who really wanted to get as much experience as possible in a certain type of school, interviewees tended to react with skepticism; that would not, they argued, be best for their hypothetical colleague.

Even their reasoning for preferring an exposure model sometimes sounds familiar, especially when it comes to its broadening effect. The CEE statement (2005) argues, "Variety allows teacher candidates to expand their understanding of the diversity of communities and of schooling experiences in our country."

In a similar vein, Hines suggests that exposure gives teacher candidates a "better sense of what the job of English teaching is like everywhere." Rena makes a comparison to the training in another profession: "If you're a nursing major, they aren't going to let you only do the maternity ward. They're going to make you do psych and geriatrics, and you're going to get different experiences before you tailor to what you want to do." These teacher candidates maintain clear ideas about why exposure improves teacher training.

They can also articulate tangible benefits to seeing the broadest possible view of the profession. Rena says,

> In the [local school district] there's a disconnect between the 8th graders and their writing skills and then they get to 9th grade, and they're behind according to the high school teachers. So, I think that if you had more exposure even just viewing what the middle school does. What the high school does. If you get a bird's-eye view of everything that comes with different experiences, then you're going to be a better teacher in your particular placement.

Though the short CEE statement does not allow space for this sort of elaboration, one can sense that teacher candidates pick up the spirit of the exposure model: A "bird's-eye view" will make you "a better teacher in your placement."

The exposure model also offers a more prosaic benefit not noted in the CEE statement: professional flexibility. Mallory says it best: "Yes, getting experience in schools like where you want to teach is important, but it's hard because what if you don't get a job there? We're going to apply to jobs regardless of where they are because we want jobs."

If Mallory is refreshingly blunt about teacher candidates' end goals, Baily explains how limited exposure can lead to fear of even applying for jobs at unfamiliar sites. Considering her own largely middle school placements, she laments, "I talk to other people in my cohort [in high school placements], and I'm like, 'how do you deal with that?' Some of those kids are eighteen. My kids are still ten years younger than me, so they think I'm ancient."

While the possibilities of Goldhaber, Krieg, and Theobald's (2017) findings about experience and teacher effectiveness are absolutely worth considering, the exposure model comes with widely recognized benefits: professional community, broadened perspectives, grade-level transition awareness, and professional flexibility/confidence. In justifying the structure of the MBFE within English teacher education, teacher candidates' powerful voices and vivid examples might be assets with regard to this putative tension.

Though teacher candidates often affirm the CEE response to the exposure versus experience tension, a less-discussed tension, career preparation versus career decision, emerges from discussions about the purposes of exposure. Understandably, methods coursework and the MBFE are designed with future English teachers in mind. But anyone who has ever advised teacher candidates knows that, for some, the question can be as much about *if they want to teach* (career decision) as it is about *how to teach* (career education).

Interviews with teacher candidates suggest confusion and lack of coherence when it comes to how methods coursework and the MBFE address the decision/education tension. To be sure, some teacher candidates saw the tension as present but not particularly fraught. Baily, for example, thinks of the MBFE as, in part, a professional sorting process. She observes, "I think a lot of the dropouts from the secondary program realized halfway through methods, I want to teach kindergartners, like I want to be with first-graders." If anything, Baily's observations argue for potential teachers to get their field experiences as soon as possible.

Methods seems to be serving teacher candidates less well in the career decision process when the MBFE is, as explained above, hands-off. Though one might imagine beginning the MBFE with exposure and observation, a less hands-on approach does not offer as much meaningful feedback on a core question for candidates: Can I do this job? Gary explains, "I feel like without being involved in the process [of actively teaching], you don't get the actual experience of *will I make it in this* and *do I still want to do this. I don't think you can honestly tell yourself that I can or cannot teach if you're just watching a classroom*."

Thinking about how to embed support for career decisions within the MBFE brings up tough questions. For one, to what extent does observation in the MBFE serve to help early career teacher candidates make professional decisions? To draw an imperfect analogy, it is hard to say if watching an Olympic gymnast do a vault makes people more or less likely to believe they can do it themselves.

Even too-early, hands-on teaching experiences could sap confidence from promising teacher candidates, obscuring the type of teacher into which they might develop. If, as Gary suggests above, initial, hands-on field experiences help candidates think about questions like "will I make it in this" profession, the stakes of deciding what these experiences should look like are high.

Regardless of the answers to these questions, this tension diffuses throughout the coursework and MBFE. Rena explains how it has an effect even on how she is viewed in her placement:

> In my placement, all I've heard is that methods and student teaching, that's when you decide if you want to teach or not. And I thought that was weird because I'm like, "Well, I've decided I want to teach since like 7th grade, so that's why I'm here." So it was almost like a let's figure out if you're capable sort of thing where maybe I have the ego that like I know I'm capable. And

like there are doubts and you get nervous, but that's all part of persistence and perseverance. So I think that from an outside perspective it's like you fail or you pass, but I think it's like your professional development and you're a sponge and you're soaking it up.

Even Rena, a confident teacher candidate clearly looking for "professional development" (career education), feels the effects of the perception of the MBFE being "when you decide if you want to teach or not" (career decision). One can see Rena mapping her own situation, her own story, onto sometimes invisible tensions in English education. As with the rest of the analysis in this chapter, the hope is that naming and exploring some tensions will begin conversations about how to make tensions productive rather than confusing for teacher candidates.

EMBRACING TENSIONS WITH ENGLISH TEACHER CANDIDATES

The word *tension*, as this book assumes, is no dirty word in thinking about English methods courses. Tensions can generate compelling ideas and challenge fusty approaches precisely because tensions are often at the nexus of honest desires that appear to (and sometimes do) compete. One wants teacher candidates to be immersed in theory *and* practice, to be exposed to various contexts *and* experienced in specific ones, and to be preparing for a career *and* deciding if it is a good fit.

Apart from research design reasons, interviews with candidates took place as soon as possible after the methods course and the MBFE because of a desire to revise syllabi and fieldwork expectations in response to grappling with these tensions. These conversations with teacher candidates have led to two principles for revision.

First, symbiotic connections between the methods course and the MBFE were made to be as explicit as possible. Previously, it was assumed that teacher candidates would perceive as impractical any class text labeled "theory based." The interviews with teacher candidates, however, indicated that even the most theoretical text might become "hands-on" by its clear connection to the MBFE. Concomitant to a greater focus on methods course–MBFE connection will yield an increased freedom to assign generative theoretical texts. For example, an article examining connections between Louise Rosenblatt and the New Critics becomes hands-on when considered in light of a cooperating teacher's approach to reading instruction.

In a related way, revisions concerning the expectations for the MBFE included both more required connections between the MBFE and course material and more "tinkering" and "active participation" in the placement classroom. A flawed assumption, though, roundly rejected by these participants, had been that there is something inherently practical about the field placement. With the goal of activating a hands-on approach, the new fieldwork expectations document requires candidates to take some idea from the methods course, design and enact direct instruction related to that idea, and then reflect on that instruction relative to what we have discussed in methods.

A second principle for revision centers on giving candidates the language to reflect on themselves as burgeoning professionals. After many interviews, the teacher candidates wondered aloud that a conversation about, for example, "exposure" versus "experience" had let them in on some secret of their education. In truth, though, the interview questions more simply provided critical language through which they could consider how their MBFE might make sense to them in the context of their training overall.

For example, altering the MBFE expectations document in the lower-level methods course to *explicitly* specify that the first 10 hours be spent observing throughout an entire English department for "exposure" to many teaching styles and levels of class while the second 10 hours be spent gaining "experience" in one specific context was helpful. While teacher candidates' work happens only within the contexts of one school, introducing possibly generative language might help candidates reflect on, and take advantage of, their training in a broader sense.

This chapter argues, at a basic level, for the importance of including as many voices as possible in thinking and making decisions about the tensions in methods coursework and the MBFE. Especially in the case of the MBFE, so much is in the head and hands of the teacher candidates themselves—much more than, one might argue, the traditional classroom setting in which methods often operates. It is crucial to elicit and consider teacher candidates' experiences.

Given that, when teacher candidates articulate the meaningfulness of tensions like hands-on versus hands-off work, exposure versus experience, and education versus decision, it behooves all involved to embrace their grappling. For English teacher educators, that embrace, of course, does not mean tearing up trusted methods syllabi and fieldwork expectations documents. But that embrace does imply a simpler promise: a shared commitment to reflect on and converse about tensions.

NOTES

1. These interviews are part of a larger study examining the MBFE from a variety of perspectives: teacher candidates, cooperating teachers, field instructors, methods instructors, and English teacher education program administrators.

2. It is important, I would argue, to capture teacher candidates' perspectives on their MBFE in the middle of it all. Soliciting their perspectives after student teaching or after they have their first job allows for a sort of whole-cloth recollection—how does the MBFE fit with everything else? But I am wary of losing those raw, in-the-moment experiences that, first, color

how candidates react to the MBFE and, second, might slip away as candidates form a larger narrative about their professional training.

3. Belief statement 14, about the intentional structuring of field experiences, suggests that these field experiences "culminat[e] in the student teaching/internship placement" ("What Do We Know"). It's important to note that, while the CEE consideration of the field experience seems to include the student teaching placement, this chapter only addresses the MBFE.

4. All teacher candidates' names are pseudonyms.

5. The CEE statement on field experiences within the methods course *does* include language about the student teaching placement (in belief statement 14). It seems possible, then, that their argument about exposing teacher candidates to a "range of placements" might extend to the student teaching experience. For example, if teacher candidate X wanted to teach in a small rural high school but hadn't yet had a placement experience in large urban middle school, would the authors of the CEE statement plump for a placement in the latter in the name of getting the "range"? Even if it gave X less immersion in the small rural environment (and thus potentially made X less "effective" as a teacher)?

REFERENCES

Atwell, N., & Merkel, A. A. (2016). *The reading zone: How to help kids become skilled, passionate, habitual, critical readers* (2nd ed.). New York: Scholastic.

Conference on English Education (CEE). (2005). What do we know and believe about the roles of methods courses and field experiences in English education? Position statements. Retrieved from http://www2.ncte.org.

Goldhaber, D., Krieg, J. M., & Theobald, R. (2017). Does the match matter? Exploring whether student teaching experiences affect teacher effectiveness. *American Educational Research Journal, 54*, 325–359.

Orzulak, M. J. M., Lillge, D. M., Engel, S. J., & Haviland, V. S. (2014). Contemplating trust in times of uncertainty: Uniting practice and interactional awareness to address ethical dilemma in English teacher education. *English Education, 47*, 80–102.

Pasternak, D. L., Caughlan, S., Hallman, H. L., Renzi, L., & Rush, L. S. (2018). *Secondary English teacher education in the United States: Responding to a changing context*. New York: Bloomsbury.

Smagorinsky, P., & Whiting, M. E. (1995). *How English teachers get taught: Methods of teaching the methods class*. Urbana, IL: Conference on English Education and National Council of Teachers of English.

Whitney, A. E., Olan, E. L., & Fredricksen, J. E. (2013). Experience over all: Preservice teacher and the prizing of the practical. *English Education, 45*, 184–200.

A Response to Chapter 7

Laura A. Renzi

As an educator who has worked with teacher candidates for the past nineteen years, I have had many conversations about field experiences. These conversations continue be a source of consternation for teacher educators as we work to figure out what is the best way to integrate field experiences and methods courses to create the most meaningful learning experiences for our teacher candidates. How varied should the placements be? What types of assignments should accompany these field experiences? And as you can imagine, the questions go on and on.

In this chapter, Chris Parsons takes the approach of engaging the teacher candidates in these questions surrounding the field experience. The anxiety around field experiences that the author experiences upon beginning his position as a teacher educator is a situation I face at the beginning of every semester, and I am sure is very familiar to most (if not all) teacher educators. The author identified two main tensions that his teacher candidates experienced before and during their methods-based field experience: (1) the hands-on versus hands-off approach, or nature of field experiences; and (2) tensions revolving around exposure, experience, and career decisions related to their field experience.

In Parsons's study, one teacher candidate, identified as Troy, stated, "I consider the work I do in the collegiate classroom to be teacher work because I think that teachers have to stay up to date on research. . . . I consider theory to be practice-ish, if that makes sense." Yes, Troy, I would say that does make sense!

Theory provides a space for teacher candidates to imagine and practice their interactions before engaging students in learning. This *practice* allows for the perfect context with the perfect students to ponder and consider why this theory might work and what the results may be. Consider this question:

Would imagining the perfect performance of a lesson provide teacher candidates with the awareness to reflect and adjust their teaching in a real setting? A teacher needs to consider the students and educational context, and adapt the implementation of theory. If a teacher candidate has performed in the ideal context, does that allow them more reflection before they implement in the real context?

The second tension identified in this chapter is the following question: Should teacher education programs expose teacher candidates to a wide range of schools providing diverse settings and students, *or* should placements more closely match their imagined first teaching job? Overwhelmingly, Parsons's students preferred the exposure model of field experiences as stated by Rena: "If you get a bird's-eye view of everything that comes with different experiences, then you're going to be a better teacher in your particular placement" (p. 110).

Other candidates expressed the concern about the possibility of not obtaining a job in their preferred districts. Parsons's candidates understand the need for a wider view of teaching, but I am curious about their view beyond the setting they envision as their perfect job. What if the teacher candidates don't have a placement with a mentor teacher that mirrors their teaching philosophy or preferred methods?

The movement in teacher education to a more clinical model would provide teacher candidates with one longer placement where they would complete their student teaching. This yearlong placement in a clinical model would allow teacher candidates to become comfortable in a classroom context, while experimenting and developing their own teaching identity with the same students. There is something to be said for spending more time in the same classroom to become accustomed to not only the school context but also the community environment in which these students live their lives. This yearlong placement would also allow for the teacher candidates to be mentored by one cooperating teacher throughout the course of one year.

When considering a more diverse field experience, or the *exposure* method, that Parsons's students preferred, teacher candidates need the time to become acquainted with school and community context—more so than in a placement that on the surface represents the more familiar school context they might seek out for their first teaching job. Providing *exposure* to various placements allows the opportunity for teacher candidates to grow in themselves as people and as teachers.

However, placements not reminiscent of teacher candidates' own schooling experience beg for more interaction among the methods or placement instructor, the mentor teacher, and the teacher candidate to provide space for teacher candidates to question, reflect, and ultimately feel discomfort as they explore the schooling context. It is in the discomfort that teacher candidates find the most value and stretch themselves to question their own assumptions and philosophy.

Field experiences revolve around so many moving parts; research can rarely provide overarching results. Rather, I think research on field experiences often raises more questions and avenues for continued exploration. In this chapter, Parsons seeks out information on field experiences from probably the least considered and most affected stakeholders in teacher education: teacher candidates. In questioning how teacher candidates see and understand the connection between their methods and education courses and the move into the field experience is a needed perspective in teacher education research. As teacher educators, we often *know* what teacher candidates need to become successful teachers. Rather, perhaps we should take a cue from what we teach our teacher candidates in the first place: Start with what your students know and are engaged in and move forward from there.

REFERENCES

Pasternak, D. L., Caughlan, S., Hallman, H. L., Renzi, L., & Rush, L. S. (2018). *Secondary English teacher education in the United States: Responding to a changing context.* New York: Bloomsbury.

Part III

Communities of English Education

Chapter Eight

English Education Methods Courses as Sites of Induction Into English Teacher Communities of Practice

James Cercone and Kristen Pastore-Capuana

This chapter explores conceptualizing English education methods courses as sites of induction into English teacher communities of practice (CoPs) and the impact such a conceptualization has on preservice teacher learning and identity development. First, we authors provide an overview of current challenges facing English teacher education programs and the teaching of English in secondary schools. The chapter then explores James Cercone's work to confront these problems by reconceptualizing his English teacher education program as a regional hub designed to encourage and support the meaningful teaching of English language arts in the Buffalo-Niagara region through the development of an English teacher CoP. The chapter then details Kristen Pastore-Capuana's methods course, which has been conceived as a site of induction into this CoP. An examination of the impact this approach had on her preservice teachers follows. The chapter concludes with suggestions for implementing this approach and a reflection on related challenges.

ISSUES FACING ENGLISH TEACHER EDUCATION

English teacher education programs continue to face ongoing challenges affecting the development of the next generation of teachers and the advancement of English teaching in schools. Declining enrollments, a growing emphasis on teacher education accountability measurements, and alternative pathways to teacher certification, along with a growing reliance on part-time instructors across higher education, among other factors, have a wide-ranging impact on the work being done to develop and support new teachers (Cochran-Smith et al., 2018; Henning, Dover, Dotson, & Agarwal-Rangnath, 2018; Madeloni & Gorlewski, 2013; Tuck & Gorlewski, 2016).

Ongoing neoliberal reforms, including teacher accountability measures, standardized testing, and mandated curricula, have a wide-ranging impact on the teaching and learning of English language arts in secondary classrooms. Limited definitions of literacy continue to drive English teaching in schools, and new teachers often feel pressure to enact traditional models of instruction that privilege the printed word, expository forms of writing, and summative assessments (Anagnostopoulos, Smith, & Basmadjian, 2007; Athanases, Caret, Canales, & Meyer, 1992; Feiman-Nemser & Buchman, 1985; Kelchtermans & Ballet, 2002; Smagorinsky, Rhym, & Moore, 2013).

COMMUNITIES OF PRACTICE IN ENGLISH TEACHER EDUCATION

To confront the internal and external issues facing teachers today, English teacher education programs can position themselves as regional hubs or centers for English teaching, in their geographic areas. In doing so, programs can draw from sociocultural perspectives on teaching and learning for a long-term, systemic approach that provides preservice teachers with meaningful learning opportunities and ongoing support throughout their careers. In exploring such an approach, this chapter draws from theoretical frameworks of learning within communities of practice (Wenger, 1998), a sociocultural framework for understanding learning as a social practice.

Lave and Wenger (1991) describe communities of practice as "a set of relations among persons, activity, and world over time [that involves] participation in an activity system about which participants share understandings concerning what they are doing and what that means in their lives and for their communities" (p. 98). Referring to initial learning within these communities as "legitimate peripheral participation," they sought to explain how new participants work initially on the periphery of a given practice and over time become full participants within that practice. Wenger has since explored the concept in greater detail examining how "newcomers" learn through participation and interactions with "old-timers" of a given practice. In doing so, he notes that a community of practice,

> can be viewed as a social learning system. Arising out of learning, it exhibits many characteristics of systems more generally: emergent structure, complex relationships, self-organisation, dynamic boundaries, ongoing negotiation of identity and cultural meaning, to mention a few. In a sense it is the simplest social unit that has the characteristics of a social learning system. (2010, p. 179–180.)

Communities of practice provide a way for English teacher education programs to implement a systematic approach to teacher education that draws from sociocultural perspectives on learning, explored in the next section through the application of this concept of a "social learning system" to the English education program at SUNY Buffalo State.

DESIGNING SOCIAL LEARNING SYSTEMS IN ENGLISH TEACHER EDUCATION

To confront issues such as diminished enrollments in English education programs, decreased availability of cooperating teachers for field placements, and localized pressures for standardized curricula in the Buffalo-Niagara region, Cercone revised the English education program at SUNY Buffalo State, conceiving of it as a regional hub, a center for English teaching in Western New York. The program focuses on providing powerful learning opportunities for preservice teachers through relevant coursework and clinically rich classroom experiences, while advocating for the meaningful teaching of English in the region and supporting in-service teachers throughout their careers. To accomplish this, the program has implemented a variety of socially embedded initiatives designed to develop and support communities of practice for both preservice and in-service English teachers' participation.[1]

Since 2012 the program has been the home of the Western New York Network of English Teachers (WNYNET), a not-for-profit, teacher-driven professional organization focused on encouraging and supporting the meaningful teaching of English language arts throughout the greater Buffalo-Niagara region (Cercone, 2009; 2014). Both WNYNET and the English education program at Buffalo State advocate for inquiry-based (Beach & Myers, 2001; Fecho, 2004; Gustavson, 2007; Smith & Wilhelm, 2002; 2006) models of literacy instruction that draw from work in cultural studies (Fecho, 2003; Gaughan, 1998; Webb, 2014), critical literacy (Freire, 1972), and workshop approaches to reading and writing instruction in secondary classrooms (Atwell, 2014; Hicks, 2009).

Through its work with WNYNET, the English education program sponsors ongoing professional development conferences and related activities for preservice and in-service teachers across the Buffalo-Niagara region. Employing a "classroom-up" approach to educational reform, English teachers are invited on campus to share instructional practices and resources, to engage in curriculum development, and to participate in ongoing conversations about the profession with other teachers, school administrators, English teacher educators, and preservice teachers from across the region.

Past conferences have focused on a variety of topics, including taking a social justice stance on English teaching, teaching English 12, middle school ELA, technology in the English classroom, and inquiry-based models of instruction.[2] Additionally, WNYNET sponsors an active Facebook group (with more than 400 members) where teachers in the region share resources, ask questions, and engage in discussions about the profession.

The English Education Student Association (EESA) was created to provide an affiliated CoP for English education students at SUNY Buffalo State similar to or in alignment with WNYNET. Among many events on campus, EESA sponsors an ongoing speaker series featuring education faculty, classroom teachers, alumni, and national scholars. Additionally, EESA works alongside WNYNET to co-plan English teacher conferences and two major end-of-the-year events. The first, the annual WNYNET Youth Voices Conference, invites middle school and high school students and their teachers to campus to present the work they have engaged in during the year in their English classrooms. The second, the annual English Education Spring Banquet, is a celebration of English teaching in Western New York where EESA officers recognize graduating students, cooperating teachers, and other members of the community. The banquet also features the WNYNET English Teacher Awards for new and experienced teachers (see website for recent honorees). An English Education Alumni Award (most recently presented to Nancie Atwell, 2017, and former editor of *English Journal*, Julie Gorlewski, 2018) is also presented by the English Education Alumni Network.

Through the various events and initiatives sponsored by these connected organizations, the program seeks to create multiple opportunities for students to engage in the *legitimate peripheral participation* Lave and Wenger (1991) describe. English education students attend EESA and WNYNET events throughout the academic year as part of their ongoing coursework. Attendance at these events is a requirement for multiple courses in the program, and students earn participation credit for attending. During these events, preservice teachers participate in a dialogue around current issues in English teaching through classroom teachers' presentations and workshops. In these instances, preservice teachers often participate in small-group activities and discussions with classroom teachers from across the region. Furthermore, EESA officers work closely with WNYNET officers, and all middle and high school English teachers, to co-plan events and initiatives.

Next follows an exploration of Pastore-Capuana's approach to teaching ENG 463: Methods, Materials, and Professional Development for Teachers of English and how it aligns with CoPs as part of the regular coursework her students engaged in and the impact this participation had on their learning and identity development.

ENGAGING IN THE SOCIAL LEARNING PROCESS THROUGH IMMERSION IN COMMUNITIES OF PRACTICE

The English education program at Buffalo State offers undergraduate and postbaccalaureate certification (for students with a BA or BS) as well as an MSED program for certified English teachers. The final methods course in the sequence for both undergraduate and postbaccalaureate students is ENG 463: Methods, Materials, and Professional Development for Teachers of English. This six-credit course is offered in both the fall and the spring, followed by a semester of student teaching.

Pastore-Capuana taught high school English for many years prior to working in teacher education and thus approaches this course as an induction into the CoP and an exploration into a range of theoretical, pedagogical, and professional topics pertinent to the teaching of secondary English language arts. Drawing from a critical inquiry model of English teaching (Dewey, 1910; Fecho, 2004; Freire, 1972; hooks, 1994; Smith & Wilhelm, 2006; Wilhelm, 2007), students engaged in a variety of readings, activities, and projects while also participating in numerous conferences and related events offered through the CoP.

The course drew from scholarship in English education, using Beach and colleagues' (2016) *Teaching Literature to Adolescents*, Smagorinsky's (2008) *Teaching English by Design: How to Create and Carry Out Instructional Units*, and Tovani's (2000) *I Read It, but I Don't Get It* as core texts. Supplemental readings were used throughout to study reading and writing workshop approaches to English language arts (ELA) instruction (Atwell, 2014), backward design planning (Wiggins & McTighe, 2005), classroom discussion strategies (McCann, Johannessen, Kahn, & Flanagan, 2006), and culturally sustaining teaching practices (Delpit, 2006; Ladson-Billings, 2014; Paris, 2012; Paris & Alim, 2017) that respect students' unique linguistic, cultural, and literacy identities.

Course materials, assignments, and discussion boards were housed on schoology to familiarize students with a learning management system used in many schools. Preservice teachers explored teaching personae and reflected on how their own identities shaped how they might teach their future students. Preservice teachers worked to develop teaching philosophies and résumés and engaged in collaborative and individual lesson and unit planning activities around texts read in the course and those encountered in related fieldwork.

Throughout the course, Pastore-Capuana modeled instructional practices she engaged in as a classroom teacher. In order to help students understand the importance of classroom discussion, for instance, the class viewed Kwame Alexander's "Take a Knee" spoken word piece and engaged in a subsequent Harkness Method Discussion. Pastore-Capuana recorded and transcribed a portion of it for students to analyze, where they noted patterns of dialogue to explore ways discussion fostered self-text-world connections. An exploration of possible follow-up classroom activities concluded the process.

In order to demonstrate how secondary students can take up various lenses to engage in deep critical readings of literature, the class read Jamaica Kincaid's "Girl" and used the critical lenses outlined in *Teaching Literature to Adolescents* (Beach, Appleman, Fecho, & Simon, 2016) to analyze the text in small groups. Groups presented their analysis on poster paper. Students then engaged in a gallery walk, adding responses to each poster. Rooted in critical literacy and sociocultural approaches to learning, this activity reflected the types of instructional practices discussed in various WNYNET conferences and engaged in on a regular basis in CoP teachers' classrooms.

Alongside these modeling activities, preservice teachers read, responded, and engaged in fieldwork in partner teachers' classrooms while examining and practicing instructional strategies for use with their future students. Throughout each semester preservice teachers intentionally shifted identities among being English education students, teachers, and secondary ELA students as they examined inquiry-based teaching valued by the CoP.

Clinical Residency

As part of their work in ENG 463, students completed a total of 50 (60 for postbaccalaureate students) hours of fieldwork in at least one mentor teacher's classroom. The clinical residency program provided students with an opportunity to contextualize their coursework in real classrooms, consult with classroom teachers, and participate in organized instructional support activities, experiences teacher candidates did not have when fieldwork was assigned prior to the CoP model.

In these placements, students conducted classroom observations, helped facilitate group work, provided one-on-one tutoring support for students, and provided other aspects of instructional support. Methods students were strategically placed, with the exception of a few participants who had travel constraints, in classrooms with teachers who participated in the CoP. The methods instructor and field experience coordinator worked specifically with cooperating teachers on how to gradually build preservice teacher participation throughout the semester. Cooperating teachers received the methods course syllabus and an overview of the teaching framework along with activities preservice teachers were working on throughout the course. Students conducted this fieldwork throughout each semester, and their experiences were integrated into coursework through assigned reflections and class discussions.

Cooperating teachers received three check-in emails to elicit feedback on the methods students and to share areas of strengths and weakness. Since cooperating teachers knew and collaborated with the methods course instructor at previous WNYNET and program events, they were already comfortable sharing information and discussing the work in their classrooms. The check-in emails provided invaluable insight to support preservice teachers' fieldwork experiences and also reinforced areas where students needed additional support. Unlike previous fieldwork placements where students were randomly placed without communication between the methods instructor and cooperating teachers, this approach focused on finding placements that fit the needs of the students while providing specific assistance on mentoring that supported the program's approach for English language arts instruction.

Methods students were required to plan, teach, and video-record two lessons in their partner teacher's classroom to gain teaching experience and engage in self-reflection. During this clinical residency, a partner teacher could determine, in consultation with the methods instructor, if the student they worked with was mutually beneficial for their classroom and school. If so, the student remained in that teacher's classroom for one student teaching placement the following semester. If not, another student teaching placement was obtained for the student.

Students in methods created a long-range unit plan with lesson plans for their final methods project. This unit plan, which was the instructional foundation for their first student teaching placement, was developed with the guidance of both the methods instructor and the cooperating teacher. Since students were placed with cooperating teachers that were part of the CoP and familiar with the pedagogy discussed in the methods course, the unit plan project facilitated a meaningful, collaborative planning experience that merged theory and pedagogy with authentic teaching contexts.

Building a Course Community

Initial activities in ENG 463 focused on building a classroom community to support critical dialogue around the larger ideas, themes, and issues impacting the profession. Students initially engaged in narrative writing reflecting on why they wanted to become English teachers and examining their previous experiences as students in secondary schools. They also engaged in an identity activity drawn from Teaching Tolerance to unpack their own cultural, ethnic, and racial identities. Additionally, students completed a critical media analysis of teachers and students in popular culture.

For each activity students were asked to share their experiences in small- and whole-group discussions as they explored preexisting beliefs about teaching and learning. These initial activities became critical points of reference for the course as students engaged in productive, but sometimes tense, conversations about teaching and the intersection of race, class, gender, socioeconomics, sexual orientation, and other aspects of identity. Developing a course-based community allowed students to build relationships with one another that then supported their learning and engagement throughout the semester.

For example, the class viewed excerpts from the film *Freedom Writers* to analyze popular media's representation of urban education. A discussion developed around Hilary Swank's character (a white female teacher working in an urban school) and the lack of representation of teachers of color in the media. When Laura Innes,[3] a white student, suggested the teacher in the film had "good intentions," Naya Mitchell, one of three students of color in the course, suggested during a class discussion that "as white folks, you really have to think about why you are teaching in a certain place and what you really think about those kids."

The discussion between Laura and Naya was tense; Laura cited that some of the "pedagogy in the clip was better than some I have seen in local schools." Naya countered that the teaching persona perpetuated the "white savior" motif that suggested white teachers view urban schools through a deficit lens and see themselves saving their students from their uncaring communities.

For Naya, much of her desire to become a teacher was rooted in wanting to work with students of color who, she passionately explained, "may never have had a teacher that looks like them." After a heated but respectful conversation about teaching, race, and identity, Naya offered to buy milkshakes for the class during their scheduled break so they could continue their discussion while enjoying refreshments. When the class resumed, Laura used her background in drama to process the conversation with her peers, demonstrating a variety of instructional strategies (a check-in activity, a group-bonding activity, and a decompressing activity) her peers could use to process similar conversations with their future students.

Critical discussions around a variety of issues related to English teaching became a regular part of the course. Spending early sessions building a course-based community allowed students the opportunity to talk openly and honestly with one another. Moreover, these conversations reflected the types of conversations taking place in the larger CoP, and in various English education discourse communities that make up the profession as a whole. Developing this new course-based community made eventual participation in the larger CoP less intimidating for students as they began interacting with the community of English teachers surrounding them.

CONNECTING TEACHING METHODS TO COMMUNITIES OF PRACTICE

Various members of the CoP visited the course to discuss scheduled topics and relate their experiences as classroom teachers. During these visits, teachers shared materials and instructional strategies with preservice teachers. Importantly, they also discussed tensions in their own work and the processes they followed as they developed into more experienced teachers and leaders in the professional community.

When exploring the reading and writing workshop, Dennis Wojtaszczyk (a retired experienced teacher and former English education professor) visited the class to discuss his experiences as a workshop-based instructor. Dennis led an extended writing workshop demonstration for students and shared resources he relied upon throughout his career. To prepare for this class, ENG 463 students read excerpts on the workshop model (Atwell, 2010; Hicks, 2009). Following the presentation and demonstration lesson, participants engaged in a discussion of the readings and their workshop experience.

The workshop model is an important component of how many teachers in the CoP approached writing instruction in secondary education classrooms. Unfortunately, such instructional practices are not always reflected in district-mandated writing programs. Hearing from an experienced teacher whose career was based on such an approach, and who successfully navigated the various changes in his district's stance toward writing instruction over time, was an important opportunity for students to learn how they could implement a writing workshop in their own classrooms and advocate for it over time.

Deborah Bertlesman (an experienced English teacher working in a large, urban public school system in the area and president of WNYNET) visited class to discuss inquiry-based approaches to English teaching and her commitment to urban education. Deb reflected on tensions in her work, including her struggles as an inquiry-based teacher working in a system that followed a top-down approach to curriculum and instruction. She shared an inquiry unit and related student work that explored the following questions: What do you believe in? What are you willing to risk for those beliefs? How do our experiences and social positions affect the action we take to change the world?

For this unit her students read *Fahrenheit 451* and analyzed a variety of other works, including popular media and other nontraditional texts. During her talk, Deb argued that "teaching for social justice is not just materials or texts but your methods," meaning that social justice must be embedded in every instructional choice teachers make. Preservice teachers returned to this insight throughout the semester as they reflected on their clinical experiences. Deb's visit to methods served as a powerful contrast to some of the traditional, lecture-based teaching students observed in field observations and became a model of enacting progressive teaching practices in the face of systemic pressures for standardized curricula in schools.

Methods students were also paired with Deb's high school students to provide noncontiguous feedback on their writing and presentations for the WNYNET Youth Voices Conference in May 2018. Using Google Drive, methods students worked alongside Deb as she provided feedback to her students. As the semester continued, methods students took up this role, supporting Deb's students writing on their own through Google Drive. Many ENG 463 students also attended Deb's after-school workshops for students participating in Youth Voices to provide additional support.

In another visit, middle school teachers Alyssa Moretti (a second-year teacher working at a local urban charter school) and Shannon Burke (WNYNET vice president and an experienced teacher working at a different urban charter school) discussed their approaches to unit planning with a particular focus on engaging middle school students through essential questions. Alyssa discussed using *Understanding by Design* (Wiggins & McTighe, 2005) and shared a unit organizer she developed to help scaffold this process. Together with Alyssa, the class brainstormed a unit for *The House on Mango Street* using her organizer and referencing our class discussions. Reflecting on this process, Mark, one of the spring semester students, stated that Alyssa "read my mind" by creating such a usable tool for someone new to instructional design. Her unit organizer became an additional part of the course repertoire of strategies and ultimately assisted with the final course unit plan project.

Shannon also spoke about planning by sharing her Wikispace filled with units and daily lesson plans from her eighth-grade curriculum. Shannon shifted her workshop approach to include more weekly literature circles, citing a desire for her students to take on more leadership identities and develop more of their own questions and analyses around the books they read in class. While Shannon presented, Alyssa shared that she had wanted to try out literature circles in her own classroom and was thankful Shannon shared her resources. Preservice teacher Stephen remarked that Shannon's website was "a resource I will keep going back to." He stated that seeing actual examples of daily plans and handouts from a teacher was invaluable in helping him think through how he would approach his own planning.

These course visits provided access to various resources being used by classroom teachers who reflected the type of teaching being advocated for in the methods course and program. Importantly though, the teacher-presenters also provided methods students with an opportunity to participate in critical discussions with classroom teachers and teacher-leaders of the CoP around important ideas, themes, and issues affecting the profession.

Participation in CoP Events

Preservice teachers in methods were also inducted into the CoP through participation in a variety of WNYNET and EESA events. The teacher candidates in methods attended the WNYNET Fall/Winter Conference on English 12, which featured presentations by English teachers from local urban, suburban, and rural schools. Presentations showcased innovative ELA work with high school seniors, including teaching for social justice, the impact of top-down educational reforms on urban students, moving beyond scripted curriculum in urban contexts, the study of popular music in the English classroom, inquiry-based learning, digital video composing, and others. Through participation in this conference, preservice teachers were able to hear from presenters about their teaching. These teacher candidates also collaborated directly with other English teachers and conference attendees in small-group activities and discussions.

Furthermore, students attended EESA's Brown Bag Speaker Series featuring Dr. Tiffany Nyachae's presentation "To Truly Reflect, Teach, and Act for Social Justice: A Conversation With Future Teachers." Nyachae explored how English teachers working in urban schools must fully commit to students. Nyachae's talk helped Naya process and critique some of the rhetoric she was encountering as she began her methods clinical residency in a large urban school district. As a young woman committed to urban education, some of the teaching she encountered was disheartening. In her discussion board post reflecting on Nyachae's talk, she wrote,

> [Dr. Nyachae] . . . has me thinking that these students deserve better and if teachers like us aren't willing to help . . . then what? I've heard so many different things since I started my field observations . . . : "Oh that will be good on your resume"; "You can get a job anywhere if people see you worked there"; or "It's only a few months." Not once has someone asked me if I am going to go back to help or teach students with needs. . . . I think as future teachers we could all use some reflection about the impact we can make and not only what we can take from these communities.

In the spring semester, preservice teachers attended EESA's Alumni Speaker Series featuring Alyssa Moretti's talk "Making the First Years Meaningful: Getting Started in Your Own Classroom." Having already learned how English teachers can approach planning from Alyssa's prior class visit, students were able to learn about her work integrating creative arts into the classroom. Preservice teachers also attended and assisted with the Youth Voices Conference, an annual event sponsored by WNYNET that invites local teachers and their students to campus to present the work they engaged in throughout the year.

In 2018, the conference featured TED Talk–style presentations, spoken word and musical performances, research presentations, and other work by 45 middle and high school students from across the region. In this context, teacher candidates were able to witness firsthand the powerful end result of the pedagogical and theoretical frameworks they had studied throughout the year.

Clinical Residency: Bridging Methods and Student Teaching in the CoP

Many of the cooperating teachers who work with preservice teachers in the methods clinical residency program identify as members of the CoP. Teacher candidates often had profound experiences in these mentor teachers' classrooms during both their methods fieldwork and subsequent student teaching. For Edel, student teaching with Alyssa was an important opportunity for her to explore her interest in arts integration. Alyssa and Edel co-planned a "class symbol—portrait project" in connection to their unit exploring the inquiry question, What are you willing to stand up for? Alyssa and Edel's students displayed their resulting projects at the spring Youth Voices Conference.

Stephen Milano created an inquiry-based unit on teenage identity for his spring student teaching placement in Mike Lester's seventh-grade classroom. Several of Stephen's students presented their resulting "This I Believe" projects at the 2018 Youth Voices Conference. Mark Bell, a methods student, was scheduled to complete his required fieldwork in Mike's room while Stephen was student teaching.

There were initial concerns about having a teacher candidate observe a student teacher, but Stephen was open and enthusiastic about the idea. Mark also embraced the opportunity and eventually completed his course requirement by observing and working with Stephen. Importantly, Mark assisted Stephen in multiple after-school workshop sessions as they prepared students for their Youth Voices presentations. Not only did Mark gain experience with inquiry-based teaching in a middle school classroom, but also his assistance in the after-school workshops proved to be an essential component of Stephen's efforts to prepare his students for their presentations.

Mike Lester, a newer member of the Buffalo State CoP, approached teaching in more traditional ways than did Stephen and Mark but remained a supportive collaborator for this endeavor. After witnessing their work using inquiry-based learning, multimodal composing, and critical literacy with his seventh-grade students, Mike became interested in changing his instructional approaches, commenting, "This is what English teaching should be."

While students in these placements still faced the typical challenges associated with student teaching, the CoP served as a support structure for them and their cooperating teachers throughout the experience and opened up possibilities of learning and professional growth that would not have occurred without it.

Impact of the CoP on Teacher Candidates

Throughout the 2017–2018 academic year, the Buffalo State CoP provided powerful learning opportunities for students in ENG 463. The variety of events, clinical experiences, guest speakers, and opportunities to work alongside in-service teachers extended learning by connecting preservice teachers to a dense network of resources that reached beyond the context of the course. Furthermore, the CoP expanded course learning by aligning topics addressed in class with a variety of clinically rich experiences and events.

As noted throughout this chapter, reconceptualizing methods as a site of induction into English teacher communities of practice had a powerful impact on teacher candidates. For Naya and Laura, interacting in legitimate, meaningful ways with teachers who were pushing back against scripted curricula and other top-down educational reforms became a significant part of their own professional identity development. Both noted how talking with teachers like Deb, seeing their curriculum and student work, reinforced their own commitment to making English meaningful and relevant to students in urban schools.

For other students, like Stephen, the opportunity to gather resources for use in their own classroom was incredibly important. Stephen also commented that having his seventh-grade students from his student teaching placement participate in the Youth Voices Conference was an important opportunity for him to bridge theory and practice: "In college, we spend a lot of time reading and thinking about theory. . . . With Youth Voices, I was able to create an inquiry-based writing workshop space where I could finally test out what I've been thinking about for four years. . . . Through Youth Voices, my students were able to see the value and power of their voice."

COP AND ENGLISH EDUCATION: PROBLEMS AND POSSIBILITIES

While not a cure-all for the challenges facing the profession of teaching English, connecting methods coursework to English teacher communities of practice supported teacher candidates' learning and identity development in powerful ways. Through participation in the CoP, students gained access to various instructional resources and began the process of developing their own agentive teaching identities through participation in meaningful discourse with more experienced members of the profession.

Still, there are challenges facing this approach. As Gee (2004) points out, communities of practice imply membership and resulting statuses of inclusion. Some preservice teachers discussed in this chapter had prior insider status in the CoP through their active involvement in EESA and WNYNET, which supported their learning and growth over multiple semesters. Other preservice teachers did not become involved in these organizations earlier in the program and initially identified as outsiders. Race, social class, sexual orientation, and other aspects of identity affect perceptions of membership and must be at the forefront when working to connect CoPs in teacher education. The Buffalo State English education program has worked to address these issues of membership and identity by making related issues a focus of many teacher-led conferences and invited talks and actively seeking out diverse voices in its membership.

Additionally, not all preservice teachers were able to work with members of the CoP as part of their clinical residency. In these instances, students depended on public transportation, which often limited them to field and student teaching experiences at schools near campus, where members of the CoP were not teaching. In these cases, teacher candidates were more likely to encounter English teaching that did not always reflect the type of instruction advocated by the program.

Preservice teachers in these placements were more likely to encounter scripted curriculum and other aspects of top-down educational policies. Connecting with new and experienced teachers in these schools to better support their work and advocating for the meaningful teaching of English remains a focus of the work discussed in this chapter. Connecting methods coursework to the CoP, however, did provide teacher candidates with meaningful interactions with mentor teachers that were engaging in the type of instruction being studied in the course.

Certainly, developing this approach takes time and the efforts of many individuals. The organizations and resulting social learning system discussed here have been decades in development. In that time, members of the Buffalo State CoP have developed close professional relationships that sustain their efforts. Furthermore, the program continually works to stay connected to graduates as they become classroom teachers. In doing so, teacher candidates have become colleagues and now serve as mentor teachers and CoP leaders who open up their classrooms to future methods cohorts and other preservice teachers in the program. The work to find required field experience placements, student teacher placements, and research opportunities is lessened by the meaningful, long-term relationships that develop in the CoP between teachers and their schools and English teacher education programs.

Re-envisioning programs as centers for English teaching and working to connect like-minded teachers through the development of teacher-driven regional networks is an essential first step. Empowering preservice teachers through their own campus-based organizations and connecting that work to classroom teachers in their region are also important steps in this process, as is the linking of those networks to methods coursework. The time and effort that goes into developing English teacher CoPs should be seen as not a burden but rather part of the DNA of English teacher education.

NOTES

1. Throughout this chapter we refer to the Buffalo State community of practice as a group of in-service and preservice English teachers, English educators, building administrators, and other members of the educational community connected through the English education program and the various initiatives of the Western New York Network of English Teachers, the English Education Student Association, and the Buffalo State English Education Alumni Network.
2. For detailed information on past conferences, events, and other WNYNET initiatives, please visit http://www.wnynet.org.
3. All names of preservice teachers are pseudonyms.

REFERENCES

Anagnostopoulos D., Smith E. R., & Basmadjian, K. G. (2007). Bridging the university-school divide: Horizontal expertise and the "two-worlds pitfall." *Journal of Teacher Education, 58*(2), 138–152.

Athanases, S. Z., Caret, E., Canales, J., & Meyer, T. (1992). Four against "the two-worlds pitfall": University-schools collaboration in teacher education. *English Education, 24*(1), 34–51.

Atwell, N. (2010). The case for literature. *Education Week, 32*.

Atwell, N. (2014). *In the middle: Writing, reading, and learning with adolescents*. Upper Montclair, NJ: Boynton/Cook.

Beach, R., Appleman, D., Fecho, B., & Simon, R. (2016). *Teaching literature to adolescents* (3rd ed.). New York: Routledge.

Beach, R., & Myers, J. (2001). *Inquiry-based English instruction: Engaging students in life and literature*. New York: Teachers College Press.

Blackmore, C. P. (Ed.). (2010). *Social learning systems and communities of practice*. London: Springer.

Cercone, J. (2009). We're smarter together: Building professional social networks in English education. *English Education, 41*(3), 199–206.

Cercone, J. (2014). Communities of practice: Bridging the gap between methods courses and secondary schools. In J. Brass & A. Webb (Eds.), *Reclaiming English language arts methods courses: Critical issues and challenges for teacher educators in top-down times* (pp. 109–122). New York: Routledge.

Cochran-Smith, M., Carney, M. C., Keefe, E. S., Burton, S., Chang W. C., Beatriz Fernández, M., Miller, A. F., Sánchez, J. G., & Baker, M. (2018). *Reclaiming accountability in teacher education*. New York: Teachers College Press.

Delpit, L. D. (2006). *Other people's children: Cultural conflict in the classroom*. New York: New Press.

Dewey, J. (1910). *How we think*. Boston: Heath.

Fecho, B. (2003). Untangling our predicaments: Inquiring into methods courses. *English Education, 36*(1), 86–89.

Fecho, B. (2004). *"Is this English?": Race, language, and culture in the classroom*. New York: Teachers College Press.

Feiman-Nemser, S., & Buchman, M. (1985). Pitfalls of experience in teacher preparation. *Teachers College Record, 87*(1), 53–65.

Freire, P. (1972). *Pedagogy of the oppressed*. New York: Herder and Herder.

Gaughan, J. (1998). *Cultural reflections: Critical teaching and learning in the English classroom*. Portsmouth, NH: Boyton/Cook.

Gee, J. (2004). *An introduction to discourse analysis: Theory and method*. New York: Routledge.

Gustavson, L. (2007). *Youth learning on their own terms: Creative practices and classroom teaching*. New York: Routledge.

Henning, N., Dover, A., Dotson, E., & Agarwal-Rangnath, R. (2018). Storying teacher education policy: Critical counternarratives of curricular, pedagogical, and activist responses to state-mandated teacher performance assessments. *Education Policy Analysis Archives, 26*, 26. doi:http://dx.doi.org/10.14507/epaa.26.2790.

Hicks, T. (2009). *The digital writing workshop*. Portsmouth, NH: Heinemann.

hooks, b. (1994). *Teaching to transgress: Education as the practice of freedom*. New York: Routledge.

Kelchtermans, G., & Ballet, K. (2002). The micropolitics of teacher induction. A narrative-biographical study on teacher socialization. *Teaching and Teacher Education, 18*(1), 105–120.

Ladson-Billings, G. (2014). Culturally relevant pedagogy 2.0: A.k.a. the Remix. *Harvard Educational Review, 84*(1), 74–84.

Lave, J., & Wenger, E. (1991). *Situated learning: Legitimate peripheral participation*. Cambridge: Cambridge University Press.

Madeloni, B., & Gorlewski, J. (2013, Summer). Wrong answer to the wrong question: Why we need critical teacher education, not standardization. *Rethinking Schools*, 16–21.

McCann, T., Johannessen, L. R., Kahn, E., & Flanagan, J. M. (2006). *Talking in class: Using discussion to enhance teaching and learning*. Urbana, IL: NCTE.

Paris, D. (2012). Culturally sustaining pedagogy: A needed change in stance, terminology, and practice. *Educational Researcher, 41*(3), 93–97.

Paris, D., & Alim, H. S. (2017). *Culturally sustaining pedagogies: Teaching and learning for justice in a changing world*. New York: Teachers College Press.

Smagorinsky, P. (2008). *Teaching English by design: How to create and carry out instructional units*. Portsmouth, NH: Heinemann.

Smagorinsky, P., Rhym, D., & Moore, C. P. (2013). Competing centers of gravity: A beginning English teacher's socialization process within conflictual settings. *English Education, 45*(2), 147–182.

Smith, M. W., & Wilhelm, J. D. (2002). *"Reading don't fix no Chevys": Literacy in the lives of young men*. Portsmouth, NH: Heinemann.

Smith, M. W., & Wilhelm, J. D. (2006). *Going with the flow: How to engage boys (and girls) in their literacy learning*. Portsmouth, NH: Heinemann.

Street, B. (1993). The new literacy studies. *Journal of Research and Reading, 16*(2), 81–97.

Tovani, C. (2000). *I read it, but I don't get it: Comprehension strategies for adolescent readers*. Portland, ME: Stenhouse.

Tuck, E., & Gorlewski, J. (2016). Racist ordering, settler colonialism, and edTPA: A participatory policy analysis. *Educational Policy, 30*(1), 197–217. http://doi.org/10.1177/0895904815616483.

Webb, A. (2014). A Cultural Studies Approach to Literature Methods. In J. Brass & A. Webb (Eds.), *Reclaiming English Language Arts Methods Courses: Critical issues and challenges for teachers in top-down times* (pp. 190–202). New York: Routledge.

Wenger, E. (1998). *Communities of practice: Learning, meaning, and identity*. Cambridge: Cambridge University Press.

Wenger, E. (2010). Communities of practice and social learning systems: The career of a concept. In *Social learning systems and communities of practice* (pp. 179–198). London: Springer.

Wiggins, G., & McTighe, J. (2005). *Understanding by design* (2nd ed.). Alexandria, VA: Association for Supervision and Curriculum Development (ASCD).

Wilhelm, J. (2007). *Engaging readers and writers with inquiry*. New York: Scholastic.

A Response to Chapter 8

Amber Jensen

One of the long-standing challenges we face as English educators is helping preservice teachers grow into their professional identities while navigating complicated shifts among university and school settings, their roles as student and teacher, and their emerging knowledge about and commitments to theory and practice. James Cercone and Kristen Pastore-Capuana call our attention to the ways English education programs—and English methods courses, in particular—can create and integrate meaningful partnerships with teachers and networks beyond the university as a way to engage preservice teachers as active participants in and contributors to ongoing and dynamic professional communities of practice (CoPs).

My response draws on my own experiences as a former high school English teacher and, now, as an English teacher educator to affirm the ways that induction into and participation within CoPs can empower, develop, and sustain preservice teachers in their transition into their teaching careers. I also address likely challenges and offer possible entry points others may consider when establishing and integrating CoPs in their English teacher education programs. Finally, I extend the conversation to ask questions and invite further discussion about how this approach enriches our understanding of English education at large.

Classroom-based fieldwork is already a significant component of most English education programs, wherein preservice teachers receive support and direction from a mentor teacher through observing, teaching, and reflecting on practice (Caughlan, Pasternak, Hallman, Renzi, Rush, & Frisby, 2017). A CoP approach extends beyond fieldwork placements, however, in ways that bring together preservice and in-service teachers in authentic and dynamic disciplinary discourse. These interactions challenge and elevate teachers' individual and collective knowledge and practice in reciprocal ways; they invite discussion on the values and priorities most pertinent to teachers' professional growth.

This important distinction, as Cercone and Pastore-Capuana point out, draws upon the kinds of lasting and sociocultural-based learning models that ultimately connect "preservice teachers with meaningful learning opportunities and ongoing support throughout their careers" (p. 122). The program they describe in their chapter takes up a key element of Lave and Wenger's (1991) CoP framework by bringing together *newcomers* and *old-timers* in ways that honor the participation of both to nurture their evolving identities and different roles within the community over the course of their careers.

The authors' argument that induction to these communities engages preservice teachers in professional conversations and relationships throughout their careers resonates with my sense of how such communities of practice affected my own teaching career. While I did not find or realize I even needed a community of practice beyond my school until well into my teaching career, I can attest that I stayed in the profession as long as I did due in large part to a grassroots community of secondary school writing center directors I collaborated with in the early years of founding and directing the writing center at the high school at which I taught.

What started as informal resource sharing and problem solving via email and an occasional face-to-face meet-up eventually evolved into a more structured community that hosted events such as an annual Secondary School Writing Center conference and the formulation of a group that conducted research to present at regional and national conferences. Because of the professional and personal connections we forged as English teachers and early proponents of high school writing centers, I expanded my own vision of the directions a career in English teaching could entail, found a voice as an advocate for peer tutoring programs focused on writing at the school and county levels, collaborated on creating a new English elective course, and began to contribute to a wider public and professional conversation about writing and writing instruction in high school and college.

What began as a local group of high school English teachers working together to envision a new model of peer learning and tutoring focused on writing ultimately evolved into what is now known as the Secondary School Writing Centers Association (SSWCA), a professional community still led by English teachers working to professionalize and advocate for peer-led writing tutoring programs at the high school level. I can only imagine how forging these kinds of cross-level and cross-institutional connections during my preservice teacher education would have deepened my roots and catalyzed me in my earliest years as a teacher to find my footing and establish my teaching values alongside mentors and colleagues.

In my current role as an English teacher educator, I grapple with a range of competing priorities and demands of educating preservice teachers, many of which are addressed in the chapters of this book. Still, I am compelled by the CoP approach to professional identity building Cercone and Pastore-Capuana outline, even if its implementation raises challenges for the workload and construct of English teacher education programs.

As the authors note, building a regional hub of English educators and students across career stages and institutions has been a long-term and evolving endeavor requiring resources, time, and institutional commitments that many English educators may not currently have. Yet, even without these kinds of established networks, I see opportunities for English education programs to build on existing relationships to integrate elements of communities of practice to benefit preservice teachers.

Key aspects of the programs in Cercone and Pastore-Capuana's CoP model include teachers teaching teachers (e.g., WNYNET Conference, Brown Bag Speaker Series, and Alumni Teacher Series), learning from youth (e.g., Youth Voices Conference), and honoring preservice and in-service teachers alike (e.g., English Education Spring Banquet). A starting point for programs considering implementing some of these practices may be to ask some of the following questions: How does (or might) our program/course foster dialogue between preservice and in-service teachers using a *classroom-up* approach, even beyond clinical field experiences? Where are (or might there be) opportunities for preservice teachers to celebrate and learn from youth? How does (or could) the program honor teachers to acknowledge meaningful teaching and elevate possible learning opportunities? Finally, are there existing communities with which the English teaching program or methods class could partner?

For some programs, established school-university partnerships might be a useful entry point. As my university's network of professional development schools (PDS) has grown, so have opportunities for preservice and in-service teachers to collaborate on teaching initiatives in ways that deepen and extend participants' teaching experiences and identities. Kristien Zenkov, the English education program director and PDS program coordinator at George Mason University, ensures preservice teachers in methods courses participate in ongoing opportunities to collaborate, coteach, and reflect on the realities, opportunities, and challenges of literacy education alongside school-based mentor teachers at partner schools.

One such example, drawing on a collaborative photovoice project Zenkov facilitated at one PDS, is illustrated in an article he coauthored with three of the project's participants. A mentor teacher, a recent program alumna, and a high school student wrote about the ways their cross-context partnership helped to "inform one another's personas" and "explore the notions of literacy and writing instruction approaches" (Zenkov, Taylor, Angle, & Nzita, 2016). Integrating these kinds of extended field-based experiences within

English methods courses at George Mason University has been one way to build and model CoPs with preservice teachers.

Another possible context for collaboration is with a National Writing Project (NWP) site, which connects literacy educators through a variety of teacher-led programs and events building on principles of teachers teaching teachers, including youths' perspectives, and honoring teachers. Many universities' writing project sites are integrated within their English education programs, making possible opportunities for rich and lasting interactions between preservice and in-service teachers.

Our local NWP site, however, has an institutional home in a different department than our English education program, which means the programs have historically run along parallel, but not intersecting, paths. Integrating preservice teachers as part of this existing and vibrant community of writing teachers would likely benefit both programs by connecting teachers along a range of career stages.

But forging the connections that Cercone and Pastore-Capuana describe requires more than onetime interactions such as preservice teachers attending the annual one-day Language and Literacy Conference for K–12 writing teachers, which is something we have encouraged in recent years. It would instead mean creating inroads for preservice and in-service teachers to collaborate more authentically, perhaps by coleading a conference presentation with a practicing teacher or even by helping to plan the conference itself. Finding ways to foster lasting and meaningful, rather than onetime, connections with existing CoPs could be a next step for our program and for other teacher education programs considering implementing some of the practices written about by Cercone and Pastore-Capuana.

By drawing on existing partnerships and, perhaps, creating new ones, methods course instructors can integrate experiences and practices of the diverse English teaching communities they engage in through their course activities. Linking course topics and experiences with authentic and clinically rich experiences is where Cercone and Pastore-Capuana's framework is most insightful, albeit, in their case, highly labor intensive. Rather than looking *inward* at the methods course as a stand-alone point along a trajectory or as a launchpad into a future professional English teaching community, Cercone and Pastore-Capuana provide a model for how a methods course might instead look *outward* in ways that integrate preservice teachers as contributing members of these communities, to act in professional roles, and to engage in meaningful learning and sharing alongside a range of their current and future colleagues and students.

REFERENCES

Caughlan, S., Pasternak, D., Hallman, H. L., Renzi, L., Rush, L., & Frisby, M. (2017). How English language arts teachers are prepared for 21st century classrooms: Results of a national survey. *English Education, 49*(3), 265–297.

Lave, J., & Wenger, E. (1991). *Situated learning: Legitimate peripheral participation.* Cambridge: Cambridge University Press.

Zenkov, K., Taylor, L., Angle, D., & Nzita, A. N. (2016). Writing our identities together. *Journal of Adolescent and Adult Literacy, 60*(3), 345–348.

Chapter Nine

Tensions in ELA Field Experiences

Service-Learning Initiatives in Rural Contexts

Allison Wynhoff Olsen

> How does a ninth grader actually write? Is this normal? I know I was a better writer than this when I was in high school. —anonymous preservice teacher in English teacher education

With four weeks remaining in the semester, as preservice teachers (PSTs) were drafting inquiry papers, it was time to prepare lessons on 5–12 student writing and feedback (with a particular focus on ninth-grade essays). The intent was to foster discussions about how to provide feedback to peers (writer to writer) and to 5–12 students (teacher to writer), serving PSTs' current writing needs while supporting them for their student teaching the following semester. Their responses to the 5–12 student essays were surprising.

The PSTs simultaneously panicked, called out linguistic errors, asked to see the assignment, and positioned themselves incapable of evaluating these essays because they didn't know how to gauge them. As questions filled the classroom, it was concerning to think that the PSTs were less than a month away from student teaching and they—future English teachers—did not position themselves as capable of reading and evaluating student writing.

Needing to quell the panic in the room, the conversation was redirected to a discussion more generally about writing, what makes effective text, and how writers experience helpful feedback. Questioning their experiences during their three-credit practicum course (field experience) as well as other times they engaged with youth, the conversation reverted to what they already knew. This provided a clear picture of this English, PST cohort: The students were strong in English content, knew how to create curriculum, and shared an inclination to teach with a social justice focus. However, they also lacked interactive moments with youth in schools and felt anxiety about how to teach and evaluate writing. While typical for PSTs to not feel *ready*, the program could dampen some panic and also help build a more robust community of English teachers across the state. This chapter details programmatic shifts made to attend to both aims.

PROGRAM BACKGROUND

The English education program described here is housed in the English department at a large land-grant university in the West. With courses across departments, English education majors take *methods classes* as a three-part sequence: two courses within English (Teaching Writing in Secondary Schools and Teaching Reading and Literature in Secondary Schools) and one course within education (Methods: 5–12 English). If PSTs are on track, they take the three-part methods during their junior year.

English requires two English education courses outside of the methods block: Language for Teachers and Capstone. Language for Teachers is centered on sociolinguistics and discourse analysis. Capstone is a seminar that synthesizes pedagogies and theories and focuses on teacher inquiry. Instructors in the education department on campus coordinate a three-credit practicum course that is aligned to field placement requirements for licensure.

Recent graduates of the program have expressed dissatisfaction with their education to become English teachers in two domains: (1) they report that they lacked sufficient opportunities to work with *real* students while learning teaching strategies; and (2) they report that they were not adequately educated to teach in rural contexts.[1] While the majority of the schools in the state are rural, the required field experiences are not. PST practicum placements typically occur near the university, and the proximal schools offer little resemblance to the majority of schools in the state.

COLLABORATIONS INFORMED BY SERVICE LEARNING

Local and digital collaborations with English/writing teachers and their students were formed to address the concerns that the PSTs expressed about experience with *real* students in rural contexts over the past three years. Two key questions framed the collaborations: (1) How can in-service teachers, PSTs, and English education scholars collaborate in mutually benefitting ways? (2) What might English teachers need/want from a flexible university partnership?

The reasoning for labeling these collaborations *service learning* was to help set them apart from PSTs' required practicum experiences and to foreground key values (Butin, 2010; Giles & Eyler, 1994). The service-learning experience centered learners and their environments and provided PSTs with experiential moments to generate interest and awaken curiosity. The program explicitly works to create community across levels, and the ways service-learning positions people within communities fit its aims: "Students must begin to understand their role *within* the community, rather than seeing themselves as outsiders *giving* to a community in need" (Thornton, 2014, p. 68). Service-learning collaborations were also opportunities for change, with the purpose of helping PSTs imagine how teachers, learners, writing, school, and community may intersect in mutually benefitting ways (White & Reid, 2008; Zeichner, 1992).

This process for collaboration simultaneously established and solidified relationships with teachers and schools across the state, while repairing disconnects. The disconnects traditionally stemmed from a one-way partnership rich with logistics and a university agenda (Zeichner, 2010), with little opportunity for teachers to dialogue with English education professors or allow PSTs to simply be in school spaces, interacting with youth and learning about the communities at play. New conversations with teachers revealed that they wanted their student writers to write for varied audiences as much as they yearned for help in providing feedback to stacks of student drafts.

The program's priorities were to connect PSTs with writers and classrooms, thereby exposing the PSTs to varied writing pedagogy and messy student processes. Additionally, the program wanted PSTs to interact with youth in school situations without such reliance on university tasks. Typically, in methods class, PSTs consider a pedagogy, text, or approach by setting it alongside their own school experiences. They notice whether they have tension or alignment and begin to make decisions on value and future use. While this may be beneficial in helping PSTs develop their own stances, it may result in PSTs lacking awareness or empathy toward students and contexts unfamiliar to them. Service learning added layers to their classroom and student narratives and helped avoid a "single story" (Adichie, 2009) of school and English teaching.

Methods Collaborations

For three years, the program infused service-learning initiatives into English methods syllabi. Table 9.1 provides a glimpse into the collaborations and how they changed, depending on methods course scheduling and collaboration opportunities.

English instructors infused service-learning initiatives into methods through local collaborations. During year one, a local teacher came into class and modeled how to provide essay feedback, PSTs partnered up and led after-school tutoring, and PSTs facilitated writing groups or led writing sta-

Table 9.1. Service Learning Sequence for English Preservice Teacher Cohorts

AY year & methods course link	Partnership	Activities	Mode	Length of time
2013–2014 ENG 339 & 445 (3-hour methods block)	Local English teacher	Essay conversations & feedback	In-person (Teacher came to our class)	1 day
	Local HS	After-school tutoring	In-person (PSTs went to HS)	10 weeks
	Local HS	Writing group facilitations or writing station managers	In-person (PSTs went to HS)	3 visits
	Local community college: Writing 101 professor	Writing group facilitations	In-person (PSTs went to class at the community college)	4 visits
2014–2015 ENG 339 & 445 (2 methods courses during spring semester)	MT rural English teacher	Essay collaboration	Online (Google Docs)	2 weeks
	MT English teacher	Essay collaboration	Online (Google Docs)	3 weeks
	Local community college: Writing 101 professor	Writing group facilitations	In-person (PSTs went to CC's class)	4 visits
2015–2016 ENG 339 & 445 (yearlong methods sequence)	Out-of-state rural English teacher	Essay collaboration, reading group members, & college mentoring	Online (Edmodo, Google Docs, Skype, & FaceTime)	26 weeks
	MT rural English teacher	Essay collaboration	Online (Google Docs) In-person (Teacher came to our class as a guest lecturer)	2 weeks

tions with high school or college writers (schedule depending). In year two, PSTs facilitated writing groups with college writers and collaborated online with high school writers in rural schools. During year three, all collaborations were rural, online collaborations: one for a two-week unit and the other for 26 consecutive weeks.

Each year, PSTs' participation in service learning was required but not graded. Removing grading pressure helped focus PSTs on the students, teachers, and schools rather than on achieving tasks set by a university agenda; not grading also helped the program embody a culture of community beyond the English education cohort. PSTs kept a service-learning field journal where each entry summarized the purpose of the session, instructional moves, learner responses, and reflections on the PSTs' shifting self-efficacy and teacher identity. Using their journals as prewriting, PSTs debriefed and shared experiences during class, which allowed all the PSTs exposure to the various collaborations. The journals also became their self-authored texts to set alongside other methods work and to carry into their research capstone the following year.

Across the collaborations, three key patterns emerged: (1) PSTs experienced academic and emotional wobble (Fecho, 2011). (2) In-service teachers were interested in pairing their students with college mentors, particularly through productive, online conversations based on curriculum (in this case, writing). (3) A community of critical English teachers afforded strong collaborations in methods classes and made visible the growth and development of teachers over time. This chapter will illustrate the first pattern: academic and emotional wobble, and how it has framed the program's service-learning initiatives and facilitated a shift into online collaborations with rural classrooms.

WOBBLE AND PRESERVICE ENGLISH TEACHERS

The concept of *wobble* (Fecho, 2011; Fecho, Graham, & Hudson-Ross, 2005) articulates teachers' tensions and shifts as they navigate their professional growth. In this case, the PSTs experienced their wobble during these collaborations. Wobble, a space of uncertainty within one's beliefs or figured worlds (Holland, 1998), is a destabilization that "signals or calls attention to a shift in balance" (Fecho et al., 2005, p. 179). As PSTs experience wobble, learning can be achieved, particularly if they use the wobble to "notice, understand, and appreciate . . . for what it might tell them about themselves as teachers and their ongoing practice" (p. 179). The wobble's demand for a response creates space for meta-awareness and meta-dialogue that can produce heightened understanding.

As PSTs interacted with *real* students and teachers, they experienced disconcerting moments of wobble that decentered their preconceived beliefs about teaching and learning. This wobble required them to regain balance in order to function as teachers within school systems by reexamining those beliefs in this new context. Working through these tensions, PSTs experienced varied tolerances to the instances that resulted in their wobble, both academically and emotionally. The experiences that resulted between wobble and balance were significant, particularly given that "those who could tolerate longer instances and greater degrees of wobble were rewarded with fresh and significant new perspectives on practice" (Fecho et al., 2005, p. 184).

Academic Wobble

Moments of academic wobble occurred as PSTs explored writing across theories and pedagogies while providing feedback to real student essays. One PST used her field journal to frame a disconnect she experienced when talking about writing with a student: "She wasn't concerned with how she felt about the material or what she wanted to say. . . . She was stuck in the mindset that she was writing to get the grade and wasn't writing for herself at all. . . . I realized how powerful the school system can be in shaping students' beliefs to reflect what she was experiencing when trying to write her assignment." Though this PST felt confident talking about writing in general, she was unsure how to handle schooled writing.

The following illustrations of academic wobble occurred during a service-learning collaboration. Ms. Blue,[2] a local high school English teacher, was teaching three AP courses. About to collect 65 essay drafts, she was frustrated that she could not connect with her writers more often.[3] An English education professor—recalling this struggle from personal experience teaching high school English—talked with Ms. Blue about creating a mutually beneficial service-learning initiative and asked, "Is there any way that PSTs can help you read and provide feedback on these upcoming students' drafts?" As a result, Ms. Blue scheduled to come to English methods class the day she collected the essays.

At this point in the program, PSTs completed a minimum of two university writing classes and some identified as writers. Prior to Ms. Blue's visit, PSTs studied Newkirk and Kent's (2007) *Teaching the Neglected 'R': Rethinking Writing Instruction in Secondary Classrooms*. In reading about writing genres, PSTs wondered how/if *real* student writing would fit as neatly within genre lines as the Common Core suggests, or if they should teach for blurred boundaries that were more aligned with their composition courses. They also wondered how they could individualize feedback while maintaining standard expectations.

When Ms. Blue came to methods, she provided a detailed context on her school and AP classes, provided a short presentation on the essay assignment, and handed each PST three or four papers. As PSTs began to read, a key question emerged: "How much grammar correction is too much to make or to suggest?" Ms. Blue explained that the essays were drafts and she wasn't concerned about correctness; however, if the PST readers were distracted by grammatical errors or noted patterns, they should comment. This was difficult direction for the PSTs because their eyes kept seeing errors and they wanted them fixed.

While reading the essays, the PSTs literally squirmed and sighed in frustration. They made visible an academic wobble, as their expectations of what students should be able to do as high school writers were clashing with the *real* student products. This wobble demanded a response because the PSTs were expected to provide meaningful feedback, but they were stuck within their own expectations for writing quality and their awareness that negative feedback would likely shut down writers.

Connected Feedback

Ms. Blue suggested that it might help PSTs to read all the essays in their stack to gauge how students were attending to the assignment (or not) and to help them think across writers. Reading across could also help them recalibrate expectations, an area where PSTs experienced the largest benefit to Ms. Blue being with them while they were giving feedback.

"Did my student try?!" "How can she say something like this?" "This student was way off; what do I do?" As these questions flooded the classroom, Ms. Blue sat next to PSTs and told them about the student who wrote the essay. She offered key details: "She has refused to write all year; this is the first essay I've received, so I need you to be encouraging." "You're right; this is not his best. You can press him with your comments; he needs it." And, "This is the *best* piece of writing he's ever done; I know it may not look like much to you as is, but this student has improved *so much*, and I couldn't be more proud of this draft."

During these conversations, PSTs were able to work through their wobble with Ms. Blue, gaining equilibrium as she disrupted their predetermined expectations for the essays by contextualizing them for each writer. One PST's compliment reveals the empowering approach of Ms. Blue: "What I really appreciate and admire is how much you knew your students—and how you used that information to their benefit rather than against them."

Though this service-learning initiative was brief (less than a full methods class block), the PSTs and high school students continued communicating. Ms. Blue had her students write thank-you notes to the PSTs that outlined what they appreciated about the writing feedback they received. PSTs were asked to respond to the thank-you notes to continue the dialogue between the participants.

Emotional Wobble

The English education program teaches PSTs to embody their classrooms (hooks, 1994), and the service-learning initiatives provided concrete illustrations of teacher vulnerability, particularly as PSTs shared that emotional responses often got in their way. The PST's emotional wobble was a continual presence and the topic of meta-conversations.

Emotions About Positioning and Identity

Three key moments illustrated how PSTs grappled with their positioning and identities during service-learning. These moments vacillated between providing interactions with youth in schools and teaching English content, allowing PSTs to interact with youth as college student mentors and future teachers.

In the first instance, English education instructors, responding to the expressed needs of the high school English teachers and the high school principal, created a schedule for a rotating pair of PSTs to offer after-school tutoring at a local high school. English teachers encouraged students to attend, delivered all-school announcements, and called parents to let them know that university PSTs were going to be in the building to offer additional support. During the 10-week collaboration, PSTs primarily helped students with math, history, and science homework, with just a few requests for help with essays or English-related topics.

One PST wrote about his positioning, "I was set back into math, the bane of my existence, and I was failing at it from the start." Out of their disciplinary element, worried and frustrated about how much they were (not) helping, PSTs were able to consider how they were interacting with youth in a school space. The English professor used methods class meetings to reframe, shifting the focus away from English content and into how PSTs spoke to and with the students. PSTs also discussed how they felt when the students expected them to have facility with various subjects because of their college student status. Both topics helped broker conversations about how people perceive education and enact schooling, as well as what it means to feel like a failure within a schooled task.

In another school partnership, PSTs entered an English/history combination course as writing group facilitators or writing station managers. The course had 60 students, two teachers, and two student teachers, so the PSTs went to class on four select days to join that team and help students get their writing questions answered. PSTs were overwhelmed with the number of students and the fast pacing; one PST remarked,

> I was very nervous going into the classroom. We went through the handout in class with the students and I felt like I got eaten alive with all their questions. I was sweating very hard because these questions were something, I, as an English major should have been able to answer. These questions went something like this, "Isn't the subjective clause in that sentence functioning adjectively?"

This collaboration made visible the kind of knowledge PSTs wobble over because they think they should know the answers as an English teacher and feel unsure about their own competence.

A third partnership relied on online collaborations with high school writers. Online, PSTs had to do different work to be noticed and heard. They learned the importance of building community in small doses, using Skype or FaceTime (when methods class and high school class times aligned) as well as short paragraphs of written introduction, accompanied by a photograph (most used an informal headshot or an action shot of the PST engaged in a typical activity they thought may be of interest or connection to the students). In their introductory paragraphs, PSTs wrote short personal biographies; most positioned themselves as students learning how to teach (not as teachers). Many of the high school students gravitated to the PSTs as co-learners, offering some of their own personal stories in response.

Some PSTs continued to insert conversation as they began on-task work with the students. For example, one PST's approach was a simple two-line note: "I have been reading your narratives and I am about ready to make some comments. :) I know you are getting ready for basketball tournaments, so enjoy and have a safe and fun weekend." This conversation is evident throughout this interpersonal work; PSTs noticed how taking time to build relationships with the high school students—albeit briefly—created more productive online work groups. For some PSTs, this caused an emotional wobble because they felt that as teachers their role was to instruct. They struggled with time spent "just talking" because they worried it was entering a friend or parent spectrum and they wanted to maintain their professional identities. For others, it affirmed that teachers teach students rather than content.

Emotions About Students' Writing

One online collaboration focused the PSTs on high school juniors' personal narratives. While this writing assignment exposed PSTs to complex student realities, it also caused emotional strain for PSTs and the partnering teacher. In the midst of the feedback cycle, a PST emailed the following to her English instructor: "The language [that my high school student] uses [in her essay] is so inappropriate and makes me feel uncomfortable. . . . I do not want to work with this/her until she completely redirects her essay because the content makes me so angry." Within an hour the high school teacher was looped in via email and responded to the instructor and PST. The teacher validated the PST's need for a break from the offending essay and explained that she had given the student permission to use vulgarity for the purpose of "developing a character," noting that the student writer went too far. The teacher had not read the student's essay before it was shared with the PST, and she praised the PST's initial comments to the student (written directly within the student's essay document) for being "professional and commanding." The teacher also articulated her insecurities in a separate email to the English professor where she apologized, asked questions about how to allow for writer's choice without censoring language, and wondered how to proceed. She also considered her student's situation and expressed, "I think things are a little rough at home."

While it comes as no surprise that teaching is emotional and taxing, the visceral emotions PSTs experienced with these personal narratives affirmed that placing service-learning initiatives within English methods class is well timed. PSTs need time to reflect on their emotional responses to teaching situations before they are expected to lead or perform as teachers. Programmatically, it was also beneficial for the English professor to extend mentorship to the high school teachers, thereby building and sustaining relationships in the statewide community of English teachers.

SERVICE-LEARNING INITIATIVES: FOCUSING ON RURAL CONTEXTS

The program's shift from local to rural service learning was purposeful. Reflecting on the successful, local partnerships allowed English instructors to articulate key practices to try to emulate in online spaces with rural schools. English instructors desired to move PSTs away from a deficit, singular notion of rurality, so building collaborations within rural schools made sense. Shifting service-learning initiatives into rural schools also created opportunities for more durative partnerships. This section highlights the partnerships from the third year (see Table 9.1), explaining moments of wobble and reciprocal benefits to rural teachers and PSTs.

The program connected PSTs to Mr. Haufbrau, a 6–12 teacher in a small rural school in the state. Given the school's small size, Mr. Haufbrau taught two to seven students per grade level. The majority of his students were monolingual and identified as white. During a two-week collaboration with the eighth-grade class, PSTs provided feedback to the students' essays via Google Drive, a typical platform for schools in the state. Giving PSTs "editing rights" within Drive allowed entry into the high school classroom without being too disruptive; it also helped PSTs learn how to use the commenting features in Drive and observe students' writing processes as they revised.

A yearlong (26-week) partnership had high school students taking community college courses for credit connected the PSTs to Ms. Mueller, a rural high school English teacher. The majority of Ms. Mueller's students were bilingual high school students who were taking a community college class for credit for the first time. PSTs were positioned as college mentors and co-learners. Using the online platforms Edmodo and Google Drive, Ms. Mueller divided her students into groups and assigned PSTs to comanage a group with a partner. This partner structure supported PSTs with their academic and emotional wobble because they were not expected to lead a group of students alone. Throughout the year, the high school students and PSTs read the same novel, engaged in literature conversations, shared writing, and cocreated a project.[4]

PSTs took ownership within this partnership more than the program observed in previous, shorter collaborations, yet they still experienced wobble. One key aspect of wobble occurred around scheduling. When service-learning initiatives intensified, the English instructor adjusted the occurrence of class meetings, giving PSTs flex time. Though adjustments were communicated, the lack of a fixed, a priori schedule caused PSTs some duress.

For instance, student writers sometimes missed deadlines, which resulted in PSTs either rearranging their schedules or telling a student he or she was too late for feedback. Partnering teachers also had to shift plans due to schooling interruptions (e.g., "It is tournament week so who knows when I will actually have any classes" or "The lab was overscheduled so students did not get a chance to upload their essays"). PSTs had a range of emotions to these changes, with irritation and discomfort being those expressed by the majority.

Numerous times PSTs entered methods class angry and confused about why and how the youth were completing assignments. Sometimes caught in their frustration, PSTs would rebuff scholars and class texts. When they experienced youth who did not meet their assignment deadlines, the PSTs experienced additional frustration with some classroom and teaching norms that many experienced teachers face. In a moment of irritation, one PST blurted out, "Why can't this teacher just make her students do the work?!" An assertion that many PSTs express in their naïveté.

It was here, in the midst of service learning, that the instructor paused methods class and addressed the PSTs' disrupted expectations to help them understand the notion of wobble and the learning that could follow if PSTs were willing to use the wobble generatively. Collectively, the class leaned into the wobble and normalized it, allowing PSTs time to feel, reflect, respond, fail, and repair. PSTs learned how to identify students and instances that destabilized them amid their academic and emotional wobble. They practiced asking for help diffusing situations, and collectively the PSTs were given opportunities to study English methods from varying mentor teachers, high school students, textbooks, and scholars over time.

As the partnership continued, frustration with student writers remained present, yet PSTs moved away from venting within the methods class and began facilitating sustained conversations directly with the student writers (e.g., "Students, I am concerned by these outlines") and Ms. Mueller (e.g., "What should I do/expect if my group members do not post on time or at all?" "How do you handle the violence when teaching *In Cold Blood*?").

Since starting service-learning initiatives within the English education program, graduates request collaborations. This opportunity for sustained relationships allows the program to see how PSTs develop into teachers, while supporting networks for them that enrich the larger English education community. This connection is of particular importance for graduates who move into teaching positions in rural and remote parts of the state and beyond. As single-person departments (each is often the sole English teacher, grades 6–12), they yearn for conversations with and support from other English teachers. The service-learning initiatives resulted in more reflective teaching practices and additional mentoring roles during their early years in the field.

NOTES

1. In this chapter, the service learning initiatives occurred in rural locations and the discussion of them considers the needs of the PSTs who engage in these partnerships.

2. This name is a pseudonym, as are all names used in this chapter.

3. I want to be clear that I find Ms. Blue's frustrations a typical expression of writing teachers (particularly those who teach multiple writing courses or who teach in larger school districts). I am in no way suggesting that she was not doing her job well. Her willingness to partner with us and to share her pedagogy and feedback values is just one illustration of her expertise and professionalism.

4. This chapter focuses on the opportunities created on the program and not the specific assessment projects created by the PSTs and their high school collaborators.

REFERENCES

Adichie, C. N. (2009). *The danger of a single story* [video file]. Retrieved from http://www.ted.com.

Butin, D. W. (2010). Service-Learning in Theory and Practice: The future of community engagement in higher education. New York: Palgrave Macmillan.

Fecho, B. (2011). *Teaching for the students: Habits of heart, mind, and practice in the engaged classroom*. New York: Teachers' College.

Fecho, B., Graham, P., & Hudson-Ross, S. (2005). Appreciating the wobble: Teacher research, professional development, and figured worlds. *English Education, 37*(3), 174–199.

Giles, D. E., Jr., & Eyler, J. (1994). The theoretical roots of service-learning in John Dewey: Toward a theory of service-learning. *Michigan Journal of Community Service Learning, 1*(1), 77–95.

Hallman, H., & Burdick, M. (2014). Service-learning and the role of "teacher": An initiative working with homeless youth. In V. Kinloch & P. Smagorinsky (Eds.), *Service-learning in literacy education: Possibilities for teaching and learning* (pp. 117–130). Charlotte, NC: Information Age.

Holland, D. C. (1998). *Identity and agency in cultural worlds*. Cambridge, MA: Harvard University Press.

hooks, b. (1994). *Teaching to transgress: Education as the practice of freedom*. New York: Routledge.

Newkirk, T., & Kent, R. (Eds.). (2007). *Teaching the neglected 'R': Rethinking writing instruction in secondary classrooms*. Portsmouth, NH: Heinemann.

Thornton, M. G. (2014). An authentic, curriculum-based approach to service-learning. In V. Kinloch & P. Smagorinsky (Eds.), *Service-learning in literacy education: Possibilities for teaching and learning* (pp. 65–84). Charlotte, NC: Information Age.

White, S., & Reid, J. (2008). Placing teachers? Sustaining rural schooling through place-consciousness in teacher education. *Journal of Research in Rural Education, 23*(7), 1–10.

Zeichner, K. (1992). Rethinking the practicum in the professional development school partnership. *Journal of Teacher Education, 43*(4), 296–307.

Zeichner, K. (2010). Rethinking the connections between campus courses and field experiences in college- and university-based teacher education. *Journal of Teacher Education, 61*(1–2), 89–99.

A Response to Chapter 9

Jamie M. Collins

Upon graduating with my doctorate in literacy curriculum and instruction, I was asked to teach the English language arts methods course for graduate and undergraduate students at my degree-granting institution. After accepting this offer, I asked my recently retired advisor to meet with me because he had taught the course several times in the past. The numerous assumptions I carried into the conversation about what preservice teachers (PSTs) needed and should know were challenged at the close of our conversation when my advisor calmly said, "Keep in mind, as the semester progresses, student loyalty shifts from the university to their student teaching schools." When I asked, "What should I do?" he responded, "Listen and help them make sense of it."

As I read Chapter 9, "Tensions in ELA Field Experiences: Service-Learning Initiatives in Rural Contexts," I was reminded of that conversation and challenged anew to consider how *those who are preparing future English educators* might listen to what PSTs are saying and respond accordingly. The following response explores the concepts and implications of how leaning into uncertainty might support more effective preparation in professional education programs. I conclude with suggestions for adjustments to professional education programs that could support the development of lifelong educators.

LEANING INTO PRESERVICE TEACHER WOBBLE IN SERVICE LEARNING

In Chapter 9, Allison Wynhoff Olsen explores the academic and emotional wobbling (Fecho, 2011; Fecho, Graham, & Hudson-Ross, 2005) of preservice teachers within extended service-learning project experiences. By bringing the experiences of the service-learning projects into the methods course, PSTs were not only interacting with various communities and individuals within schools (Boyle-Baise & Sleeter, 2000) or being challenged to change a deficit perspective (Sleeter, 2000); they were also being invited to develop their identity in practice (Holland, Lachicotte, Skinner, & Cain, 2001) as they documented experiences, collaborated with peers and instructors, and understood their experiences in connection to their developing teacher identities.

Based on the work of Fecho and colleagues (2005), we know veteran teachers can experience a friction within themselves as they collaborate with colleagues, explore various resources, or experience professional development. This internal friction or *wobble* is "an authored space of uncertainty that lies between and among figured worlds" (p. 175). These figured worlds are varying understandings experienced teachers carry of what they have experienced, what they are learning, and what they will do in their classrooms as a response.

While we have documented instances of experienced teachers encountering a wobble, little research exists regarding how PSTs experience their own wobbling as they negotiate the figured worlds of early career teaching. Many PSTs experience a collision of sorts between what they know or assume and what they learn or experience as they matriculate through their professional education programs. This chapter invites us to see this collision or wobble of PSTs as a generative experience that can support the development of an effective teacher identity.

Toward the end of the chapter, we read that the methods course instructor paused class in response to PSTs' expressed frustrations. The instructor "addressed the PSTs' disrupted expectations to help them understand the notion of wobble and the learning that could follow if PSTs were willing to use the wobble generatively" (p. 153). In this part of the chapter, Olsen shows the recursive, complex, and often problematic process (Fecho et al., 2005) of becoming an effective teacher as we read of the instructor choosing to make the university classroom a safe but curious space for individual and collective wobbling. The instructor chose to listen and help the PSTs make sense, as my advisor suggested, of the uncertain and uncomfortable experiences the PSTs faced.

Some might treat the PST wobble as amateur jitters or uncomfortable but necessary obstacles that will simply subside over time and do not need much attention, especially if attention means valuable instruction time will be sacrificed in the university course. However, this chapter encourages those of us in teacher education to make space for uncertainty and see how we might position wobbling as an opportunity for PSTs to become authors of their own ever-developing teacher identities.

The teacher preparation program in this chapter created multiple opportunities for students to engage with students in rural schools, defining the experiences as service-learning opportunities. The conversation of how and what to do with service learning within teacher education programs is ongoing and varied in its interpretations. The experiences outlined in this chapter could arguably be seen as service learning because of the rural setting or could also be seen as additional field experiences in teacher education because the collaborations focused on students' required school-based learning and writing. Regardless, PSTs were offered multiple and varied experiences to engage with students over time and in various ways, which provided mutually beneficial partnerships and a large collection of experiences for PSTs to explore.

In my experience working with service-learning initiatives within teacher preparation programs, required documentation often involves keeping a log of hours and collecting signatures to prove completion of the requirements. The focus is typically how to make curricular adaptations for a specific student population, developing familiarity with a school's community programs, or working with students in an extracurricular activity. For the extensive, multisemester project described in this chapter, PSTs kept personal journals, engaged in online collaborations, and participated in face-to-face meetings with teachers and students. Instead of the focus being on curriculum or school resources and activities, the focus of the chapter was on how PSTs might better understand their own developing teacher identities. The extended timeline, types of documentation, and focus of the experience cultivated a contextual exploration involving the PST's personal journey of integration and future professionalism in the field.

APPLICATIONS AND FUTURE DIRECTIONS

As I composed this response, I considered some of my colleagues who may be tired and frustrated with too little time and too much to accomplish groaning at the thought of trying to cram yet another component into an already packed PST program. Therefore, as I turn to future considerations and applications, I seek to strike a challenging balance between practicality and possibility by including a few final thoughts, questions, and suggestions.

Our professional education courses might better serve students in the field if the courses make a concerted effort to create a simultaneously safe and curious space in which PSTs can collaboratively engage in professional conversations around balancing the academic and emotional components of wobbling. Might PSTs be better prepared to become lifelong educators if professional education programs listened intently and made them aware of the friction they might feel, the shifts in loyalty that might arise, and the opportunity for growth that can come from pressing into the uncertainty instead of dismissing it as inevitable speed bumps along the well-marked path of effective teaching? I think so.

In response to Olsen's chapter, I find the need to do some of my own shifting and continue my current pursuit to create a space for what Alsup's terms *borderland discourse*, a space of discursive exploration in which PSTs have the opportunity to "negotiate conflicting subject positions and ideologies while creating a professional self" (Alsup, 2006, p. 6). Over the last two years, I have experienced my own wobbling as I have sought to adjust my classroom and rethink my coursework to provide opportunities for my PSTs to create their own conceptions of the professional self.

For the classroom, I sit down with my students at their tables, and they share what is happening in field experiences and what they are learning from their courses. Then, we collaboratively problem-solve and complicate the various issues and ideas woven within and sitting at the edges of the issues discussed. After a few minutes, we start asking each other what role the issues have in broader conversations concerning learning and schooling. We then finish by exploring how our discussion connects to our understanding of who we are as teachers and learners.

For coursework, I offer students specific positions to occupy, such as positions of scholar practitioner or effective classroom teacher, and then ask them to explore how those various positions affect their relationship to the content or the project's meaning. When it comes to feedback on coursework, I strive to provide specific commentary concerning practice or application as well as conceptual commentary concerning assumptions or possible interpretations. I also include questions and an invitation for students to converse with me further about the ideas. My goal is to frame teaching as a complex personal and professional exploration of meaning and identity development.

Too much wobbling at early stages of teacher development could be detrimental, and we must be careful not to impose too much of an agenda on a service-learning project. I suggest we revisit our university's goals in teacher preparation programs and, within reason and application to each places' specific culture and communities, (1) explore ways to educate preservice teachers for and create safe environments in which wobbling is a positive part of teacher preparation, and (2) develop ways to honor service-learning opportunities and intentionally emphasize their potential as places where further teacher identity development can occur.

Uncertainty can either be seen as an obstacle to effective teaching or an authentic learning opportunity where teachers can develop "fresh and significant new perspectives on practices" (Fecho et al., 2005, p. 184). Our purpose in all of the listening and responding is to create lifelong career educators who learn to see their ever-evolving identity of a teacher strengthened by uncertainty and enriched by intentional engagement of and connection to the places and communities in which they serve.

REFERENCES

Alsup, J. (2006). *Teacher identity discourses*. New York: Routledge.
Boyle-Baise, M., & Sleeter, C. E. (2000). Community service learning for multicultural education. *Educational Foundations, 14*(2), 33–50.
Fecho, B. (2011). *Teaching for the students: Habits of heart, mind, and practice in the engaged classroom*. New York: Teachers' College.
Fecho, B., Graham, P., & Hudson-Ross, S. (2005). Appreciating the wobble: Teacher research, professional development, and figured worlds. *English Education, 37*(3), 174–199.
Holland, D. C., Lachicotte, W., Skinner, D., & Cain, C. (2001). *Identity and agency in cultural worlds*. Cambridge, MA: Harvard University Press.
Sleeter, C. E. (2000). Strengthening multicultural education with community-based service learning. In C. R. O'Grady (Ed.), *Integrating service learning and multicultural education in colleges and universities* (pp. 263–276). Mahwah, NJ: Erlbaum.

Chapter Ten

A Teaching Mythology

Disrupting the Tutor/Teacher Dichotomy

Heidi L. Hallman and Melanie N. Burdick

Portes and Smagorinsky (2010) remind us that the dominant model of classroom teaching into which English teachers are socialized is one that adheres to the teacher role as one of "teacher as authority." Thonus (2001), similarly, reflects that the dominant model for socializing writing tutors is one that differentiates tutor and teacher, with a tutor's role being distinct and different from a teacher's. Yet Thonus notes that this is indeed a tutoring mythology—a mythology that constrains the tutor's role, limiting it to "issues of personality and strategies of interpersonal interaction" (p. 61). Similarly, the teacher role as one of "teacher as authority" bolsters a teaching mythology that constrains beginning teachers' views of an appropriate teacher's role.

Yet beginning teachers seem to be consistently drawn to inhabiting the *teacher as authority role*. In this chapter, we grapple with the best ways to mentor preservice teachers into the roles of tutor and teacher. The chapter explores the perceptions that preservice teachers have when they assume the role of tutor as a component of a field experience connected to an English language arts methods course.

By experiencing the work of a tutor, preservice teachers can be guided toward productive and complex understandings of the work of both tutors and teachers while also offering preservice teachers an opportunity to apply their knowledge in real tutoring situations. The authors also move toward exploring how program curriculum in the field experience moved from tutoring to service learning. Throughout the chapter, the discussion of the teacher role is expanded to contexts outside of the school day and classroom.

First, this chapter describes the context in which the study work took place. Next, it moves toward featuring preservice teachers' understanding of their experience. The chapter concludes by posing questions about field experiences that are premised on one-to-one tutoring relationships, tutoring, and service learning, aiming to see connections across the tutor and teacher roles.

As part of the course, Teaching English in Middle/Secondary Schools, we envisioned that a tutoring experience, as a component of the course, would present beginning teachers with opportunities to tutor youth in reading and writing, better understand youth's in-school and out-of-school literacies, and provide a context for preservice teachers' ongoing identity formation. Throughout the past several years, this tutoring experience for preservice teachers has been implemented as a component of a secondary English language arts methods course at Green State University (GSU).

In this chapter, preservice teachers' voices are featured through showcasing excerpts of interviews and conversations that were had with them as part of larger research projects (see Hallman & Burdick, 2011; 2015). Exploring the views of preservice teachers assisted us in better understanding how preservice teachers perceive teacher education and their experience within the GSU teacher education program.

CONTEXT OF THE TUTORING EXPERIENCE AND THE ELA METHODS COURSE

GSU (all names of people and places are pseudonyms) is a large, Midwestern university located in a community of 90,000 people. Because the university is also situated 45 miles from Marshall City, a large metropolitan area of just over 2 million, the relative proximity of Marshall City to Green State University offers teacher education students the ability to attend the state's flagship institution yet complete field experiences and the final student teaching experience in schools located in the state's largest metropolitan center. GSU, also surrounded by rural communities and towns, gives teacher education students the option to complete field experiences and student teaching in any or all of urban, suburban, and rural contexts. As part of the teacher education program at GSU, diverse field experiences might contribute to preservice teachers' preparedness to work in a variety of contexts.

The course, Teaching English in Middle/Secondary Schools, is part of a traditional teacher education program that consists of general education coursework, English coursework, and professional education coursework in the School of Education. This chapter describes the field sites in the local community that sought preservice teachers to tutor adolescents, specifically in the areas of reading and writing. These sites included an after-school program at Cloverleaf Middle School, a local middle school, and a tutoring program for English language learners at Walnut Grove High, a local high school. Cloverleaf Middle School[1] and Walnut Grove High[2] were, respectively, the community's most diverse middle and high schools. The portrait that this diversity created mirrored a reality as documented in research literature (e.g., Haddix, 2008)—a reality that recognizes that a majority white teaching force (such as is the group of preservice teachers who constitute the majority of preservice teachers at GSU) will work in increasingly diverse school contexts.

The field experience that the preservice teachers undertook at the two sites, Cloverleaf Middle School and Walnut Grove High School, was structured primarily through one-on-one tutoring between preservice teacher and adolescents. Preservice teachers involved in Cloverleaf's after-school program assisted students with completing homework or led students in book clubs and other language arts–related activities. For example, screenplay writing was of high interest to many students who attended Cloverleaf's after-school program.

Walnut Grove High School's English as a second language (ESL) tutoring program took the form of one-on-one tutoring before the school day started. One frustration that several preservice English teachers expressed over the course of their work at Walnut Grove High was their lack of desire to assist ESL students with homework outside the domain of language arts. Preservice teachers often asked, "Why is it beneficial to me as a future teacher to help students with their homework in math when I will be teaching English?" It is these kinds of questions that constitute a dilemma. How can we assist beginning teachers in seeing the bridge between tutoring and teaching work? How can we work alongside the dominance of a teaching mythology—and discuss its limitations in productive ways with beginning teachers?

WHAT IS A TEACHING MYTHOLOGY?

As stated at the chapter's opening, a teaching mythology is a trope that constrains teaching to a particular conception of *teacher as authority* (Portes & Smagorinsky, 2010). Several preservice teachers were bound to the teaching mythology, as they had a strong preference for assuming the work of a teacher directing whole-group lessons in an English classroom. Preservice teachers often became disgruntled by the stymied position they felt in the tutoring context.

At both Cloverleaf Middle School and at Walnut Grove High, preservice teachers perceived they were in a clearly defined hierarchy consisting of *teacher* and *tutor* while working within their sites, with teachers possessing the specialized knowledge that allowed them authority and autonomy in the classroom. The expressed teacher/tutor juxtaposition became a focal point in preservice teachers' narratives and reflections. This chapter explores some of these reflections, illustrating both a confirmation of and disruption of a teaching mythology.

Preservice Teachers' Understandings of a Teaching Mythology

One preservice teacher, Erin Stiller, described the relationship between *teacher* and *tutor* by saying, "I see myself as a tutor and a tutor is more like a friend but still has some authority. The teacher is mainly an authority figure and the person who ultimately makes the choices." Such decision-making duties were ones that signaled being an authority in the classroom. Erin referenced her role at her field site when she said that "teachers set the framework of assignments while a tutor must work within that framework."

Erin's comments were based, in part, on her perception that a tutor resides in a lower-status role to that of a teacher. Interestingly, despite acknowledging a tutor's so-called lower status, several preservice teachers still processed the job of a tutor as more complex than the job of a teacher. Because of the lack of autonomy to make decisions in the classroom, many preservice teachers embraced the idea that a tutor needed more patience when working with students.

Sam Archer, a preservice teacher who worked within Cloverleaf's after-school program, expressed the difficulties of possessing patience with the seventh-grade students he worked with. Sam said, "When I was at the school I wished that I could slow down the class and allow that the student I was mainly working with to get the help he needed. But, that is how it is. Teachers are moving forward and tutors are slowing down."

Several preservice teachers told us that they had limited agency in changing those conditions. When listening to the comments such as those made by Erin and Sam, one can see the uneasiness in preservice teachers' observations. This uneasiness stemmed from their perception that they were en route to becoming a teacher and therefore were ready to shed the role of tutor. This location of being a *not-yet* teacher placed them at an identity point difficult for them to define. Not only were they asking, "Who are the students I am working with at my tutoring site?" but also they were asking, "Who am I at my tutoring site?"

This unease with their roles was confirmed by several other preservice teachers who described a *transitional state* of identity while engaged in tutoring. Through their experience, they reflected on their positions of authority as these contrasted with the needs of their students. Because tutoring required close relationships through one-on-one relationships, preservice teachers were not positioned in a *traditional* teacher role, standing in front of a (passive) class and extolling information. This different positioning with students placed the preservice teachers closer to students and further from curriculum, loosening up the authoritarian, traditional role. They were not creating curriculum but rather working through another teacher's curriculum with the students as they tutored. One preservice teacher, Maria Collins, discussed this change in position when she wrote,

> The experience I am having tutoring is teaching me more than I had anticipated. I expected to gain knowledge of students' skills and how to help the students. I am gaining that, but I am also gaining more. When tutoring at Cloverleaf school, I am learning that students are individual people and they need individual attention. Each student I work with at Cloverleaf needs something different from me. Some need help with homework, others want to play a game, and some even seem as if they simply want a friend. Since I am not their teacher, I can be all three to them.

The story Maria tells reflects her negotiation with her teaching role while working with individual students and how this, to her, was not an entirely academic role. However, she reported that she was able to assume this role because she was *not their teacher*—because a teacher, in her mind, must fulfill the traditional, authoritarian stance of curriculum creator and dispenser.

Interacting with students as individuals and valuing their individual needs was not congruent with Maria's idea of a teacher's role. Stepping outside the traditional role of teacher provided an opportunity for Maria to interact with students in ways that valued their individual perspectives and needs. Further, it was not a part of the traditional teacher identity in which a teacher creates and shares curriculum with a homogenous group of students. Understanding that students have different needs and are bringing these needs to the classroom was a positive recognition by Maria and signaled a step toward a willingness to negotiate students' experiences within the school space.

BACK TO THE METHODS COURSE: A DISCUSSION OF THE PRESERVICE TEACHER'S ROLE

After this particular semester of placing preservice teachers in tutoring field experiences at Cloverleaf Middle School and Walnut Grove High, we initiated more discussion in the English language arts (ELA) methods course about the roles of tutor and teacher. We drew upon an article by Alsup, Conrad-Salvo, and Peters (2008) that features the benefits of peer tutoring in a writing center environment. This article stresses the *real-world* experience that tutoring work presents to preservice teachers, as opposed to the sometimes-disconnected and mostly observation-based work that often takes place in traditional field experiences in secondary schools. Alsup and colleagues also highlight the freedom that can come with a tutoring experience; instead of being held under the close watch of a supervisor or mentor, a preservice teacher can carve out his or her own pedagogical space in a tutoring context.

In the ELA methods class, the article by Alsup, Conrad-Salvo and Peters (2008) was used in connection with the experiences preservice teachers had at Cloverleaf Middle School and Walnut Grove High. The article became a springboard for discussing the contrasts in the roles of teacher and tutor, and discussions in class, as well as reflections about the field experience, asked preservice teachers to question theory and practice and think about the pedagogies drawn upon within the tutoring experience. Some preservice teachers articulated the benefits of questioning as a pedagogical tool while others talked through the needs of their *focal students*—or the students they chose as case studies for their tutoring assignments throughout the semester. The chapter turns now to the service-learning innovations that came about as a result of the tutoring field experience.

SERVICE LEARNING: A FURTHER DISRUPTION OF THE TRADITIONAL TEACHER ROLE

Over the following years, we moved from including tutoring experiences as part of the ELA methods course to developing field experiences that were premised on service learning. In contrast to the tutoring field experiences, some of the service-learning experiences that were connected to the methods courses included extensive work with a day center for homeless youth and the development of a creative writing workshop for foster children who resided at a foster home (see Hallman & Burdick [2015] for a more thorough discussion of this work). We were optimistic that service learning would assist beginning teachers in breaking down the tutor/teacher dichotomy and saw this as a related goal to the breaking of the server/served dichotomy discussed in service learning, a relationship where some people are cast as the knowledgeable servers while others are cast as the "clients, patients, or the educationally deficient—the served" (Flower, 1997, p. 96).

A server-served dichotomy is often perpetuated in service learning's connotation. Flower's (2002; 2008) exploration of service learning problematizes the server-served dichotomy that service learning often creates and articulates a more complex picture of the potential role-reversals present in the act of service-learning. Her work features *reciprocity*—a concept that refers to both the interchange in roles between teacher and student and the interchange between university and community partnerships—as central to service learning's definition, thus seeking to reverse the long-standing practice of the academy using the community for the academy's own ends (Zlotkowski, 1996).

Such tenets guided our work throughout the integration of service learning into the ELA methods course. Of the many preservice teachers who worked in the methods class in tutoring and service-learning work, those who desired to complete field experiences in service-learning contexts often expressed the widest range of perceptions about their role as teachers while participating in the field experience.

Some beginning teachers found that youth at Family Partnership, the program for homeless families, recognized students from GSU as *teachers* within the context of the Family Partnership organization. Sometimes, though, GSU students were acknowledged as *volunteers*. While some beginning teachers believed they could make certain moves with their students because they were not positioned as teachers, other preservice teachers equalized the roles of teacher, tutor, and volunteer in their written reflections.

Although this equalizing view of a teacher's role was distinctly different from many others' views that endorsed the view of teacher as authority, this perspective, nonetheless, affirmed the idea that preservice teachers' identity-building process resided on a continuum that was affected by certain experiences with students. The continuum subtly carried a progress narrative, one that told preservice teachers they would increasingly gain more knowledge over time and move from a role of student to a role of tutor and, eventually, to a role of teacher. This narrative of *progress* of the teacher mirrors, in many ways, the manner in which Popkewitz (1998) references the way "personal salvation and redemption [are] tied to personal development and 'fulfillment,' words that signaled religious motifs but placed them in secular discourses of science and rational progress" (p. 24). Prospective teachers' construction of progress narratives became a way for them to seek authority while covertly maintaining the teacher-as-authority trope.

In a reflection authored by preservice teacher Anne Chisholm, we can see the pervasiveness of the teacher-as-authority paradigm in shaping beginning teachers' perceptions of the teaching act. Anne wrote, "Mostly I feel that I'm practicing the role of being a tutor while I'm at Family Partnership. It has been rare that I'm really teaching the students something and it is more likely that I'll be working with them on their homework. I'm fine with that but I know I'm itching to get into an English classroom and really practice developing that teacher presence." Anne's comments, and especially her lukewarm evaluation of her role through her expression "I'm fine with that," suggests that she looked upon the experience at Family Partnership as distinctly not teaching. Through such a view, Anne subscribed to a teaching mythology. Other preservice teachers were also bound to a teaching mythology and, as a result of this perspective, identified the ways in which they felt stymied in their field site. Sarah Emerson, another student who worked with homeless youth at Family Partnership, wrote,

> I've been in limbo this semester. I feel that I have learned things at Family Partnership, but I have not really learned about what it takes to be a teacher in a classroom. I see the role more as a tutor or a mentor and not really a teacher. I've done a lot of tutoring and mentoring so I feel that I'm already good at those things. Family Partnership did teach me about the reality of homeless kids' lives.

Surely, reading such comments feels somewhat discouraging, and we often honed the presentation of how service learning and the work at Family Partnership was presented to our students. We created this conversation with our beginning teachers as part of the methods course and developed questions that were posed to preservice teachers. The questions included the following:

- What have been your initial impressions of the work you are doing at Family Partnership?
- What themes that were pertinent in the training are arising in your work at Family Partnership?
- Describe the youth who you are working with at Family Partnership. What do you see as their strengths? In what ways are you working with them on activities related to literacy learning?
- Youth at Family Partnership can be considered *at risk* of school failure because of homelessness. What are your thoughts about the at-risk status and how you perceive the students with whom you work?
- How might you define your role as a *teacher*, *tutor*, or *mentor* with youth at Family Partnership?
- Are there aspects of your work that have surprised you? In what ways is the experience different than you may have anticipated?

Through discussion of the questions above, we encouraged preservice teachers to articulate their understanding of their work as teachers, the process of students' learning, and the perceptions they held of the students with whom they worked. We encouraged beginning teachers to think more carefully about the purposes of teaching and learning, and urged them to define their role as teachers at the same time as they pivoted to the other side of the teaching act—a view of the students.

FORWARD THINKING: CONTINUING TO DISRUPT THE TEACHING MYTHOLOGY

Now, after several iterations of placing preservice teachers in both tutoring and service-learning experiences as part of the English language arts methods course, the landscape must be surveyed. Our goals of promoting tutoring work and service-learning experiences for preservice teachers are twofold.

First, tutoring and service-learning experiences must have a goal of viewing "self" and "other" as ultimately intertwined. A breaking of the self-other dichotomy through the act of tutoring and service learning is essential for beginning teachers' reflections on "self" as well as for their recognition of their prior, and perhaps limited, understandings. Second, the act of tutoring and service learning must be pursued alongside a process of inquiry.

Flower (2008) notes that inquiry must begin by "confronting the conflicts within the everyday practice of outreach" (p. 154). These two tenets, as applied to the methods course and to teacher education, broadly, are embodied within any well-planned field experience. Field experiences, as inquiry, do not become a series of interventions or programs but instead are treated as a situated sociocultural activity—an activity that is always socially, culturally, and historically located.

Still, we know that many preservice teachers hold tightly to the "teacher as authority" trope and still witness preservice teachers who flail in the pedagogical freedom that might reside in the tutoring space. Instead, they yearn for a clearly articulated curriculum that they can adhere to completely. However, even in this, we remain steadfast in the belief that early and diverse field experiences—such as those premised on tutoring and service learning—will push preservice teachers to question the relationship among teacher, pedagogy, and students. This perspective will, hopefully, instill a curiosity within preservice teachers, pushing them to question the "teacher as authority" trope and the progress narrative that undergirds the tutor to teacher pathway.

NOTES

1. Cloverleaf Middle School (grades 6–8) is known in the community as the most diverse of the city's four middle schools, and using the figures from the 2017–2018 school year, the school reported that 60% of its students were economically disadvantaged. The school consisted of 50% white students, 5% African American students, 2% Asian students, 10% Hispanic students, and 9% labeled as two or more races. A large portion of the students that the school reports as two or more races are Native American students, as the community is also home to a federally funded Native American university (NCES, 2017–2018).

2. Walnut Grove High School's student body of 1,591 students, as reported for the 2017–2018 school year, is 65% white, 13% African American, 9% Hispanic, 3% Asian, and 10% two or more races. And 43% of students at Walnut Grove High are economically disadvantaged (NCES, 2017–2018).

REFERENCES

Alsup, J. (2006). *Teacher identity discourses: Negotiating personal and professional discourses*. Mahwah, NJ: Erlbaum.

Alsup, J., Conrad-Salvo, T., & Peters, S. J. (2008). Tutoring is real: The benefits of the peer tutor experience for future English educators. *Pedagogy: Critical Approaches to Teaching Literature, Language, Composition, and Culture, 8*(2), 327–347.

Flower, L. (1997). Partners in inquiry: A logic for community outreach. In L. Adler-Kassner, R. Crooks, & A. Watters (Eds.), *Writing the community: Concepts and models for service-learning in composition* (pp. 95–117). Washington, DC: American Association for Higher Education Press.

Flower, L. (2002). Intercultural inquiry and the transformation of service. *College English, 65*(2), 181–201. doi:10.2307/3250762.

Flower, L. (2008). *Community literacy and the rhetoric of public engagement.* Carbondale, IL: Southern Illinois Press.

Flower, L., Long, E., & Higgins, L. (2000). *Learning to rival: A literate practice for intercultural inquiry.* Mahwah, NJ: Erlbaum.

Haddix, M. (2008). Beyond sociolinguistics: Toward a critical approach to cultural and linguistic diversity in teacher education. *Language and Education, 22*(5), 254–270.

Hallman, H. L., & Burdick, M. N. (2011). Service learning and the preparation of English teachers. *English Education, 43*(4), 341–368. Retrieved from http://search.proquest.com.

Hallman, H. L., & Burdick, M. N. (2015). *Community fieldwork in teacher education: Theory and method.* New York: Routledge.

National Center for Education Statistics (NCES). (2017–2018). Lawrence High School, Lawrence, KS; Liberty Memorial Central Middle School, Lawrence, KS. Retrieved from https://nces.ed.gov.

Popkewitz, T. S. (1998). *Struggling for the soul: The politics of schooling and the construction of the teacher.* New York: Teachers College Press.

Portes, P. R., & Smagorinsky, P. (2010). Static structures, changing demographics: Educating teachers for shifting populations in stable schools. *English Education, 42*(3), 236–247. Retrieved from http://www.jstor.org.

Thonus, T. (2001). Triangulation in the writing center: Tutor, tutee, and instructor perceptions of the tutor's role. *Writing Center Journal, 22*(1), 59–82.

Zlotkowski, E. (1996). A new voice at the table? Linking service-learning and the academy. *Change, 28*(1), 21–27.

A Response to Chapter 10

Terri L. Rodriguez

> Field experiences, as inquiry, do not become a series of interventions or programs but instead are treated as a situated sociocultural activity—an activity that is always socially, culturally, and historically located. (Hallman & Burdick [Chap. 10], p. 171)

The direction of this response will be to connect with the authors from my current context in preservice teacher preparation, affirm the many strengths of their work, and extend their discussion of preservice teachers' identity negotiations during service-oriented, community-based field placements. Throughout, I will argue that Heidi L. Hallman and Melanie N. Burdick's findings help us reimagine English teacher education within traditional programs where preservice teachers' lives are often far removed from the realities of their K–12 students' lives. Envisioning field experience as inquiry rather than a *series of interventions or programs* would be, I think, an important tenet to guide our work.

Like the authors, I teach in a majority white institution that prepares teachers for racially diverse schools. Further, my department is approaching our Council for the Accreditation of Teacher Preparation (CAEP) accreditation visit and state board of teaching review. Questions about school partnerships and field experiences are paramount in this process. Through the inquiry about our English teacher education requirements, we are asking questions like the following:

- How do we develop complex partnerships in ways that support and sustain teachers across many points of their career paths, including the preservice teachers enrolled in our program as well as the mentor teachers with whom we collaborate?

- How might we better design mutually supportive relationships with schools and other community organizations while sharing resources that target and promote student learning and success?
- How do these experiences provide opportunities for our teacher candidates to demonstrate their emerging knowledge, skills, and dispositions as professional educators?

Our work tends to be complicated by the need to provide opportunities for preservice teachers to demonstrate teaching competencies as outlined by external Standards of Effective Practice (SEPs) in observable and measurable ways. We limit ourselves to becoming observers of preservice teachers' practices in ways that equate *good teaching* with technical skills. Such a focus limits our ability to remember the relational core of teaching and learning that is, as Hallman and Burdick remind us, always socially, culturally, and historically situated. Teacher and student identities and the roles they inhabit are central to this process.

Importantly, Hallman and Burdick find that the tutoring experience positioned preservice teachers closer to K–12 students and allowed them opportunities to interact with them as individuals. Rather than assuming the authoritative stance of a teacher delivering curriculum to a homogenous group of students, one preservice teacher in particular, Maria, recognized that students have different strengths and needs. This realization opened the possibility for her to negotiate students' experiences in school from multiple positions defined by Maria as *all three* (homework helper, game partner, and friend). She came to understand students as "individual people [who] need individual attention," an important part of her teaching identity and role.

Like others in Hallman and Burdick's study, Maria came to see the benefits of questioning as a pedagogical tool as she discussed the strengths and needs of focal students in her tutoring assignments. Her case resonates with those of preservice teachers discussed in an earlier publication (Hallman & Rodriguez, 2015) as she begins to more broadly conceptualize her own and youths' literate identities, knowledge, and practices and to conceptualize them as pedagogical resources.

Despite the possibilities, Hallman and Burdick note that redesigning field placements to focus on identities, roles, and relationships in nontraditional sites is not without its challenges. The view of teacher-as-authority could be temporarily suspended for some preservice teachers who were willing to take on the role of tutor but continued to see their own development as somewhere on a continuum from "student to a role of tutor and, eventually, to a role of teacher" (p. 169).

Hallman and Burdick call this a progress narrative that covertly affirms preservice teachers' conception of the teaching mythology. Such mythologies, or grand narratives, are difficult, if not impossible, to interrupt, especially in light of the ways in which schooling, as an institution, is designed to work against a model of teaching as relational and centered on individual learners.

Nevertheless, I am hopeful, alongside Hallman and Burdick, that when we encourage preservice teachers to think more carefully about the purposes of teaching and learning and urge them to redefine their role as teachers, we can bring them to the other side of the teaching learning act—to a place where the student, as an individual learner with unique strengths, interests, needs, and experiences, is in full view and pedagogy truly becomes a place of inquiry.

REFERENCES

Hallman, H. L., & Rodriguez, T. L. (2015). Fostering community-based field experiences in teacher education. In E. Hollins (Ed.), *Rethinking field experiences in preservice teacher preparation: Meeting new challenges for accountability* (pp. 99–116). New York: Routledge.

Index

academic modes of writing, xviii, 67
accreditation, 27, 175
activist ally, 22, 24, 34
Adichie, Chiamanda Ngozi, 147
aesthetic: dimensions, 29; efferent-aesthetic, 91, 92; experience, 93, 96, 97; response, 7
agency, 22, 24, 25, 33, 168
Alexander, Kwame, 127
All American Boys, 81
apprenticeship of observation, 61
The Autobiography of Malcolm X, 18

backwards design planning, 13, 127
Ball Don't Lie, 81
Becoming Naomi Leon, 78
borderland discourse, 162

career decision v. career preparation, 106, 108, 112
CCLS. *See* Common Core Learning Standards
CCSS. *See* Common Core State Standards
CEE. *See* Conference on English Education
clinically rich, xix, 125, 135, 142
Common Core Learning Standards, 18, 150
Common Core State Standards, 5
Communities of Practice, xix, 123, 124, 125, 135, 139, 140, 141

Community Teaching Strand, 55–56
Conference on English Education, 107, 111, 116n3, 116n5
Conference on English Education Position Statement (2005), 108, 111, 112
constructivism, 4, 9, 23, 27, 28, 29
cooperating teacher, 6–7, 8, 12, 106, 107, 110, 114, 115n1, 125, 126, 128–129, 134
CoP. *See* Communities of Practice
critical: conversations, 38, 39, 40, 49, 50, 54; inquiry model, 127; language awareness, 38, 49; lenses, 24, 77, 128; literacy, 38, 92, 125, 128, 134; media analysis, 129; pedagogies, 29; pragmatism, xvi, 4, 8, 9–11, 14, 17, 18, 19; praxis, 14; stance, 38, 48; theory, 88; transactions, 93, 97, 98
critical reflection, 9, 40, 44, 48; journals, 149, 161; notebooks, 12
cross-cultural, 92
CTS. *See* Community Teaching Strand
cultural studies, 125
culturally responsive pedagogy, 49, 92, 93, 101
culturally sustaining pedagogies and teaching practices, 19, 127

democracy, xvi, 4, 9, 98
digital natives, 61

EESA. *See* English Education Student Association
efferent aesthetic stances, 91, 92, 102
egocentric-sociocentric view of reading, 78, 87, 88, 89, 97
EngageNY, 18, 19
English Education Alumni Network, 126
English Education Student Association, 126
English Journal, 126
English language learners, 9, 166
English language arts (ELA) methods course, 91, 92, 101, 170, 171
English Language Arts Teacher Educators (ELATE). *See* Conference on English Education
equity, 14, 22, 43, 49, 92, 98, 101; literacy, 22
exposure, 106, 111, 112, 118

FCMN. *See* Family and Community Mentor Network
Family and Community Mentor Network, 55
field experience and work, xiii, 105, 107–108, 109, 111, 116n3, 128, 136, 141, 145, 161, 165, 170, 173; tensions with, 4, 9–11, 12
Fahrenheit 451, 131
Feed, 78
figured worlds, 149, 160
First Part Last, 84
formalism, 102
Freedom Writers, 130

The Great Gatsby, 98

hands-on v. hands-off, 106, 108, 109, 111
Harkness Method Discussion, 127
Harry Potter, 78
hegemony, 46
hierarchy, 45, 167
Home of the Brave, 83
The Hunger Games, 77

I Read It, but I Don't Get It, 127
identity, 22, 24, 39, 40, 42, 124, 129, 130, 134, 135, 159, 168; development, 123, 126, 135, 140, 162, 166, 171; teacher identity, 118, 149, 160, 162, 169, 175, 176
inquiry, 22; community of, 12; inquiry-based teaching, 125, 126, 127, 128, 131, 133, 134, 135
in-service teachers, xix, xx, 13, 14, 40, 125, 128, 137n1, 139, 141, 142, 146, 149

Kincaid, Jamaica, 128

legitimate peripheral participation, 124, 126
Like Water on Stone, 83
Literature as Exploration, 91, 102
literary: criticism, 83; critic, 78, 87, 91, 98, 102; response, 91, 96, 97

The Man Who Walked Between the Towers, 95
mentor: college, 149, 152, 154, 155; community, 56; teacher, 14, 118, 128, 134, 136, 139, 140, 141, 155, 169, 172, 175
metacognition, xv, 74, 75
MBFE. *See* Methods-Based Field Experiences
Methods-Based Field Experiences, 105–106, 111, 115n1–115n2, 117
microteaching, 21, 25, 26, 27, 28, 30, 33
Miracle Boys, 78
motif, 130, 171
multimodal, xiv, 61, 62, 63, 65, 66, 67, 73, 74, 149; composing, 61, 65, 66, 67, 68, 69, 74, 134

National Council of Teachers of English, xi, 26, 27
National Writing Project, 142
NCTE. *See* National Council of Teachers of English
neoliberal reform, 17, 124
New Critics, New Criticism, xviii, 87, 88, 91, 101, 102, 114
new literacies, 69
No Child Left Behind (2001), 5
No Ordinary Day, 78
NWP. *See* National Writing Project

PDS. *See* professional development, schools
pedagogy, xiv, 18, 22, 23, 26, 29, 49, 59, 63, 94, 95, 129, 145, 173, 177; parallel, 64, 66–67, 74; tools, 170, 176
Persepolis, 68
PLC. *See* Professional Learning Communities
positioning, 44, 92, 93, 97, 98, 152, 168
practicum experiences, 6, 7, 8, 9, 12, 13, 19, 145, 146
pre-service teachers, 3, 17, 21, 37, 38, 59, 77, 123, 165; dispositions, xvii, 21, 22, 25, 60. *See also* teacher candidates; PSTs
professional development, xix, xx, 8, 113, 125, 126, 127; schools, 141
professional learning communities, 5
prophetic pragmatism, 9
PSTs, 145, 159. *See also* preservice teachers; teacher candidates

racial identities, 38, 129
racial literacy, 38, 40
The Reader, the Text, the Poem: The Transactional Theory of Literacy Work (1978), 91
The Reading Zone, 110
reader response: reader-as-self, 78, 79; reader-as-character, 78, 80; reader-as-literary critic, 83; reader-as-teacher, 81; reader-as-writer, 82; theory, 77, 83, 87, 88, 92, 96, 97, 101, 102
reciprocity, 170
remedial reading classes, 7
Rosenblatt, Louise, 91, 101, 114
rural, 9, 34, 40, 107, 116n5, 133, 146, 154–155, 156n1; service learning in, 161, 166

Secondary Schools Writers Association, 140
SEPs. *See* Standards for Effective Practice
service-learning, 146, 147–149, 159, 161, 170–171, 172
"single story," 147
sociocultural, xx, 9, 26, 78, 83, 92, 101, 124, 125, 128, 140, 173; activity, 173

social: justice, 21–22, 23, 24, 27, 33, 34, 38, 92, 98, 101, 124, 131, 133, 145; learning system, 124, 125, 136
Southern Poverty Law Center, 54
SPLC. *See* Southern Poverty Law Center
SSWA. *See* Secondary School Writing Centers Association
standardization, xiii, 3, 133, 135, 136
Standards for Effective Practice, 24, 26

teacher as authority, xx, 165, 167
teacher candidates, xiv, xv, 21, 24. *See also* pre-service teachers; PSTs
teacher education: as a conceptual home base, 4, 5, 8, 13
teaching approach: differences, 3, 4, 7–8
Teaching English by Design: How to Create and Carry Out Instructional Units, 127
Teaching Literature to Adolescents, 127, 128
teaching mythology, 165, 167, 171, 176
Teaching the Neglected 'R': Rethinking Writing Instruction in Secondary Classrooms, 150
Teaching Tolerance, 46, 50, 129
threshold concepts and writing, 61
To Kill a Mockingbird, 12, 98
transactional, 91, 92, 101, 102
The Transactional Theory of the Literary Work (1978), 91
trope, 167, 171, 173
tutor, 128, 140, 147, 148, 152, 165–166; one-on-one tutoring, 167; teacher and tutor, 167, 168
Tyrell, 79

Uglies, 84
Understanding by Design, 132
Understanding Poetry, 102

video analysis assignment, 42, 49

Western New York Network of English Teachers, 125–126, 129, 133, 137n2, 141
Will Grayson, Will Grayson, 78
Winter Girls, 78

WNYNET. *See* Western New York Network of English Teachers
wobble, 34, 149–150, 152, 160
workshop, 13, 125, 127, 131, 132, 135, 170
writing for the 21st century, 59, 60, 62

young adult literature, 23, 78, 87, 88
Youth Voices Conference, 126, 132, 133, 134, 135, 141

About the Editors and Contributors

Heidi L. Hallman is professor of English education in the Department of Curriculum and Teaching at the University of Kansas. Hallman's research interests include studying "at-risk" students' literacy learning as well as how prospective English teachers are prepared to teach in diverse school contexts. Her work has appeared in *English Journal, Teaching Education, English Education,* and *Equity and Excellence in Education,* among others. In 2018, she was a corecipient of the National Council of Teachers of English's (NCTE) English Language Arts Teacher Educators (ELATE) Richard A. Meade Award for her coauthored book *Secondary English Teacher Education in the United States* (2018).

Donna L. Pasternak is professor of English education and director of the University of Wisconsin–Milwaukee Writing Project. She studies the integration of technology into the teaching of English and English language arts teacher education in urban contexts. Pasternak's scholarship has been published in a variety of journals and edited volumes. In 2018, she was a corecipient of the National Council of Teachers of English's (NCTE) English Language Arts Teacher Educators (ELATE) Richard A. Meade Award for her coauthored book *Secondary English Teacher Education in the United States* (2018).

Kristen Pastore-Capuana is assistant professor of English education at Buffalo State College where she teaches undergraduate English language arts methods courses and coordinates field experiences and community partnerships. A former high school English teacher in Western New York, Pastore-Capuana's 14 years of experience informs her work as a researcher and teacher educator. Her research interests include critical literacy pedagogy, secondary English language arts teacher development, and teacher advocacy. She is also the assistant director of the Western New York Network of English Teachers.

* * *

Robert Brooke is John E. Weaver Professor of English at the University of Nebraska, Lincoln, where he directs the Nebraska Writing Project. His most recent book is *Writing Suburban Citizenship: Place-Conscious Education and the Conundrum of Suburbia* (2015). Research interests include teachers' public advocacy, secondary writing, and place-conscious education especially for the Great Plains.

Melanie N. Burdick is associate professor of English and serves as director of the Center for Teaching Excellence and Learning at Washburn University. Her recent publications have been included in journals such as *Writing Program Administrators Journal*, *English Journal*, and *English Education*. Her research focuses on the teaching of writing in high school and college, community-based learning, and literacy acquisition of traditionally underserved student populations.

James Cercone is associate professor and English education program coordinator at SUNY Buffalo State. His research focuses on developing communities of practice in teacher education and inquiry-based approaches to English language arts instruction. His published works include "We're Smarter Together: Building Professional Social Networks in English Education" (2009), "Being Great for Something: Composing Music Videos in a High School English Class" (2012), "Communities of Practice: Bridging the Gap Between Methods Courses and Secondary Schools" (2014), and "Standing at the Crossroads": Content Creation in the 21st-Century English Classroom" (2017). Cercone is the director of the Western New York Network of English Teachers and the Center for English Teaching at SUNY Buffalo State.

Jamie M. Collins is lecturer and field experience coordinator for the Department of Curriculum and Instruction at the University of Arkansas. She is part of the Elite Directions faculty team with the Center for the Professional Education of Teachers, Teachers College Columbia University. Collins's research currently focuses on university students' identity development within their teacher preparation programs, culturally responsive secondary teaching, and the meaning-making process of adolescents' in-school writing practices.

Lauren Gatti is associate professor of English education at the University of Nebraska, Lincoln. Her book on teacher learning and teacher education, *To-*

ward a Framework of Resources for Learning to Teach: Rethinking U.S. Teacher Preparation*, was published in 2016. Her peer-reviewed work has appeared in a number of journals including *Teaching and Teacher Education, English Journal, Urban Education, English Teaching: Practice and Critique*, and *Journal of Higher Education Outreach and Engagement*. Gatti's research interests include democratic education and teacher education policy and practice.

Crag Hill is associate professor of English education at the University of Oklahoma. His recent work in critical literacy includes an edited collection of essays on young adult literature, *Coming of Age: The Critical Merits of Young Adult Literature* (2014), and on comics, *Teaching Comics Through Multiple Lenses: Critical Perspectives* (2016). His latest project, *Critical Approaches to Teaching the High School Novel: Reinterpreting Canonical Literature*, coedited with Victor Malo-Juvera, will appear in 2019.

Amber Jensen is a doctoral candidate in writing and rhetoric and a graduate instructor in the secondary English education program at George Mason University. Her research interests in multimodal and digital writing, teacher advocacy, and secondary school writing centers reflect her own teaching experiences as a former high school English teacher, writing center director, and National Writing Project teacher consultant. Jensen's dissertation explores preservice teachers' conceptions of 21st-century writing and pedagogy throughout their teacher education programs and into their first years as classroom teachers.

Jessica Masterson is a postdoctoral researcher at the University of Nebraska, Lincoln. Her work examines the literate practices of youth from marginalized communities and informs her approach to teacher education. Her scholarship can be found in *English Teaching: Practice and Critique*, with forthcoming pieces in *Pedagogy* and AERA's *Review of Research in Education*.

Mike Metz is assistant professor of English education at the University of Missouri. A former middle and high school English teacher on the south side of Chicago, Metz brings his 15 years of classroom experience to his role as a teacher educator and researcher. His research examines linguistically informed approaches to grammar and language instruction as a way to counter systemic linguistic discrimination in English classrooms. His scholarship appears in journals including *Research in the Teaching of English, Teachers College Record, Linguistics and Education*, and *Urban Education*.

Allison Wynhoff Olsen is assistant professor of English at Montana State University and director of the Yellowstone Writing Project. Her research examines student writing development over time and the experiences of rural English teachers. Thus far, her writing scholarship emphasizes the social and relational processes within the teaching and learning of argumentative writing, and her work appears in a coauthored book: *Teaching and Learning Argumentative Writing in High School English Language Arts Classrooms* (2015) as well as peer-reviewed journals: *Written Communication*, the *Journal of Adolescent and Adult Literacy*, and *Research in the Teaching of English*. Her scholarship about the experiences of rural English teachers examines teachers' professional practices, teachers' emotional strain, and preservice teacher preparations for rural contexts.

Christopher M. Parsons is assistant professor of English and coordinator of secondary English education at Keene State College. His research focuses on the salience of ideologies about gender and literacy in secondary English classrooms as well as on teacher candidates' field experiences in university-based teacher preparation programs. Previously, he taught high school English in North Las Vegas, Nevada.

Sue Ringler Pet is assistant professor at the Isabelle Farrington College of Education at Sacred Heart University in Fairfield, Connecticut. She specializes in secondary English education and literacy in K–12; adolescent and children's literature; and multicultural education. Ringler Pet's research interests include examining preservice English teachers' developing identities as readers and future teachers as well as reframing the scholarship of Louise Rosenblatt as pivotal for promoting socially conscious transactions with literature.

Laura A. Renzi is professor of English at West Chester University of Pennsylvania. Her recent works include *Secondary English Teacher Education in the United States* (2018). Renzi's research interests include teacher education and field experiences, as well as LGBTQI young adult literature.

Terri L. Rodriguez is a former secondary English teacher and currently associate professor of education at the College of St. Benedict and St. John's University in St. Joseph, Minnesota. Her recent work appears in *English Education* and *Literacy Research and Instruction* and includes *Supporting Muslim Students: A Guide to Understanding the Diverse Issues of Today's Classrooms* (Rowman & Littlefield, 2017). Her research explores issues of social justice, equity, and diversity in U.S. schools.

Melissa Schieble is associate professor of English education at Hunter College of the City University of New York. Her work investigates critical literacy practices in English education and has appeared in numerous literacy and teacher education journals. She is coauthor of *Observing Teacher Identities Through Video Analysis* (2016). She is currently working with Amy Vetter on a Spencer-funded research project to investigate critical conversations in English language arts classrooms.

Rachael Wendler-Shah is assistant professor of English at University of Nebraska, Lincoln, where she teaches classes on writing pedagogy and public rhetorics. Her recent work appears in *College Composition and Communication*, *Reflections*, and the *Michigan Journal of Community Service Learning*. Shah's current book project explores community member perspectives of university-community literacy partnerships.

Sarah Thomas is assistant professor of practice in English education at the University of Nebraska, Lincoln, where she teaches classes on adolescent literature, content area reading, methods, and undergraduate and graduate curriculum studies foundations. Her recent work appears in *English Teaching: Practice and Critique* and the *Michigan Journal of Community Service Learning*. Thomas's research interests include teacher induction, educative mentoring, and teaching for creativity and critical literacy.

Amy Vetter is associate professor in English education in the School of Education at the University of North Carolina, Greensboro, where she teaches undergraduate courses in teaching practices and curriculum of English and literacy in the content area, and graduate courses in youth literacies, teacher research, and qualitative research design. She has published articles in *English Education*, *Journal of Literacy Research*, *English Teaching: Practice and Critique*, *English Journal*, *Qualitative Research in Education*, *Teacher Education Quarterly*, *Journal of Adolescent and Adult Literacy*, *Changing English*, *Journal of Teacher Education*, and the *Urban Review*. She presents regularly at the National Conference for Teachers of English and the Literacy Research Association Conference.

www.ingramcontent.com/pod-product-compliance
Lightning Source LLC
Chambersburg PA
CBHW022012300426
44117CB00005B/156